THE ARCHITECTURE OF DESIRE

FAMILIES, LAW, AND SOCIETY SERIES

General Editor: Nancy E. Dowd

Justice for Kids: Keeping Kids Out of the Juvenile Justice System
Edited by Nancy E. Dowd

Masculinities and the Law: A Multidimensional Approach
Edited by Frank Rudy Cooper and Ann C. McGinley

The New Kinship: Constructing Donor-Conceived Families
Naomi Cahn

What Is Parenthood? Contemporary Debates about the Family
Edited by Linda C. McClain and Daniel Cere

In Our Hands: The Struggle for U.S. Child Care Policy
Elizabeth Palley and Corey S. Shdaimah

The Marriage Buyout: The Troubled Trajectory of U.S. Alimony Law
Cynthia Lee Starnes

Children, Sexuality, and the Law
Edited by Sacha Coupet and Ellen Marrus

A New Juvenile Justice System: Total Reform for a Broken System
Edited by Nancy E. Dowd

Divorced from Reality: Rethinking Family Dispute Resolution
Jane C. Murphy and Jana B. Singer

The Poverty Industry: The Exploitation of America's Most Vulnerable Citizens
Daniel L. Hatcher

Ending Zero Tolerance: The Crisis of Absolute School Discipline
Derek W. Black

Blaming Mothers: American Law and the Risks to Children's Health
Linda C. Fentiman

The Ecology of Childhood: How Our Changing World Threatens Children's Rights
Barbara Bennett Woodhouse

The Politicization of Safety: Critical Perspectives on Domestic Violence Responses
Edited by Jane K. Stoever

Living Apart Together: Legal Protections for a New Form of Family
Cynthia Grant Bowman

Social Parenthood in Comparative Perspective
Edited by Clare Huntington, Courtney G. Joslin, and Christiane von Bary

The End of Family Court: How Abolishing the Court Brings Justice to Children and Families
Jane M. Spinak

The Architecture of Desire: How the Law Shapes Interracial Intimacy and Perpetuates Inequality
Solangel Maldonado

The Architecture of Desire

*How the Law Shapes Interracial Intimacy
and Perpetuates Inequality*

Solangel Maldonado

NEW YORK UNIVERSITY PRESS
New York

NEW YORK UNIVERSITY PRESS
New York
www.nyupress.org

© 2024 by New York University
All rights reserved

Library of Congress Cataloging-in-Publication Data
Names: Maldonado, Solangel, author.
Title: The architecture of desire : how the law shapes interracial intimacy and perpetuates inequality/Solangel Maldonado.
Description: New York : New York University Press, 2024. |
Series: Families, law, and society | Includes bibliographical references and index.
Identifiers: LCCN 2023049420 (print) | LCCN 2023049421 (ebook) | ISBN 9781479812356 (hardback) | ISBN 9781479859665 (ebook) | ISBN 9781479850808 (ebook other)
Subjects: LCSH: Interracial marriage—Law and legislation. | Race discrimination—Law and legislation. | Minorities—Legal status, laws, etc. | Equality before the law. | Racially mixed people—Legal status, laws, etc. | Miscegenation. | Interracial dating. | Intimacy (Psychology) | Freedom of association.
Classification: LCC K3242 .M323 2024 (print) | LCC K3242 (ebook) | DDC 342.08/5—dc23/eng/20231023
LC record available at https://lccn.loc.gov/2023049420
LC ebook record available at https://lccn.loc.gov/2023049421

This book is printed on acid-free paper, and its binding materials are chosen for strength and durability. We strive to use environmentally responsible suppliers and materials to the greatest extent possible in publishing our books.

Manufactured in the United States of America

10 9 8 7 6 5 4 3 2 1

Also available as an ebook

CONTENTS

Introduction: Intimacy, Law, and Choice   1

1. A Gendered Racial Hierarchy in the Intimate Market   13

2. How Law Regulated Interracial Intimacy and
   Its Effects Today   37

3. Freedom of Association versus Discrimination in
   Intimate Spheres   66

4. How Law Shapes Opportunity for Interracial Intimacy   91

5. Perpetuating Inequality: The Psychological, Economic,
   and Social Consequences of Racial Preferences   112

6. Working toward Equality   130

   Acknowledgments   149

   Notes   151

   Index   219

   About the Author   234

Introduction

Intimacy, Law, and Choice

When Beth Humphrey and Terence McKay sought to get married in Louisiana in 2009, they did not expect that a judge would refuse to perform the ceremony. They were not related to one another, they were not married to other people, they were not of the same sex (marriages between persons of the same sex were not legally recognized at the time), and they were not minors. Thus, they did not violate any of the statutory marriage restrictions in effect in Louisiana or any other state at the time. However, Justice of the Peace Keith Bardwell refused to marry them because, in his view, Beth and Terence's children, if they had any, would be social pariahs. He also expected their marriage to end in divorce.[1] Judge Bardwell did not know Beth or Terence or the quality of their relationship, but he based his predictions on one fact: Beth is White (Caucasian) and Terence is Black (African American).[2]

Judge Bardwell is not alone in his views on interracial marriage. In 2011, a church in Kentucky voted to ban interracial couples from membership.[3] That same year, a poll found that 46 percent of registered Republicans in Mississippi believed that interracial marriages should be illegal.[4] More recently, in 2019, the owners of an event hall in Mississippi refused to host a wedding for an interracial couple stating that "mixed-race" marriages go against their Christian beliefs.[5]

Beth and Terence did eventually get married. There are currently no laws prohibiting marriages across racial lines, and Beth and Terence soon found another judge to marry them. As recently as 1967, however, couples like them were prohibited from marrying in sixteen states and faced criminal punishment for attempting to do so. Forty-one states prohibited marriages between Whites and African Americans at some point in our nation's history.[6] Some states also prohibited marriages between Whites and persons of Asian descent and between Whites and

American Indians.[7] Proponents of these laws prohibiting interracial intimacy (known as "anti-miscegenation laws") claimed that such laws were necessary to protect the children of such unions who would be rejected by both White and non-White communities.[8] The true purpose of these laws, however, was the preservation of perceived White racial purity. As the California Supreme Court declared in *Perez v. Sharp*, the 1948 case striking down California's anti-miscegenation law, these laws were enacted by individuals who believed they had to protect "the Caucasian race from being contaminated by races whose members are by nature physically and mentally inferior to Caucasians."[9] *Perez v. Sharp* involved an African American man and a Mexican American woman who wished to marry but were prevented from doing so by California's anti-miscegenation law. Although anti-miscegenation laws typically applied only to marriages between Whites and non-Whites (and did not prohibit non-Whites from marrying members of other non-White groups), at the time, the law classified individuals of Mexican ancestry as White, due to a treaty between the United States and Mexico.[10]

After the California Supreme Court's decision in *Perez*, many other states repealed their own anti-miscegenation laws. Still, such laws remained in effect in almost one-third of states until 1967, when the U.S. Supreme Court, in a case aptly named *Loving v. Virginia*,[11] held that anti-miscegenation laws violated the constitutional right to marry and to equal treatment. After more than 300 years of laws prohibiting interracial marriage (and interracial sex in some states), individuals across the United States were finally free to marry without regard to race.

Interracial relationships are much more common today than when *Loving* was decided. In 1967, just 3 percent of marriages in the United States were interracial.[12] In 2019, 19 percent of new marriages were between persons of different races.[13] Social norms against interracial intimacy have also evolved. Our country has come a long way toward accepting interracial love, although holdouts such as Judge Bardwell and the Mississippi Republicans described above remain. In 1958, only 5 percent of Whites supported marriages between African Americans and Whites.[14] By 2021, however, 93 percent of Whites reported that they approve of marriages between Blacks and Whites.[15]

These shifts in intermarriage rates and social norms do not mean that race does not play a role in our intimate choices. Researchers have found that if couples across the United States were randomly matched without regard to race, 44 percent of all marriages would be interracial.[16] The actual intermarriage rate of 19 percent suggests that despite the absence of *direct legal* barriers to interracial intimacy, race continues to influence our intimate choices. But the extent to which race affects our intimate choices may depend on an individual's racial and gender identity.[17] More than one-third of U.S.-born Asian Americans and Latinos, as well as a majority of American Indians, marrying today marry out.[18] In contrast, only 18 percent of African Americans marry out.[19] The contrast is starker when one considers gender. U.S.-born Asian American women are three times as likely as African American women to marry someone of a different race.[20]

Social scientists have long believed that intermarriage is an indicator of social distance between groups—specifically, that lower rates of intermarriage indicate greater social distance.[21] If that is true, African Americans might be more isolated than other groups. The difference in intermarriage rates may be attributable, in part, to the legacy of slavery and anti-miscegenation laws.[22] African Americans are the only group that was enslaved because of race and the only group that was prohibited from marrying Whites under every state's anti-miscegenation law. Yet, as I will show in subsequent chapters, this history alone does not explain why more than half a century after the Supreme Court's decision in *Loving v. Virginia*, marriages between African Americans and Whites lag behind those of other groups.

Structural impediments such as residential segregation and limited access to educational and economic opportunities significantly reduce opportunities for interracial intimacy. After all, as Elizabeth Emens has noted, "One will not befriend, bed, or marry someone whom one never meets."[23] But groups facing similar hurdles have higher rates of interracial intimacy. Like many African Americans, many Latinos live in segregated neighborhoods, attend segregated schools, and have limited educational and employment opportunities. Moreover, Latinos and Asian Americans are more likely than African Americans to be immigrants, or the children of immigrants, and to speak a language other than English at home.[24] Yet, Latinos and Asian Americans are significantly more likely than African Americans to have a spouse or partner of a different race. Structural inequality may discourage interracial coupling, but it is not the only reason that some groups are less likely than others to have a romantic partner of different race.

During college, I, a Latina of Dominican descent, dated a fellow student named Ricky for several years. I brought Ricky, who was not Latino, home to meet my family on Thanksgiving. Ricky had been high school valedictorian, played college football, and planned to go to medical school. In the eyes of many parents, he was a "catch." My father, though, disapproved of the relationship, and hardly spoke to Ricky all afternoon—it was an uncomfortable Thanksgiving. During my three year relationship with Ricky, I endured negative comments from family members and friends about our racial and cultural differences and predictions about how physically unattractive our "mixed" children would be. In contrast, when my sisters brought home non-Latino romantic partners a few years later, my family welcomed them warmly. I wanted to think that my family had grown more open to interracial intimacy. But I suspect not. Ricky was African American. My sisters' romantic partners were White.

Each person's racialized romantic preferences and society's attitudes toward some interracial unions influence the individual's choice of a romantic partner in varying degrees. Americans today are more likely than ever before to express romantic interest in persons of a different race. Yet, an explicit and implicit racial hierarchy exists in the dating market. Most individuals, regardless of race, are willing to date Whites. In fact, many heterosexual Asian American and Latina women have stronger romantic preferences for White men, at least for long-term committed relationships, than for men of their own racial or ethnic background.[25] The majority of Whites, Asians, and Latinos, however, reject African Americans as long-term romantic partners. This racial hierarchy is gendered. Most heterosexual White men exclude African American women, but do not exclude Asian American or Latina women as potential romantic partners. Heterosexual White women, in turn, reject Asian American men at higher rates than they do Latino or African American men. A similar hierarchy exists in the gay male dating and marriage market, at least when seeking a long-term relationship.

Parents have similar preferences. My father's rejection of my African American boyfriend and his acceptance of my sisters' White boyfriends are not uncommon. Studies have repeatedly found that parents' approval or disapproval of a child's interracial relationship often depends on the race of the partner.[26] Parents are less likely to object when the child's love interest is White, regardless of the race of the parents and the adolescent or adult child. In fact, some Latino and Asian American parents express approval when they learn that their child's love interest is White.[27] These same parents discourage their children from dating African Americans.[28]

Romantic preferences for individuals of certain races might seem at odds with our country's expressed commitment to racial equality,[29] but some Americans do not view these positions as inconsistent. They make a distinction between racial preferences in the public realm such as the workplace, where race-based preferences are prohibited, as most Americans believe they should be, and the intimate sphere of the bedroom, where, in their view, individuals should be able to express and exercise their race-based preferences freely. Other individuals deny having any racial preferences when seeking a romantic partner. Yet, their behaviors on online dating platforms suggest otherwise. While some individuals may not be fully truthful about their race-based choices, others have *implicit* preferences of which they are not consciously aware. When asked to explain their reasons for rejecting members of particular racial groups, individuals often reject any suggestion that race may have influenced their choices. They explain that they are simply not attracted to, or have little in common with, individuals of certain races. Although studies suggest that race has little or no effect on the likelihood that two people will be compatible,[30] some individuals believe that members of certain racial groups are unlikely to possess the traits they seek in a romantic partner. These beliefs are sometimes based on racial stereotypes.

The law treats romantic preferences as private, free of legal influence, and outside the realm of law. Indeed, many of us assume that the law plays no role in matters of the heart and family formation generally. The truth, however, is that the law encourages certain family forms, such as marriage and marital childbearing, and discourages others, such as cohabitation and nonmarital childbearing. The law shapes parenting norms and gender roles in intimate relationships, and it even influences whether couples decide to divorce and the type of child custody arrangement they agree on.[31]

While the law no longer prohibits interracial intimacy, it continues to influence whom we find to be desirable and suitable long-term intimate partners.³² In this book, I argue that the law influences our choices of long-term intimate partners in ways that perpetuate racial hierarchy and societal inequality. The law limits, on the basis of race, individuals' prospects for committed relationships, and this, in turn, constrains opportunities for economic and social mobility. Through slavery and through anti-miscegenation and segregation laws, the law facilitated the residential, economic, and social distance between groups that historically shaped and continues to shape romantic preferences today. The law has continued to influence intimate choices by supporting the creation of public spaces with well-defined racial boundaries. As a result of legally sanctioned residential segregation and exclusionary zoning practices, many public spaces across America have a distinct exclusionary racial identity. As police officers have freely admitted, they would stop "four or five Black guys . . . in a white neighborhood" because "they are not supposed to be there."³³ By facilitating the creation of racialized spaces, the law limits opportunities for interracial interaction and intimacy.

The law further shapes preferences and reinforces racial hierarchy in romantic choices by guarding an artificial line between public (unlawful) and private (lawful) discrimination. From exceptions to housing and employment discrimination laws to the absence of laws prohibiting what Sonu Bedi refers to as "sexual racism" in online dating platforms,³⁴ the law signals that racial preferences are legitimate in intimate spaces. A homeowner who occupies one unit in a three-family home and rents out the other two units can legally reject a potential tenant on the basis of race. A parent seeking a nanny for their child can refuse to hire an applicant on the basis of race. Dating platforms provide race filters that allow members of minority groups to find each other easily, but these filters also allow Whites to exclude entire racial groups from consideration as potential partners. By permitting these practices, the law facilitates discrimination against members of groups that the law itself historically treated as inferior and subjected to state-sanctioned discrimination.

The law's influence over individuals' intimate choices contributes to racial inequality in our society. Whether one partners and *whom* one partners with are among the most important decisions an individual will ever make. Social scientists and government researchers have identified numerous benefits of marriage, including increased happiness, health, wealth, and better outcomes for children.³⁵ While these benefits may be the result of selection bias—wealthier, happier, and healthier people may be more likely to partner in the first place—romantic preferences, as influenced by law, may limit racial minorities' prospects for marriage or marriage-like commitments and their related benefits.

The law's influence over individuals' intimate choices also impacts future generations. As a result of economic and social inequality, children who have at least one White parent tend to have greater access to safe neighborhoods, high-quality schools, economic resources, intergenerational transfers of wealth, and the intangible opportunities that result therefrom, than the children of racial minorities. Racial preferences may limit not only the pool of intimate partners available to racial minorities but also the resources they may be able to provide to their children. Given the large income and wealth disparities between groups, a racial minority who has the opportunity to partner with a person who is higher on the racial hierarchy may be better able to provide their children with a home in a safe neighborhood, a quality education, and a safety net than a person who is excluded as a potential partner because of their race.

Racial preferences may also provide some mixed-race children with access to what sociologist Eduardo Bonilla-Silva has termed "honorary white" status.[36] While individuals may not consciously choose their partners based on the potential privileges they may confer on their offspring, the desire to provide one's children with as many advantages as possible, including shielding them from racial discrimination, might unconsciously strengthen individuals' attraction to White or honorary White partners. For some, however, these are conscious choices. Upwardly mobile Latino parents encourage their adult children to find a White or light-complexioned partner so that they can "improve the race,"[37] and some racial minorities in intimate relationships with Whites seek to repudiate negative stereotypes about their group through these relationships.[38] Some identify their mixed-race children as White only.[39]

To be clear, I am not suggesting that anyone should have access to interracial relationships as a means to climb the racial and socioeconomic ladder. No one has a right to "marry up," and, in my view, such considerations pervert the true essence of committed relationships—love, companionship, and emotional support. My point so far is descriptive: intimacy patterns in the United States reinforce racial hierarchy and inequality.

This book shows that our romantic desires and choices of long-term intimate partners are not purely "private" and unaffected by law. By limiting opportunities for interracial interactions and signaling that race is a legitimate consideration in our intimate relationships, the law influences our attraction and choices. A society committed to racial and social justice should be troubled by the direction of this influence and, in particular, by the gendered racial hierarchy, the economic, social, and political implications of that hierarchy, and our choices within it.

* * *

Chapter 1 explores the role that race, color, gender, education, income, and place of birth (whether a person was born in the United States or immigrated) play in partnering patterns. Relying on studies of online and offline dating preferences, this chapter demonstrates that romantic preferences follow a gendered racial hierarchy—Whites at the top; African Americans at the bottom; and (depending on skin tone) Asian Americans and Latinos in the middle. It further shows that these preferences are influenced by racial and gender stereotypes reflected in social and cultural norms.

Chapter 2 then turns to the law and its role in shaping these preferences. Part of the law's role is based in history—specifically slavery, antimiscegenation laws, and legally sanctioned segregation. This chapter draws that history into the present to help us understand the continuing influence of the law in building and reinforcing racial hierarchy in our intimate and partnering preferences. It traces how the law shaped societal assumptions about racial and ethnic groups and how these assumptions signaled, and continue to signal even today, that members of these groups are not suitable long-term partners.

Chapter 3 shows that the law currently permits racial discrimination in multiple areas of our lives, including housing, domestic employment, adoption, and dating platforms. The professed reason for permitting racial discrimination in these contexts is the constitutional freedom of association: we are allowed to discriminate in our "intimate" decisions. Those freedoms, however, are not unlimited. This chapter examines how the law has attempted to balance associational freedoms against the state's interest in equality in the housing, domestic employment, and adoption contexts and argues that the reasons for regulating discrimination in those settings apply to sexual racism on dating platforms.

Chapter 4 uncovers structural barriers to interracial intimacy. Despite numerous laws prohibiting discrimination in education, housing, and employment, the law continues to shape racialized romantic preferences by facilitating segregation in virtually every sector of our lives. Segregated neighborhoods and schools are ubiquitous as a result of legally sanctioned practices—such as redlining, racial steering, and racially restrictive covenants—in effect throughout most of the twentieth century.[40] Our current exclusionary zoning laws arguably facilitate segregation as effectively as the explicitly discriminatory policies of the past. Moreover, while workplaces are often more integrated than other institutions, racial stratification is common. A disproportionately small number of racial minorities occupy leadership positions, and the majority are clustered in lower paying jobs and sectors.[41] These structural barriers limit opportunities for individuals of different races to interact as equals and reinforce the perception that some groups are not suitable long-term partners.

Chapter 5 draws out why we should be troubled by the law's influence on our romantic preferences. First, it explores the psychic harm inflicted by racial hierarchy in the intimate sphere. In addition to the emotional harm experienced by individuals when they are rejected as intimate partners because of their race, racial preferences limit the opportunities of members of less preferred groups to find love and enter long-term romantic relationships—a social good that scholars have identified as "the single most important source of life satisfaction."[42] While scholars have argued that the opportunity for intimacy is a matter of social justice and consequently we ought to care about how this opportunity is distributed,[43] this chapter also examines the tangible harms caused by the racial hierarchy. Marriage confers substantial legal, economic, and social benefits, and sexual racism may limit an individual's opportunity to find a partner and reap these benefits. To illustrate, the pool of "marriageable" African American men is smaller than the number of African American women seeking male long-term partners. While some African American women may prefer to remain single rather than partner with a person of different race, studies show that others would consider partners of other races.[44] But that is not an option if individuals of other races engage in what Russell Robinson calls "romantic segregation" and exclude them as romantic partners.[45] Racial preferences may influence not only whom one partners with but whether one has the opportunity to partner at all. Again, I am not suggesting that romantic partnerships should be used as a mechanism for racial and economic equality; rather, this chapter demonstrates that not everyone has equal access to the benefits of committed relationships and that this lack of access disproportionately impacts certain racial groups.

In chapter 6, I propose several reforms that could reduce the pernicious effects of the law's influence on interracial intimacy. These include changes to dating platforms, as well as to housing, education, and transportation policies. While these proposals may further integration and improve the economic opportunities and status of racial minorities, I hope they will also start a conversation about the role of intimacy in the reproduction of inequality among scholars and policymakers in what might seem to be unrelated fields, such as information and technology law, property law, education law, and transportation law.

When I have discussed the ideas in this book with friends and colleagues, a few have asked why the law should care whether racial preferences influence our choices of intimate partners. After all, we discriminate on the basis of sex/gender, gender identity, age, religion, height, weight, education, income, class, and physical ability (discrimination against individuals with disabilities is common) when seeking an intimate partner. One could argue that discrimination of any type is objectionable—especially when seeking a romantic partner. Shouldn't individuals connect on a cosmic level in which love and attraction transcend race and other characteristics? In theory, yes. But "the heart wants what it wants,"[46] even if those desires are shaped by sociolegal influences. Thus, the law should attempt to influence romantic preferences *only* when it played a direct role in creating those preferences *and* those preferences are harmful to individuals and communities.[47] The law *directly* shaped preferences for partners of certain races through anti-miscegenation laws, segregation, and structural barriers to interracial intimacy, and those preferences contributed to and continue to perpetuate racial and social inequality. Therefore, the law should address the inequities stemming from its actions.

As a country, we are committed to racial equality. Consequently, the law should intervene when groups are disadvantaged by racial preferences that the law helped create. More importantly, the law should be concerned with racial hierarchy. In a world without racial hierarchy, a preference for light- or dark-complexioned individuals might be as meaningless as a preference for blue or green eyes. In the absence of racial hierarchy, our racial preferences might not have any social, economic, or political consequences. But racial preferences (or rather, the exclusion of certain individuals on the basis of race) do result in significant long-term consequences for groups at the bottom of the hierarchy. The law should further be concerned with racial hierarchy in the dating market because, as several scholars have observed, the individuals we prefer in the boardroom might resemble those we prefer in the bedroom.[48]

Social scientists have shown that intermarriage—long considered the ultimate indicator of assimilation and acceptance by the dominant group in society—was critical to the integration of European immigrants such as Italians and Irish who were once considered not White.[49] While racial minorities may not follow the same assimilation patterns as European ethnic groups, we learn a lot about equality in our society by studying interracial dating and partnering patterns and the factors that drive them.

Marriage and marriage-like relationships (long-term committed relationships of mutual interdependence) are a primary focus of this book. While some Americans, especially racial minorities and low-income individuals, are increasingly postponing or foregoing marriage,[50] many are entering marriage-like relationships. Moreover, despite the decreasing incidence of marriage, marriage is associated with substantial benefits that are currently not available through any other institution in the United States. Marriage will likely continue to be a prerequisite for a panoply of legal benefits, at least for the foreseeable future. My goal is to show how racial hierarchy limits access to marriage and its benefits, even as I question the wisdom and fairness of making legal benefits contingent on marriage.

This book is an attempt to start a conversation about the role of our racial preferences in one of the most intimate and important decisions of our lives. Although our intimate preferences may reinforce racial hierarchy and inequality in society, this book concludes that the law should stop short of encouraging interracial intimacies or "nudging" individuals to pursue partners of a different racial background.[51] First, while preferences for White partners may stigmatize racial minorities and reinforce racial hierarchy (due to our history of discrimination), racial minorities' same-race preferences do not have the same effect. These preferences are often based on a desire for a partner who shares a similar culture, language, or immigrant experience or on a desire to guard against potential fetishization by daters of a different race. Of course, Whites' same-race preferences do not always stigmatize racial minorities or perpetuate racial hierarchy. An Italian American who expresses a preference for a partner who shares their heritage, language, and culture is quite different from a White individual who will only date Whites. A preference for a shared culture and language is not the same as a categorical racial preference or exclusion on the basis of race. The former is reflected in dating platforms such as "JDate"[52] or "Latino People Meet"[53] that help individuals meet partners of similar cultural and religious backgrounds, while the latter is reflected in the now defunct dating platform "Where White People Meet,"[54] which is reminiscent of the Whites-only social clubs of the not-so-distant past.[55]

Second, there is something deeply unsettling about heavy-handed government attempts to influence our intimate choices. Our history of anti-miscegenation laws has shown us how much harm the law can do. But just as importantly, we should be free to choose whom we love and bring into our family with as little government interference as possible. Government efforts to encourage interracial intimacy are likely to backfire and sully relationships before they begin. No one wants to think that their partner chose them because the government provided incentives or nudged them to make that choice.

What the law can and should do is help us recognize how external influences and structural barriers shape our intimate preferences. This is the first step toward helping to ensure that the freedom to choose an intimate partner is not hindered by racial preferences that the law created or facilitated. We may not be able to completely eliminate the influence of law in the intimate sphere, but the changes I propose in this book might just help us recognize the law's influence so that we can seek love and intimacy without regard to race, if we so choose.

This book also challenges assumptions that racial bias and discrimination are remnants of the past. The hierarchy in the dating market demonstrates that racial biases persist. It also reveals that legal efforts to eradicate racial discrimination have not gone far enough. Neighborhoods remain racially segregated, and the structural design of public spaces limits opportunities for interactions between individuals of different backgrounds. Laws and the actions of government actors shape social perceptions, behaviors, and norms. The law's work for racial equality is far from complete.

1

A Gendered Racial Hierarchy in the Intimate Market

It was Thanksgiving 2015. One of my sisters did what I had done twenty-five years earlier. She brought her new boyfriend, Oliver (not his real name), who is African American, home to meet our parents. This time, however, my parents were much more welcoming. My father made conversation and expressed interest in Oliver's work. Maybe my father had become more accepting. Maybe he just wanted his daughters to find partners, regardless of race, who would love and respect them.

If my father has become more open-minded, he is not alone. Americans' acceptance of interracial intimacy has shifted dramatically in just one generation. In 1992, fewer than half (48 percent) of all Americans approved of marriages between African Americans and Whites.[1] By 2021, 94 percent approved of such marriages. Yet, approval is not action. Most Americans date, cohabit with, and marry individuals of their same race,[2] and when seeking an intimate partner, many individuals prefer someone of their same race, either consciously or unconsciously.[3] In fact, persons who approve of interracial relationships are not always willing to cross the color line themselves,[4] and those who are open to dating a person of a different race often have clear preferences for certain races to the exclusion of others.

The majority of Americans claims not to have any racial biases. Yet, a 2021 study found that 46 percent of all Americans believe there is "a lot" of discrimination against African Americans.[5] Thirty percent and 27 percent reported there is "a lot" of discrimination against Latinos and persons of Asian descent, respectively. Notably, African Americans, Latinos, and Asian Americans are significantly more likely than Whites to say that there is a lot of discrimination against racial minorities. The wealth of data discussed in this chapter supports this perception and helps explain how racialized and gendered notions of beauty, comfort, and status, along with familial and societal norms, influence our romantic preferences. While I am concerned primarily with the economic and social consequences of a gendered racial hierarchy in *long-term* relationships, almost all long-term romantic relationships in the United States begin with dating. Studies of dating patterns tell us a lot about our preferences, so I begin this chapter by examining the traits date-seekers want and then explore the reasons for these preferences. But first, I define a few terms and note some caveats.

There are many terms used to describe the Latino population, including "Hispanic," "Latino/a," "Latinx," "Latine," "Latin@." While many scholars reject the term "Hispanic" because it was created by the U.S. Census and does not reflect the population's roots in Latin America,[6] the terms "Latino" and "Latina" are gendered and may render nonbinary individuals invisible. Consequently, scholars and younger generations increasingly use the gender-neutral "Latinx." Most Latinos, however, prefer "Hispanic" or "Latino," and only 5 percent prefer Latinx.[7] This book uses "Latino" to include male, female, and nonbinary individuals because it reflects our multiracial Latin American origins and is the term preferred by almost 40 percent of Latinos. However, when referring to Latina women only, I use "Latina" or "Latinas."

Social scientists use "interracial" to describe marriages between different racial groups such as African Americans, Asian Americans, American Indians, and Whites of non-Hispanic/non-Latino origin, and "interethnic" to describe marriages between Latinos and non-Latinos. One should of course ask why we track rates of intimacy between Latinos and non-Latinos even though we do not engage in similar inquiries for other ethnic groups, such as Italian Americans or Irish Americans. In other words, are Latinos a racial or an ethnic group?

Some Latinos are light-complexioned and appear phenotypically White or European. Others are dark-complexioned and appear phenotypically Black. Some Latinos are descendants of the Indigenous people of the Americas (including North, Central, and South America), and many trace their ancestry to two or more races, most commonly Caucasian and Black, Caucasian and Indigenous, Black and Indigenous, or a combination of all three.[8] While the U.S. Census defines "Hispanic" or "Latino/a" as an ethnic category rather than a racial category,[9] when examining racial preferences in the dating and marriage market, I agree with scholars who juxtapose Latino identity "with Asian American, black, and white as a distinct racial group" for several reasons.[10] First, a significant percentage of Latinos identify their race as Latino/Hispanic and reject the racial categories in the U.S. Census—White/Caucasian, Black/African American, Asian American, Pacific Islander, or American Indian.[11] Admittedly, some Latinos reject these categories because they refuse to identify as Black even though based on their ancestry and/or phenotype they are considered Black under U.S. notions of race.[12] In other words, some Latinos reject the U.S. Census categories because they seek to distance themselves from blackness. These reasons notwithstanding, many Latinos genuinely believe that their race is Latino.

Second, the Latino population is increasingly compared with different *racial* groups by researchers and policymakers when studying educational, wealth, housing, employment, marriage, health, and fertility patterns, among other issues.[13] This is not the case for other ethnic groups such as Italian Americans or Irish Americans, who are classified as White. Third, Latinos have been, and continue to be, racialized as non-White.[14] Even though Mexican Americans, the largest Latino group in the United States, were for decades *legally* categorized as White,[15] they have never been accepted as *socially* White. During the Jim Crow era, Mexican Americans were denied access to schools attended by White children and were subjected to racially motivated violence, including lynching.[16] As the documentary *Bad Hombres: From Colonization to Criminalization* illustrates, even today, Latinos are targets of racial slurs and racially motivated discrimination and violence.[17]

Finally, Latinos and Asian Americans increasingly occupy the *racial* middle between African Americans and Whites.[18] Consequently, when discussing interracial intimacy, this book treats Latinos as a racial group similar to Asian Americans, African Americans, American Indians, and Whites. The term "interracial" will include relationships between a Latino partner and a non-Latino partner regardless of race, skin tone, or phenotype.

Treating Latinos as a racial group illustrates the illusion of race. There is no such thing as biological race—there are no genetic differences between African Americans and Caucasians, for example. Race is socially and legally constructed.[19] Yet, race, as socially and legally constructed, affects access to educational and employment opportunities, income, wealth, and the quality of medical care we receive.[20] It also influences whom we desire as intimate partners and who desires us. The next section shows how.

Who Dates and Marries Out?

Dating and Cohabitation

We do not actually know how many people have dated interracially. What constitutes "dating"? Is one date sufficient? Two, three? Must two people go out for one month? Three months? College students' romantic relationships increasingly start out as hookups,[21] not dates. Do hook-ups count? Despite these open questions, about half (48 percent) of Americans who participated in a Gallup poll in 2005 reported that they had dated a person of a different race.[22] Younger generations and racial minorities were even more likely to have dated interracially, and the rate of interracial dating is undoubtedly even higher today.[23] Yet, even among 18–29-year-olds, we find evidence of social distance and racial hierarchy. White college students are more likely to have dated Asian Americans and Latinos than to have dated African Americans. African American college students are similarly less likely than other racial or ethnic minorities to date or hook up with persons of other races.[24]

It turns out that not all individuals who are willing to date interracially are willing to marry interracially.[25] Americans are about twice as likely to cohabit with a person of a different race than to marry across race,[26] possibly because interracial couples enjoy less social support than same-race couples.[27] Adolescents in interracial relationships, for example, are less likely to meet each other's parents or tell their parents or friends about the relationship,[28] but they are also more likely than teens in same-race relationships to report experiencing social disapproval.

Marriage

RACE, GENDER, AND FOREIGN-BORN STATUS

Interracial marriage patterns vary widely by race, gender, and whether a person was born in the United States. The majority of American Indians marry out, primarily with Whites.[29] While rates of intermarriage vary for different Asian American and Latino groups,[30] 46 percent and 39 percent of U.S.-born Asian Americans and Latinos, respectively, and 18 percent of African Americans who married in 2015, married out.[31] Multiracial individuals who are part White are much more likely than their monoracial co-ethnics to have a White partner, but here, too, marriage patterns vary by racial background.[32] The majority of Asian/White and about half of Latino/White multiracial individuals have a White spouse or cohabiting partner.[33] In contrast, the majority of African American/ White multiracial individuals partner with African Americans.

The marriage patterns of some minority groups are also influenced by gender. U.S.-born Asian American women are almost *five times* as likely as African American women to intermarry, and African American men are twice as likely as African American women to marry out.[34] The opposite is true for Asian American men, who are half as likely as their female counterparts to intermarry.[35] American Indian men are also less likely than American Indian women to marry out.[36]

Intermarriage is considered the ultimate indicator of assimilation.[37] Immigrants, especially racial minorities who do not speak English and are not familiar with American culture, are more likely to reside near their co-ethnics and are less likely to have meaningful interactions with other groups. Not surprisingly, they are less likely than their U.S.-born counterparts to intermarry. U.S.-born Latinos, for example, are two and a half times as likely as Latino immigrants to marry out.[38]

EDUCATIONAL ATTAINMENT AND INCOME

Marriage patterns are influenced by education. Racial minorities who intermarry with Whites are more likely to have a college degree than their counterparts who marry in.[39] They are also more likely to have a college-educated spouse. College-educated second-generation (the U.S.-born children of immigrants) Latinos are almost three times as likely to marry out as their counterparts who have only a high school degree (43 percent versus 16 percent).[40]

The majority of recently married couples (interracial or same-race) share similar levels of formal education. But when African Americans and Latinos marry a White partner whose level of education differs from theirs, the White spouse tends to be the less-educated partner.[41] Research suggests that less-educated Whites trade their higher *racial status* for non-White partners with higher educational and economic status, while non-White individuals with higher education and income trade their *class status* for White spouses with higher racial status.[42]

Given the higher levels of educational attainment of racial minorities who intermarry with Whites, it is not surprising that these couples tend to enjoy substantially higher combined incomes. In 2010, for example, the median family income of Latinos who married other Latinos was 40 percent lower than that of Latinos who married Whites.[43] Asian Americans who intermarried with Whites earned higher combined incomes than all other couples—same-race or interracial.[44] There are significant income differences, however, based on the gender of the non-White spouse. Marriages between White men and African American or Latina women tend to have higher combined earnings than marriages between White men and White women.[45] White women who marry Asian American men also have higher combined earnings than White women who marry in. These patterns suggest that Whites who marry out often partner with persons with high incomes. However, because African American and Latino men earn significantly lower incomes than White men, White women who marry African American or Latino men have lower combined earnings than those who marry in.

SKIN TONE

Marriage patterns also vary by skin tone. Lighter-complexioned racial minorities are more likely than their darker counterparts to intermarry with Whites. For example, U.S.-born Latinos who identified as White on the U.S. Census were significantly more likely than darker Latinos to be married to non-Latino Whites.[46] Latinos with Indigenous ancestry were also more likely than Latinos with Black ancestors to be married to non-Latino Whites. Skin tone plays a similar role in the intermarriage patterns of U.S.-born Asian Americans. Intermarriage rates with Whites are lowest for African Americans, slightly higher for darker-complexioned Latinos, higher for lighter-complexioned Asian Americans, and highest for the lightest-complexioned Latinos.[47] Darker-complexioned individuals are more likely than their lighter—complexioned counterparts to marry Whites who are less educated than themselves.[48] This suggests that many Whites will only marry darker-complexioned racial minorities if they are marrying up—if the partner is of a higher class status than they.

Same-Sex Couples

Same-sex couples are more likely than different-sex couples to be interracial.[49] A study of 2019 U.S. Census data found that 28 percent of men in a same-sex marriage had a partner of a different race as compared to 16 percent of men in a different-sex marriage. Twenty percent of women in a same-sex marriage had a partner of a different race as compared to 16 percent of women in a different-sex marriage.[50] Yet, the same racial patterns observed in different-sex relationships are evident in same-sex pairings. Asian Americans and Latinos in same-sex relationships are significantly more likely than African Americans to have a partner of a different race or ethnicity. Sixty-seven percent of Asian Americans and Pacific Islanders and 55 percent of Latinos as compared to 33 percent of African Americans in same-sex relationships have a White partner.[51]

What Drives Interracial Intimacy Patterns?

Dating and marriage outcomes are the result of both preferences and opportunities. Thus, while rates of interracial intimacy can shed light on race relations and social distance between different racial groups, they cannot accurately measure individuals' racial preferences. After all, a Latina may find Asian American men particularly desirable, but if there are few Asian American men in her school, workplace, or social network, she may have to consider a non-Asian partner. Even if she meets an Asian American man to whom she is attracted, coupling requires mutual attraction: he has to like her, too. Dating and marriage outcomes do not explain whether opportunity, racial preferences (and if so, whose preferences), or both, are driving the different rates of interracial coupling. Moreover, as scholars have noted, "Racial preferences may be shaped by the opportunity context."[52] When an individual has limited opportunities for contact with members of particular racial groups, attraction or aversion to members of such groups may be shaped by stereotypes about those groups and by the media's and policymakers' portrayal of their members.[53]

A number of studies has attempted to address the limitations of marriage and dating outcomes by directly examining the racial preferences of individuals seeking a romantic partner. Some studies have focused on *stated* preferences—what individuals say they want in a partner.[54] These studies generally ask date-seekers to identify the traits they look for in a romantic partner, or they examine the traits individuals have identified in a dating profile. Not surprisingly, individuals may not be completely truthful when listing the traits they seek in a partner, because they fear they will be judged as superficial, elitist, or racist. We tend to answer questions in ways that will portray us favorably, but even when we are completely honest, our stated preferences may not reflect our *true* preferences. Evolutionary psychologists have found that we are sometimes not attracted to individuals who have the traits that we think we want and are instead attracted to individuals who lack those traits.[55] In other words, we do not always know what we want in a partner.

To address the limitations of stated preferences, some studies have examined the *revealed* preferences of online date-seekers by observing how they respond when contacted by daters with certain traits.[56] The majority of individuals seeking romantic partners use the internet to meet potential partners.[57] Online dating platforms allow researchers to observe date-seekers' search and response patterns without their knowledge, thereby eliminating concerns that date-seekers will alter their behavior to present themselves in a more flattering light to the researchers. Dating platforms might also provide a more accurate measure of actual preferences since date-seekers are not limited by the pool of potential partners in their daily environment. Online date-seekers might reveal preferences for or against groups with whom they do not usually come into contact in their neighborhood, school, or workplace.

What Makes Two People Click?

Studies in various fields, including economics, sociology, and psychology, demonstrate that couples in committed relationships do not randomly end up together but are the result of assortative mating—the tendency of people to date and marry individuals like themselves.[58] In the United States, we generally partner with people who are similar to us in terms of education, income, socioeconomic status, race, and physical traits such as attractiveness, height, and weight.[59] (Yes, it's true: attractive people tend to end up together.) Interestingly, people engage in assortative mating even when they are not seeking a long-term relationship. One explanation is that we spend a lot of time in the company of those with similar levels of education at school or at work. Our neighbors and individuals in our social circles also tend to be of the same race and similar socioeconomic status. However, this explanation is incomplete. Online dating studies found that even when the pool of potential mates is not limited by whom we see at school, work, or in our neighborhood, we nonetheless prefer to date our equals or as one aptly titled article noted, "In the End, People May Really Just Want to Date Themselves."[60]

No formula can guarantee that two people will be attracted to each other, but there is wide agreement on the traits that are desirable in an intimate partner. One study examined the search behaviors of almost 6,500 heterosexual online daters and found, not surprisingly, that people prefer attractive partners with high incomes.[61] The strength of these preferences varies by gender, however. Men's preferences for physically attractive partners were stronger than women's, and women's preferences for partners with high incomes were stronger than men's. Older studies have similarly found that heterosexual men value a woman's physical appearance over her intelligence and ambition but that heterosexual women (at least when seeking a partner for a long-term relationship) care more about a man's earning potential, intelligence, and social status.[62]

Racial Preferences

It is no longer socially acceptable to express racial preferences in most contexts.[63] It is also illegal to act upon such preferences in settings such as education, employment, and housing. In fact, 84 percent of online daters stated they would not date someone "who has vocalized a strong negative bias toward a certain race of people."[64] Yet, as shown below, numerous studies reveal that racial preferences play a significant role in the intimate market. Many Americans have same-race preferences, but others are willing (or prefer) to date someone of a different race. That interest in dating interracially does not extend to all races, however. Our romantic preferences reveal a racialized and gendered hierarchy that, in many ways, reflects and reproduces racial disparities in education, employment, income, wealth, and housing.

For example, a study of the search behaviors of almost 6,500 heterosexual online daters found that more than half (54 percent) of the women expressed no racial preferences in their profiles. Their *revealed* preferences, however—whom they contacted and whom they responded to when contacted—showed otherwise. The women with no *stated* racial preferences *revealed* preferences equally as strong as the 41 percent of women who had actually expressed a preference.[65]

Online dating studies further reveal a *hierarchy* of preferences. In one study, more than 90 percent of straight White men with a stated racial preference excluded African American women, while only half excluded Asian American women and Latinas.[66] Other studies have found a similar racial hierarchy.[67] This hierarchy is also reflected in straight White men's response rates when contacted by female online date-seekers. White men are most likely to respond to messages from White women and from multiracial Asian American and Latina women who are part White.[68]

White women's preferences also reveal a racial hierarchy. Almost 75 percent of straight White women in one online dating study expressed racial preferences, and a majority of those (64 percent) preferred to date White men only.[69] Although most White women with stated racial preferences expressly excluded all non-White men, they were more willing to date Latino men than to date African American or Asian American men.

Data from millions of online daters on Match (the most popular dating site in the United States for the last twenty years), OkCupid, and Date Hookup confirm this racial hierarchy. Straight White women on these sites rated Asian American and African American men as significantly less attractive than White men.[70] This hierarchy is also reflected in White women's response rates when contacted by online date-seekers. White women respond mainly to White men and tend to ignore messages from men of other races with one exception—multiracial men who are part White.[71] One study found that while more than 90 percent of White women rejected Asian American men as potential dates, they responded to messages from multiracial Asian American/White men at similar rates as they did to messages from monoracial White men.[72] They also responded to Latino/White men and African American/White men at higher rates than to their monoracial counterparts.

Online date-seekers have many preferences, including gender, age, race, body type, height, weight, education, income, and religion. But race ranks particularly high on their preferences. Although 59 percent of straight White men in one study stated a racial preference, only 23 percent expressed a religious preference.[73] For these men, a woman's race was more important than her education, religion, employment, marital status, or how much she smoked or drank. Straight White date-seekers on the online dating site OkCupid revealed similarly strong preferences for Whites even when the system's algorithm determined that their best "match," based on their responses to approximately 300 questions about their beliefs, needs, wants, and the activities they enjoy, was a person of a different race.[74]

As we saw above, college-educated individuals are more likely than their less-educated counterparts to be married to a person of a different race or ethnicity. One might assume that college-educated Americans have weaker racial preferences, but studies do not support this conclusion. The vast majority of White women, regardless of their level of education or income, have strong preferences for White men,[75] and studies have found that college-educated White men and women are *more* likely than Whites with only a high school education to exclude African Americans as romantic partners.[76] Although date-seekers with college degrees prefer college-educated partners, racial preferences trump educational preferences.[77] College-educated White date-seekers are more likely to contact and respond to messages from Whites *without* a college degree than to messages from African Americans *with* a college degree. White men without a college degree received more messages than college-educated African American and Asian American men. College-educated African American women received fewer messages than women of other races with lower levels of educational attainment.

Asian Americans and Latinos are more willing than Whites to date interracially;[78] yet their preferences tend to reflect the same racial hierarchy as Whites'. Seventy percent of straight Asian American and Latina women in one online dating study expressed a racial preference and overwhelmingly excluded minority men other than their co-ethnics.[79] The vast majority, however, was willing to date White men. Forty percent of straight Asian American women in one study refused to date Asian American men, but only 11 percent excluded White men.[80] Asian American and Latina women are also more likely to respond to emails from White men and men who are part White (Asian American/White men and Latino/White men) than to messages from Asian, Latino, or African American men.[81] Surveys of college students' dating preferences have also found that many Latinos and Asian Americans prefer Whites to members of their own group.[82]

The preferences of straight Asian American and Latino men reflect a racial hierarchy as well. One online dating study found that over 60 percent of Asian American and Latino men who expressed a racial preference stated that they would date White women.[83] Approximately 50 percent of Asian American men were willing to date Latinas, and similar numbers of Latino men were willing to date Asian American women. Fewer than 20 percent, however, were willing to date African American women.

The *stated* preferences of African American men and women do not follow the same pattern as other group's preferences. African Americans express stronger same-race preferences than Asian Americans and Latinos, and they are at least three times as likely as Asian Americans and Latinos to expressly refuse to date individuals of other ethnicities.[84] In addition, while the majority of heterosexual Asian Americans, Latinos, and Whites are willing to date Whites, the majority of heterosexual African American men and women in one online dating study expressly *excluded* Whites.[85]

There are some similarities, however, between African Americans' preferences and those of other groups. Like White and Latina women, African American women exclude Asian American men at higher rates than men of other races.[86] In addition, the *revealed* preferences of straight African American men and women suggest that they may be more willing, consciously or unconsciously, to date Whites than they admit. One study found that African Americans were ten times more likely to contact Whites than Whites were to contact them,[87] and several studies have found that African Americans are *more* likely to respond to messages from Whites and from multiracial African American/White individuals than to messages from African Americans.[88]

While White, Asian American, and Latina female online date-seekers receive messages from men of all races, African American women rarely receive messages from men who are not African American.[89] They also receive fewer messages overall, which might make it easier to respond to most messages.[90] Thus, it is also possible that African American women reply to messages from White men because it is polite and not because they are interested in each of the men to whom they reply. None of these theories, however, explains why African American women responded most often to White and multiracial African American/White men. Is it possible that African American women are more willing to date White men than they expressly indicate, but that they expressly exclude White men because they anticipate that White men will reject them, as the studies discussed above suggest?

Preferences of Gay Men and Women

Although same-sex couples are more likely than different-sex couples to be interracial, gay White men have strong preferences for White partners.[91] One study of male online date-seekers found that gay White men were three times more likely than straight White men to express a racial preference and five times more likely to express a preference for a White partner.[92] Another study found that gay White men were most likely to initiate contact with and respond to messages from other White men.[93] White lesbians, in contrast, tend to respond to messages from women of all races at roughly similar rates.[94]

Although gay White men have stronger same-race preferences than either straight White men or White lesbians, they are more likely than their heterosexual or lesbian counterparts to cohabit with a partner of a different race.[95] This inconsistency might be explained by the limited pool of gay White men: there simply are not enough gay White men for all the men (of all races) who prefer White men. Nonetheless, studies show that the racial hierarchy that exists in the heterosexual dating market is reproduced in the gay male dating market—Asian American and African American men are at the bottom of the hierarchy. Gay men of all races strongly prefer Whites and lighter-complexioned Latinos to Asian American or African American partners.[96] One-third of gay Asian American men in one study stated they would date only Whites, and only 8 percent were willing to date Asian American men.[97] Another study found that gay Asian American men preferred White men over all other races, including Asian Americans.[98] Gay men saw White men as the standard of attractiveness against which they would be judged.[99] Light-complexioned gay Latino men attempted to use these racial preferences to their advantage by highlighting their "White" appearance, such as light complexion and eyes, and their ability to "pass for White" in their dating profiles.[100]

Asian American men are often stereotyped as submissive and effeminate,[101] while African American men are stereotyped as hypermasculine and potentially dangerous.[102] Neither characterization leads to many positive responses from potential dates. Russell Robinson's study of the "hooking-up" preferences of gay men in several cities found that gay men contacted Asian American men only when their profiles indicated that they would play the sex role of a "bottom," a role that reflects and reinforces stereotypes about Asian American men as submissive.[103] Robinson further found that gay men contacted African American men only when their profiles indicated they would play the sex role of a "top," a role that reinforces stereotypes of Black men as hypermasculinized and hypersexual objects. Other studies found similar results.[104]

A Word about the Data

Most of the studies discussed above examined the preferences of online date-seekers and might not reflect the preferences of individuals who search for romantic partners offline. Americans over the age of 65 and the very poor are less likely to join online dating platforms, so their preferences might not be reflected in these studies.[105] Individuals who have not been on the dating market since the mid-1990s (when online dating sites were created) might also have different preferences.

That said, online dating studies have many advantages over other sources of data. When Pew or Gallup conduct a study, the organization is able to poll only small percentages of the population. When researchers at academic institutions conduct studies, they often use college students as subjects. Consequently, their data and conclusions are based on the needs, preferences, and experiences of college students and small percentages of the population. In contrast, the pool of online daters is exponentially greater. The co-founder of OkCupid examined the behaviors of more than one *million* online daters on three different dating platforms—a data set thousands of times larger than a typical one.[106] Individuals of all different ages, races, sexual orientations, and economic and religious backgrounds are on online dating platforms, so online studies may be better able to examine the preferences of a broader demographic. For example, the majority of individuals in the United States between the ages of 18 and 64, including racial minorities and individuals with less than a high school diploma, are online,[107] and 75 percent of those seeking an intimate partner use the internet to meet potential dates.[108]

It is possible that online daters may not be completely honest about their preferences. However, people want to appear open-minded and thus are probably more likely to *overstate* their willingness to date interracially or to respond to individuals that they have no intention of dating. Thus, to the extent that online dating studies may not accurately reflect daters' racial preferences, these studies are more likely to *underestimate* the strength of daters' preferences than to overestimate them. Moreover, all of the online dating studies found the same pattern of preferences: Whites were always at the top of the hierarchy, and African Americans and Asian American men were always at the bottom. These patterns were consistent across daters of different ages, incomes, education, geographic location (including urban versus rural dwellers), and political identities.

Offline studies have found a similar racial hierarchy. Speed-dating studies and surveys of college students' preferences found the same racial preferences as online studies.[109] While online dating studies do not definitively predict how people will behave offline, intermarriage rates mirror the racial preferences revealed online. The two groups who are least preferred by online daters—African American women and Asian American men—are also the groups with the lowest rates of intermarriage. The racial preferences we reveal *online* may tell us a lot about our preferences *offline*.

Observations about Racial Preferences

The studies discussed above show that, with the possible exception of African Americans, most date-seekers prefer Whites. Online daters' attraction to multiracial individuals might suggest that racial boundaries are weakening. Yet, daters' preferences for individuals who are part White over monoracial minorities reveals a racial hierarchy that values a light complexion and European appearance. Date-seekers consider men who are both Asian American and White desirable but reject monoracial Asian men. Date-seekers consider women with one Latino parent and one White parent as equally desirable as White women but rank Latinas who do not identify as part White as less desirable. These preferences suggest that partial Whiteness can soften the traits that make minorities less desirable romantic partners. As Christian Rudder, co-founder of the online dating site OkCupid, has noted, "Adding 'whiteness' always helps your rating."[110] These studies also suggest that while partial Whiteness can elevate Asian American and Latina women to White status, it does not have the same power for African American women. Asian American, Latino, and White men rated online profiles and photographs of biracial

African American/White women as significantly more attractive than monoracial African American women but less attractive than women of other races.[111]

These studies also illustrate how race and gender intersect. As sociologists Michael Omi and Howard Winant have argued, "Race is gendered and gender is racialized."[112] Although partial Whiteness elevated multiracial Latina/White women to White status, it did not do the same for Latino/White men. Latino/White men and African American/White men were deemed more desirable than Latino men and African American men, but not as desirable as White men.

These studies further reflect a racial hierarchy that does not merely rank some groups above others but also categorically excludes and stigmatizes members of other groups—African Americans and Asian American men, especially. Daters' reasons for excluding all African Americans and Asian American men, specifically, do not just reflect a preference for Whites but also suggest an aversion to African Americans and to Asian American men as intimate partners. Date-seekers' ratings of different profiles and rejection rates exceeding 90 percent (as described above) illustrate this aversion. Women seeking male partners tend to rate African American and Asian American men (other than their co-ethnics) as significantly less attractive than men of other races, and men of all races rate African American women as less attractive than women of other races.[113] In short, all groups reject African Americans and Asian American men at disproportionately high rates.

A survey of 381 college students at a progressive public university in California suggests that individuals make assumptions about certain groups based on gendered and racialized stereotypes. Students completed an anonymous questionnaire that asked them to describe the traits they desire in a romantic partner, whether they were willing to date someone of a different race, and if so, to rank their preferred racial groups and their reasons for their rankings. All of the male students who expressed racial preferences, except for Black students, ranked African American women last. White students, however, were significantly less likely than other groups to report racial preferences or to expressly exclude African Americans.[114] At first glance, these finding might suggest that the social distance between White and African American college students is decreasing. Students' explanations for their preferences, however, reveal a racialized and gendered hierarchy fueled by stereotypes and by family and societal resistance.

Physical Attraction and Personality

When the student participants were asked to explain their reasons for excluding African Americans or ranking them last, the most common responses were lack of physical attraction, cultural differences, African Americans' "aggressive" personality or behavior (in their view), and the social disapproval they would encounter if they dated an African American partner.[115] The likelihood of exclusion varied by gender. Heterosexual White male students were more than twice as likely as their female counterparts (67 percent versus 30 percent) to exclude African Americans as potential romantic partners. Asian American males were also more likely than their female counterparts to exclude African Americans. Male students were more than twice as likely as female students to list lack of physical attraction based on dark skin tone, hair texture, or "body type" as reasons for excluding African Americans as potential partners. For example, non-Black men wrote "Too dark," "I generally don't like curly hair or dark skin," "Because African American women are usually bigger broader physically type people," "I just don't like to date anyone who has really dark skin . . . anyone but Black."[116]

As noted earlier in the chapter, all individuals prefer physically attractive romantic partners. Beauty may be in the eye of the beholder, but throughout most of the Western world, a light complexion and phenotypically European features, such as silky hair and a narrow nose, are perceived as most attractive, especially for women.[117] These physical features are deemed desirable not only by Whites but also by all racial groups.[118] One study found that African Americans (male and female) rated lighter-complexioned African American women, but not men, as more attractive than those with darker complexions.[119] Some African Americans have internalized societal preferences for a light complexion,[120] as have Asian American and Latina women (in the United States and abroad) who spend billions of dollars on skin-lightening products each year.[121] For women, light "skin tone is a form of social capital that grants access to marriage to higher status men."[122] One need only name a few African American female celebrities considered beautiful by all racial groups—Beyoncé Knowles, Halle Berry, and Alicia Keys—to conclude that women with lighter skin and more Eurocentric features are perceived as more attractive. As the African American EGOT (Emmy, Grammy, Oscar, and Tony) award–winning actor Viola Davis retorted when a journalist referred to her as "darker-skinned and less classically beautiful" than other Black actresses, this is simply "a fancy term of saying ugly."[123]

These Eurocentric standards of beauty are reflected in the stripping industry. An ethnographic study of erotic clubs revealed that upscale clubs rarely hire dark-complexioned dancers because, as one club manager explained, "too many dark-skinned women would make the club lose money"[124]—their customers want White and Asian American dancers. Even the clubs with mostly dark-complexioned dancers feature White women and light-complexioned Latinas on their websites to entice potential customers. Customers' preferences for lighter-complexioned dancers are reflected in the larger tips they receive.

Women seeking male partners tend to prefer men with masculine traits, and men seeking female partners tend to prefer women with feminine traits.[125] Societal notions of masculinity and femininity depend on race and gender and are reflected in stereotypes and media portrayals of minority groups. Asian American women are depicted as hyperfeminine, Asian American men are portrayed as effeminate and asexual, and African American men are depicted as hypermasculine.[126] While the media has recently begun portraying African American women as desirable partners,[127] African American women have historically been depicted as matronly caregivers or as sexually immoral or emasculating and angry.[128] These images continue to predominate. A *New York Times* columnist, for example, referred to Shonda Rhimes, the producer of programs with African American characters, as "an angry Black woman."[129] The association between Whiteness and beauty reflects historical depictions of African American women as the antithesis of White femininity.[130] The image of the dark, strong Black woman was (and arguably still is) the polar opposite of the traditional feminine ideal of a woman.

Gendered and racialized stereotypes affect how individuals are perceived in the dating market. One online study found that White men who expressed a body type preference were more likely to exclude African American women, presumably because they associated African

American women with an undesirable body type.[131] Another study found that the more highly a man valued femininity, the higher the likelihood that he would be attracted to Asian American women but not African American women.[132] Similarly, the more highly a woman valued masculinity, the higher the likelihood she would be attracted to African American men but not Asian American men. Several studies have found that Americans perceive Asian Americans to be more feminine than other groups and African Americans to be more masculine.[133] Individuals are also more likely to associate feminine traits and words with Asian Americans and masculine traits with African Americans. They also associate dark skin with masculinity.[134] When White college students looked at facial photos of African American women, they sometimes mistook them for male faces but did not make similar errors when looking at photos of White women.[135] Given the importance that men place on a partner's physical appearance and the emphasis that all races place on light skin tone for women, it is not surprising that lighter-complexioned women are ranked higher in the dating market.

Stereotypes of African American men also affect how they are perceived in the dating market. Although both straight women and gay men reject African American men at high rates, African American men are rejected less often than African American women. While the stereotype of African American men as hypermasculine and sexually aggressive fuels the perception that they are threatening and dangerous, these are also traits that some date-seekers find appealing. Studies have found that a small percentage of White women, specifically those who like very tall and masculine men, have strong preferences for African American men.[136] Pornography sites are filled with images of interracial sexual encounters between dark-skinned Black men and White women, reflecting and reinforcing the stereotype of Black men as well-endowed and sexually gifted.[137] The popularity of these porn sites suggests that whom we desire in the bedroom might be quite different from whom we are willing to date in public. They also demonstrate that our sexual desires are not free of legal and societal influences but that they are instead shaped by racialized and gendered systems of subordination.[138]

Gender differences in the racial hierarchy are also apparent when one analyzes stereotypes about different groups' personalities and behaviors. Male college students in the California study were much more likely than female students to list "aggressive personality" as a reason for excluding African Americans as potential romantic partners.[139] Fifty percent of Latino males as compared to 10 percent of Latinas and 29 percent of White males as compared to 9 percent of White females cited aggressive personality and behavior when describing their reasons for excluding African Americans. Male students wrote that African American women are "abrasive" and have "attitude problems" and "large chips on their shoulders."[140] These remarks are similar to those reported in an earlier study of White college students' perceptions of African American women.[141]

Students who excluded African American women as potential romantic partners often relied on stereotypes of African American women as emasculating, domineering, and angry. Stereotypes about African American and Asian American men's personalities also affect racial preferences. Some female students reported that they would not date African American men because are aggressive—citing their "gangster style," and "tend[ency] to be violent."[142] These statements reflect cultural assumptions about African American men as dangerous.[143] Similarly, as noted above, stereotypes about Asian American men as submissive and effeminate lead both gay men and straight women to reject them as romantic partners.

Perceptions of Cultural Differences and Societal Disapproval

Many students in the California public university study expressed concerns about cultural differences and social disapproval when considering whether to date a person of a different race. These concerns might seem surprising given that the study was conducted in 2008–2009, when support for interracial marriage exceeded 95 percent among 18–29-year-olds. Nonetheless, approximately 35 percent of non-Black students cited cultural differences and fear of societal disapproval (including family disapproval) as reasons for excluding African Americans as romantic partners.[144]

Students also expressed concerns that family members and society in general would not approve if they dated African Americans. Asian Americans and Latinos were much more likely than Whites to express these concerns—55 percent of Asian Americans and 39 percent of Latinos, as compared to 10 percent of White students, who expressed racial preferences listed societal disapproval as a reason for excluding African

Americans. The likelihood of these concerns varied by gender. Asian American women and Latinas were significantly more likely than their male counterparts to express concern that parents, friends, and even strangers would disapprove and to fear that they might be subjected to discrimination if they dated African Americans.[145] Other studies have similarly found that college students fear family and societal disapproval if they marry a person of a different race.[146]

These concerns are not unfounded. Even today, individuals in interracial relationships are more likely than those in same-race relationships to face opposition or disapproval from family members and society more generally.[147] Family members express concern that the interracial couple will face societal disapproval and that neighbors, teachers, and strangers will treat them and their offspring differently.[148] They also express concern about the racial identity and psychological well-being of mixed-race children.[149]

Racial Privilege and Status

Parents' objections to their children's interracial relationships reflect a racial hierarchy. Asian American, Latino, and White parents all express greater objections to their children intermarrying with African Americans as compared to other groups.[150] Parents' objections are not based solely on concerns that their children and future grandchildren will experience discrimination. Parents are also concerned about their own potential loss of status. One study found that Latino parents express disapproval of their children's romantic relationships with African Americans because they fear jeopardizing the family's status in the racial hierarchy.[151] Latinos, including immigrants with African ancestry, are aware of African Americans' stigmatized status in the United States and their own position in the racial hierarchy.[152] They fear that a child's relationship with an African American partner will jeopardize the higher racial status that Latinos enjoy (or think they enjoy) and presume that they must distance themselves from African Americans to achieve social mobility.[153] Other studies have found that some White parents are similarly concerned about the loss of status for the family when an adult child marries a partner of a different race, especially if the partner is African American.[154]

Parents' objections to children's interracial relationships reflect not only a racialized hierarchy but also a gendered one. Their reactions to the relationship depend not only on the race of the child's partner but also the partner's gender. Families are much more likely to express strong disapproval when daughters date or marry out than when sons do.[155] For example, White women in relationships with men of other races experience greater parental disapproval than White men in interracial relationships.[156] Latino parents are similarly more likely to express disapproval when daughters date African Americans than when sons do.[157]

Societal disapproval of interracial relationships also depends on the race and gender of the non-White spouse. Relationships between African American men and White women have historically aroused stronger objections from both African Americans and Whites than relationships between African American women and White men. As recently as 2005, a Gallup poll found that 72 percent of Whites approved of a White man dating an African American woman but only 65 percent approved of an African American man dating a White woman.[158] White women with Asian American male partners also experience greater societal objections than Asian American women with White male partners. Indeed, one ethnographic study found that White men married to Asian American women could not recall a single instance of discrimination against them because of their relationship. In contrast, White women married to Asian American men reported negative comments from friends and neighbors about their choice of mate.[159]

Implicit Biases

Some White Americans believe that the United States is a post-racial society in which individuals are judged by their character and achievements and that any disparities between racial groups are the result of class inequalities and individual choices, not race.[160] Yet, studies show that race affects whom we share our bedroom, our home, and our lives with. Individuals have many reasons for preferring a partner of a certain race. Some racial minorities prefer a same-race partner who shares their cultural background or understands first-hand the challenges of navigating discrimination.[161] However, when individuals who are willing (or prefer) to date interracially exclude a particular group, it is quite possible that their preferences are motivated by racial biases. How do we reconcile a commitment to racial equality with racial preferences? For some individuals, there is nothing to reconcile, because they make a distinction between racial preferences in the public sphere (such as the workplace), where they believe race should be irrelevant, and their intimate lives, where they believe preferences of all kinds should be respected as a matter of personal taste. Other individuals do not believe that race should be a consideration when seeking an intimate partner, and they claim not have any racial preferences. Yet, their actions show that they prefer partners of certain races and exclude others. Are they lying about their commitment to colorblindness when seeking a romantic partner? Not necessarily.

Most Americans subscribe to an anti-discrimination norm, and many report having no racial preferences or biases.[162] However, cognitive bias tests repeatedly reveal that many of us (regardless of race) have implicit preferences for Whites.[163] Even Whites who are expressly committed to racial equality hold more positive attitudes about Whites than about African Americans.[164] These tests also show that most Americans have unconscious biases against minorities, even when we genuinely believe otherwise.[165] To illustrate, although individuals may honestly report having no biases against African Americans or gay men, implicit bias tests often reveal unconscious negative attitudes toward those groups. Studies show that implicit biases may influence employment decisions, disciplinary actions in grammar schools, police behavior, medical treatment decisions, and even the perception of an individual's behavior as threatening.[166] It is not only Whites who harbor unconscious negative views toward certain groups; racial minorities also hold negative attitudes against other minority groups and against members of their own group. Many Latinos, for example, have strong implicit biases against African Americans, and racial minorities often unconsciously favor Whites over members of their own group.[167]

Individuals' romantic preferences and the reactions of their families, friends, and society in general have been shaped by stereotypes and notions of racial status that reinforce a racialized and gendered hierarchy. Stereotypes hinder our ability to treat people as individuals and influence how teachers, employers, and neighbors perceive members of minority groups. They also affect an individual's status and desirability on the dating market.

*   *   *

This chapter has discussed racial preferences as shaped by society—individual preferences influenced by stereotypes, social norms, and implicit biases—without any mention of the role of law. This portrayal is incomplete. For three centuries, the law expressly prohibited interracial intimacy. Through anti-miscegenation laws, legally enforced segregation, race-based immigration restrictions, and laws that denied racial minorities access to wealth, the law helped to create and strengthen societal norms against interracial intimacy that remain today. With the stroke of a pen, the U.S. Supreme Court in *Loving v. Virginia* dismantled the *legal* barriers to interracial intimacy. But it did not and could not just as easily dismantle the societal barriers.

The law's influence on our romantic preferences is not limited to the lingering effects of its formal regulation of interracial intimacy. Even today, the law continues to facilitate residential and educational segregation that maintains both physical and psychological distance between groups. It also signals that racial discrimination in the intimate sphere is acceptable despite the psychic, economic, and social harms it inflicts on groups at the bottom of the racial hierarchy. In the following chapters, I show how law has shaped and continues to shape our intimate choices, why the resulting hierarchy is problematic, and what we should do about it.

2

How Law Regulated Interracial Intimacy and Its Effects Today

More than fifty years have passed since the 1967 U.S. Supreme Court's decision in *Loving v. Virginia* holding that legal restrictions on interracial intimacy violate the U.S. Constitution.[1] Although some states did not repeal their anti-miscegenation laws until decades later,[2] the laws that prohibited interracial relationships for three centuries are part of a history that many Americans would prefer to forget. Yet, as we saw in chapter 1, race continues to play an important role when individuals seek an intimate partner. What effect did the law's prohibition of interracial intimacy for three centuries have on our romantic preferences today? How did these laws shape, and continue to shape, whom we are attracted to, as well as whom we view as a suitable intimate partner and potential co-parent?

This chapter argues that through its project of racialization, the law created the racial hierarchy that shapes our attraction and perception of who is a desirable partner for a long-term committed relationship. The law created this racial hierarchy in at least three ways. First, the law created racial categories: it defined who was White, Black, American Indian, or Asian and, based on these categories, determined whom one could marry. As Peggy Pascoe has explained, "Miscegenation law acted as a kind of legal factory for the defining, producing, and reproducing of the racial categories of the state."[3] But state anti-miscegenation laws were not the only tools the law used to construct race and regulate intimacy. The law also constructed race through discriminatory federal immigration and naturalization laws. As Ian Haney Lopez has uncovered, from 1878 to 1952, federal and state courts, including the U.S. Supreme Court, applied arbitrary and often contradictory racial classifications to determine whether a person was White and thus eligible to become a naturalized citizen.[4] The racial classifications adopted in citizenship cases extended to matters involving the validity of a marriage under state anti-miscegenation laws and thus impacted interracial intimacy.

Second, segregation shaped our beliefs of who is a desirable romantic partner. State anti-miscegenation laws kept people of different races apart, as did federal immigration and citizenship laws that excluded anyone who was not White and stripped female U.S. citizens of their own citizenship if they married men ineligible for citizenship. Residential and educational segregation prevented social interactions that, as lawmakers feared, could lead to interracial intimacy and marriage.[5] Segregation also fueled beliefs that there are inherent differences between racial groups, thereby legitimizing stereotypes and creating psychological distance between groups.

Third, racially discriminatory policies in virtually every area—for example, marriage, immigration, education, housing, employment—legitimized and reinforced individuals' beliefs that non-White groups were inferior and created a racial hierarchy that placed Whites at the top, African Americans at the bottom, and American Indians, Asian Americans, and Latinos in the middle.

Law was, and is, at the center of our intimate preferences. White students in my race seminars, most of whom were born several decades after the *Loving* decision, have shared that they grew up believing that racial minorities were inferior to, or at minimum, different from them. The messages that the law conveys influence our attitudes and attraction toward members of groups that have long been regarded as undesirable partners. What your friends and family say or think about a potential romantic partner (or what you imagine they will say or think) may influence your attraction to that person. Their reactions to your partner are likely influenced by the messages their parents and family conveyed, which in turn were influenced by the messages their grandparents passed down.

The Court's decision in *Loving* made it possible for individuals to form intimate relationships across racial lines without fear of legal repercussions. It also empowered individuals with a partner of a different race to tell anyone who disapproved of their choice that they were wrong, at least as far as the law was concerned. But the law's expressive powers are limited. After shaping our romantic choices for three centuries, the Court's decision in *Loving* could not undo the messages that certain racial groups were not desirable or suitable partners. In a segregated society in which the majority of people do not have meaningful interactions with individuals of other races, beliefs about other groups are deeply embedded and its vestiges remain today.

Defining Whiteness: The Law's Construction of Race

At their core, state anti-miscegenation laws prohibited interracial marriage. Some also prohibited interracial sex. But these laws did a lot more. They constructed race and racial categories, as a brief review of state anti-miscegenation laws from the colonial period to the twentieth century demonstrates.

Let's start with Eleanor Butler, known as Irish Nell, who immigrated to Maryland in the late 1600s as an indentured servant. Nell would have been free once she completed her term of service, but she spent the rest of her life in servitude because she fell in love with and married Charles Butler, an enslaved Black man. At the time, Maryland law provided that a free White woman who married an enslaved Black man would be enslaved by her husband's enslaver, and so would any children resulting from the marriage.[6] When Nell's employer warned her that marrying Charles would condemn her and her children to a life of servitude, Nell replied that she would "rather have Charles than have your lordship."[7] Nell and Charles married and raised a family. Their children were all born into slavery.[8]

The 1661 Maryland law that enslaved Nell and her children was the first law in America that sought to prevent interracial intimacy, but it was by no means the last.[9] A year later Virginia passed a law punishing Whites who engaged in extramarital sex with a Black partner more harshly than Whites who engaged in extramarital sex with a White partner.[10] Interracial sex was not uncommon, however, as enslaved Blacks and White indentured servants worked side by side and became friends and intimate partners.[11] But once race-based slavery began to replace the system of indentured service, lawmakers needed clear racial boundaries to determine who could be enslaved. Mixed-race children blurred these lines. In 1691, Virginia passed a law banishing from the colony any White person who married a "negroe, mulatto, or Indian man or woman."[12] The law's stated purpose was "the prevention of that abominable mixture and spurious issue"—mixed-race children.[13] A White woman who had a child out of wedlock with a "negro or mulatto" man faced five years indentured service and enslavement of the child for thirty years.[14]

Over the next six decades, another half dozen colonies, including Massachusetts and Pennsylvania, enacted laws punishing or prohibiting interracial intimacy.[15] After the Revolutionary War, another twenty states and the District of Columbia enacted similar laws.[16] Interracial marriages were not only illegal in these states but were also null and void—the marriage was not legally valid[17]—which rendered any children from those unions illegitimate.[18] While some states repealed their anti-miscegenation laws after the Civil War, many reinstated them after the end of Reconstruction and thereby invalidated marriages that had been valid.

In 1883, in *Pace v. Alabama*, Tony Pace, a Black man and his White female partner, Mary Cox, were convicted of violating the Alabama law that prohibited Whites and Blacks from marrying or engaging in sex outside of marriage. Each of them was sentenced to two years imprisonment. Although another Alabama law prohibited sex outside of marriage with a person of the same race, the minimum penalty under that law was a $100 fine as compared to a minimum of two years' incarceration for interracial sex under the anti-miscegenation statute. Tony appealed his conviction to the U.S. Supreme Court and argued that the law's harsher penalty for interracial sex constituted race discrimination in violation of the Fourteenth Amendment of the U.S. Constitution, which guarantees equal treatment under the law. The Court rejected his claim. It held that by imposing the same punishment on both Blacks and Whites who engage in sex with a person of a different race, the law treated Blacks and Whites the same and thus did not discriminate.[19]

Following the Court's decision in *Pace v. Alabama*, many states enacted anti-miscegenation laws for the first time. In sum, forty-one states had anti-miscegenation laws at some point between 1661 and 2000, when Alabama finally repealed its (by then invalid) anti-miscegenation law.[20] Each of these states prohibited Whites from marrying a Black person or a person with a certain proportion (depending on the statute) of African ancestry. A minority of states also prohibited Whites from marrying members of other racial groups such as "Persons of Color, Indians, Mestizos, Half-Breeds, Mongolians, Chinese, Japanese, Malays, Kanakas, [K]oreans, Asiatic Indians, West-Indians, and Hindus."[21]

Shifting Definitions: The Politics of Racial Categories

Once lawmakers decided to prohibit interracial intimacy, they had to determine who was White and how to classify persons with ancestors of different races. Through this process of creating racial categories, the law communicated that Whites were a superior race and created a racial hierarchy that continues today.

Racial categories varied from state to state.[22] Alabama and Arkansas, for example, defined a person with any trace of African blood as Black.[23] Other states relied on proportions of non-White ancestry.[24] Mississippi, for example, prohibited Whites from marrying Blacks or Asians and set the limit at "one-eighth or more of negro" or "Mongolian blood."[25] Georgia prohibited Whites from marrying a person who was not White and defined a White person as one with "no ascertainable trace of either Negro, African, West Indians, Asiatic Indian, Mongolian, Japanese, of Chinese blood in their veins."[26] Courts also attempted to define the percentage of non-White ancestry that rendered a person not White.[27]

Non-White Ancestry and the American Indian Exception

Racial categories were not static—they varied depending on political and economic interests. Virginia, for example, had for over a century defined a person with "one-quarter or more non-White blood" as "colored" and made no distinction between American Indian or African American ancestry, for example, for purposes of its anti-miscegenation law.[28] Thus, a person with more than three-quarters White ancestry was legally White, irrespective of the race of their ancestors. In 1924, however, Virginia enacted a new anti-miscegenation law, titled the Racial Integrity Act, which defined a "white person" as one "with no trace whatever of any blood other than Caucasian." But it made an exception for American Indian ancestry.[29] This provision, known as the "Pocahontas exception," provided that a person who had "one sixteenth or less of the blood of the American Indian" and "no other non-Caucasian blood" was White.[30]

Scholars have long recognized that race is not a biological fact but a legal and social construction.[31] As George Martinez has observed, "Racial categories are constructed through the give-and-take of politics or social interaction."[32] The Pocahontas exception illustrates how Virginia defined racial categories based on White men's economic interests. As the Supreme Court explained in *Loving*, Virginia carved out the Pocahontas exception in order to recognize the descendants of John Rolfe and Pocahontas as White.[33] White leaders during the colonial period and westward expansion encouraged marriages between White men and American Indian women because they expected that these unions would help facilitate the transfer of tribal lands to White men.[34] As a result of these marriages, some of the most prominent families in Virginia had American Indian ancestry, and the Pocahontas exception protected their interests in a White identity and all of its privileges.[35]

Other states' treatment of American Indian ancestry illustrates how lawmakers defined racial categories to preserve the property interests of White men. Until the late nineteenth century, the laws in most states granted a husband rights to his wife's real property.[36] Judges in the 1800s generally upheld marriages between White men and American Indian women, including "Indian custom" marriages,[37] as state recognition of these relationships granted White men rights to land that belonged to their American Indian wives.[38] Although several states enacted anti-miscegenation laws that prohibited marriages between Whites and American Indians,[39] others found ways similar to those of Virginia to protect marriages between powerful White men and American Indian women and the children of these unions. Oregon, for example, amended a proposed law that would have prohibited marriages between Whites and persons with "*one-fourth* or more of negro, Chinese, kanaka [Native Hawaiian], or Indian blood" to apply only to American Indians with *one-half* or more Indian blood.[40] As with the Pocahontas exception, lawmakers in Oregon sought to, in the words of one lawmaker, protect "that class of citizen who, coming here at an early day, married Indian women and have raised families by them."[41] In other words, Oregon sought to protect White men and their children.

Asian Ancestry

Laws prohibiting Whites from marrying persons of Asian ancestry also demonstrate how the law constructed racial categories based on political considerations. Starting in 1861, fifteen states passed laws prohibiting marriages between Whites and persons of Asian ancestry.[42] In 1881, for example, California amended its anti-miscegenation law, which prohibited Whites from marrying a Black or "mulatto" person, to also prohibit marriages to a "Mongolian" person.[43] While the statute did not define who was "Mongolian," it was generally understood to include persons of Chinese ancestry. Some state officials, however, concluded that persons of Japanese ancestry were also Mongolian, despite objections from persons of Japanese ancestry.[44]

While some states' laws enumerated the groups that Whites were prohibited from marrying, such as "Asiatic Indian, Malay, Japanese, or Chinese,"[45] others, including California, sought to interpret "Mongolian" broadly to include all persons of Asian ancestry.[46] Until 1930, Filipinos and Whites could legally marry in California. Then, a marriage clerk, facing pressure from nativist groups and judges who objected to marriages between Filipino men and White women, began denying marriages licenses to couples with a Filipino partner and a White partner. Salvador Roldan, a Filipino man seeking to marry his White fiancée, sued the marriage clerk. Roldan argued that Filipinos were members of the Malay race and since California's anti-miscegenation law did not include persons of the Malay race, the clerk could not deny him and his White bride a marriage license. The state defended its policy and argued that Filipinos were members of the "Mongolian" race. The trial court agreed with Roldan and held that Filipinos were part of the Malay, not Mongolian, race and ordered the marriage clerk to issue the couple a marriage license. Although the trial court's decision was upheld on appeal, it was pyrrhic victory. Three days later, the California legislature amended its anti-miscegenation law to prohibit marriages between Whites and members of the "Malay" race.[47] Neither this amendment nor the earlier law prohibiting marriages between Whites and "Mongolians" elicited much debate among lawmakers or the public at large.

The different reactions to proposals to extend anti-miscegenation laws to persons of Asian ancestry as compared to American Indians can be explained by gender and economic interests. The majority of marriages between Whites and American Indians were between White men and American Indian women—relationships that could further U.S. interests in trade with tribes, westward expansion, and transfer of American Indian lands to White men.[48] In contrast, there were few Asian women in the United States because of U.S. immigration laws barring them from entering the country.[49] Consequently, lawmakers feared that Asian men would seek to marry White women.[50] Like the laws in colonial Maryland and Virginia that targeted intimacy between White women and Black men, laws prohibiting marriages between Asians and Whites, although gender-neutral, sought to control White women and Asian men.[51] These restrictions were not lifted until after World War II, when White men successfully fought to bring their Asian wives to the United States.[52]

Mexicans as (Legally) White

The legal construction of Mexicans as White is another example of how the law defined racial categories to further the economic and political goals of White men. Although some Mexicans are of European (Spaniard) ancestry alone, most have Indigenous ancestry,[53] and several courts have concluded that Mexicans are not White from an anthropological perspective.[54] Yet, for purposes of citizenship and marriage, the law defined Mexicans as White. Under the 1848 Treaty of Guadalupe Hidalgo, Mexico ceded more than 50 percent of its land to the United States and, in exchange, the United States granted U.S. citizenship to persons residing in those territories at the time of the treaty.[55] At the time, only Whites could become naturalized U.S. citizens.[56] Fifty years later when Ricardo Rodriguez, a Mexican man, applied to become a U.S. citizen, a federal court in Texas rejected the government's argument that Rodriguez was ineligible for citizenship because he was not White. Although Rodriguez was not a descendant of Spaniards, and "as to color, he may be classed with the copper-colored or red men," the court in *In re Rodriguez* concluded that because only Whites could become citizens at the time of the treaty's enactment, Mexicans were White for purposes of the naturalization laws.[57] As George Martinez has explained: "Through the give and take of treaty making, Mexicans became white."[58]

In re Rodriguez was a citizenship case but judges have treated Mexican Americans as White when interpreting and applying anti-miscegenation laws. In 1922, twenty-five years after the *In re Rodriguez* decision, the Supreme Court of Arizona held in *Kirby v. Kirby* that a marriage between a Black woman and a man of Mexican ancestry was void under Arizona's anti-miscegenation law because the husband was White.[59] Although the wife argued that the husband was not White because his Mexican mother had Indigenous ancestry, the court accepted the husband's claim that "he belonged to the white race."[60]

Similarly, in a case heard by the Supreme Court of California in 1948, a marriage clerk in California refused to issue a marriage license to Andrea Perez, a Mexican American woman, and Sylvester Davis, an African American man, because doing so would violate California's anti-miscegenation law, which prohibited Whites from marrying members of certain non-White groups, including African Americans.[61] As a Mexican American woman, Andrea Perez was legally White even though she was not phenotypically or socially White. Indeed, "Andrea was shocked to hear that . . . she was "White."[62] Andrea had olive skin tone and features not generally associated with Whites. Like most Mexicans and Mexican Americans at the time, she had attended school with mostly Mexican children and lived in a predominantly Mexican American neighborhood.[63] While no laws authorized segregation on the basis of Mexican ancestry, schools officials in several districts in California, as in a number of other states, required Mexican American children to attend segregated schools for children of "Mexican and Latino descent."[64] This practice continued until 1947, when a federal appellate court held in *Westminster v. Mendez* that "segregation of school children because of their Mexican blood" violated the U.S. Constitution's guarantee of equal treatment.[65]

Mexican Americans also experienced segregation and discrimination in housing and public accommodations.[66] As a result of informal segregation practices known as "Juan Crow," Mexicans and Mexican Americans were denied access to White neighborhoods,[67] and to public bathrooms, water fountains, restaurants, parks, playgrounds, and swimming pools reserved for Whites.[68] Businesses posted signs that read: "No Mexicans allowed" or "We serve Whites only. No Spanish or Mexicans,"[69] and Andrea Perez herself "had endured rejection by 'Whites Only' signs."[70] Many Americans did not consider Mexicans to be White, and many believed Mexicans were an inferior race.[71] Yet, despite their lower social status, because Mexican Americans were legally White, they could and did marry Whites. Some Mexican Americans, however, were able to marry African Americans and Asian Americans—groups that Whites were legally prohibited from marrying—if the marriage clerk determined that the Mexican American applicant had discernable Indigenous ancestry or "looked too dark to marry a White person."[72] In those cases, marriage clerks issued licenses to couples with a Mexican American partner and an Asian American or African American partner, further illustrating the arbitrariness of racial categories and their enforcement.

Andrea and Sylvester challenged the denial of the marriage license, and their case went all the way to Supreme Court of California. The court struck California's anti-miscegenation law and held that restricting a person's right to marry the person of their choice on the basis of race violated the Fourteenth Amendment's guarantee of equal treatment under the law.[73] The state had argued that California's anti-miscegenation statute was necessary to "prevent . . . the Caucasian race from being contaminated by races whose members are by nature physically and mentally inferior to Caucasians."[74] However, as Justice Roger Traynor, writing for the majority of the court, observed, the statute did not prohibit *all* marriages between Whites and members of other races.[75] It did not, for example, prohibit Whites from marrying American Indians or Hindus—groups that were not White under the law[76]—and it did not prohibit Whites from marrying Mexicans even though most were "a mixture of 'white' and 'Indian.'"[77] The statute also permitted some persons with White ancestry to marry a person who is not White—a person with seven-eighths White ancestry and one-eighth African ancestry, for example, could marry an African-American.[78] Noting that there were many racial classification systems and that the number of racial categories under these systems ranged from three to as many of thirty-four different races, Justice Traynor concluded that California's anti-miscegenation law was impermissibly vague. Specifically, it did not define the terms "'white persons,' 'Mongolians,' and 'members of the Malay race,'" nor did it address how it would apply to persons of mixed race.[79]

Justice Traynor recognized the illusion of race and arbitrary nature of racial classifications, especially when a person had mixed ancestry. He questioned whether in those cases, race would be defined by physical appearance or by ancestry and found both approaches troubling. A physical appearance test relied on the subjective impressions of the beholder and could result in siblings with identical ancestry being classified differently. A genealogical test, in turn, required determining what proportion of ancestry would make a person Black, Caucasian, or Malay under the anti-miscegenation law. In Justice Traynor's view, both the one-drop rule and the blood quantum approach were ridiculous. He explained that "to determine that a person is a [member of a particular race] because of any trace of such ancestry, however slight, would be absurd," but concluded that it would be similarly absurd to "assume that a predominance in number of ancestors of one race" determines a person's race.[80] He explained that

> a person with three-sixteenths Malay ancestry might have many so-called Malay characteristics and yet be considered a white person in terms of his preponderantly white ancestry. Such a person might easily find himself in a dilemma, for if he were regarded as a white person under [the statute], he would be forbidden to marry a Malay, and yet his Malay characteristics might effectively preclude his marriage to another white person. Similarly, a person having three-eighths Mongolian ancestry might legally be classed as a white person even though he possessed Mongolian characteristics. He might have little opportunity or inclination to marry any one other than a Mongolian, yet [the statute] might forbid such a marriage. Moreover, if a person were of four-eighths Mongolian or Malayan ancestry and four-eighths white ancestry, a test based on predominance in number of ancestors could not be applied.[81]

For Justice Traynor, these examples were proof that the anti-miscegenation statute was "too vague and uncertain" to be a valid restriction on marriage.[82] Although it would be another nineteen years before the U.S. Supreme Court in *Loving v. Virginia* would hold that anti-miscegenation laws were unconstitutional, Justice Traynor's deconstruction of California's statute demonstrates the arbitrariness of racial classifications and how these categories shift based on social, political, and economic interests. As Justice Traynor observed, the statute not only failed to define how a person's race would be determined or how the statute would apply to persons of mixed race, but it also precluded, without any scientific basis, certain non-White groups from marrying Whites while permitting other non-White groups to do so. In this manner, the statute signaled that some groups—those prohibited from marrying Whites—were "by nature physically and mentally inferior to Caucasians" and would contaminate the "Caucasian race."[83]

Congress and the Supreme Court Weigh In

The law's regulation of interracial intimacy was driven primarily by states, as state legislators set the requirements for entry into marriage, local officials enforced them by issuing or denying marriage licenses, and state courts determined whether a marriage was valid. Yet, federal immigration and naturalization laws also hindered interracial intimacy by excluding anyone who was not White from the United States.

Beginning in 1882, Congress passed numerous laws banning persons from Asia and Latin America from immigrating to the United States. The Chinese Exclusion Act of 1882 banned most immigration from China,[84] the 1908 Gentleman's Agreement significantly curtailed immigration from Japan,[85] and the Immigration Act of 1917, also known as the Asiatic Barred Zone Act, barred immigration from most of the rest of Asia.[86] Congress then passed the Immigration Act of 1924, also known as the Johnson-Reed Act, which excluded any person ineligible for citizenship from entry to the United States.[87] At the time only Whites and persons of African ancestry were eligible for naturalization. While these laws did not exclude Mexicans, who were legally White as a result of the Treaty of Guadalupe Hidalgo, that same year Congress created the Border Patrol to exclude immigrants from Mexico.[88] Five years later, Congress passed the Undesirable Aliens Act, which made it a misdemeanor to enter the United States outside an official port of entry and a felony to reenter the United States illegally after being deported.[89] The Undesirable Aliens Act was driven, at least in part, by fear of "'race mixture' between women and 'inferior races'"[90]—specifically race mixing between Whites and Mexicans.

These federal laws contributed to the construction of the racial categories and racial hierarchy that shaped interracial intimacy. Although Mexicans were legally White, in the early 1900s Congress commissioned a study on the problems created by immigration from Latin America. The Undesirable Aliens Act's legislative history is replete with examples demonstrating that lawmakers believed that Mexicans were not White. One influential congressman, for example, warned that the United States must restrict immigration from Latin America as "'blood' from a person from Latin America is 'a very great penalty upon the society which assimilates it,' because it is 'composed of mixture blood of white, Indian, and negro.'"⁹¹ As one court concluded, the Undesirable Aliens Act "solidified perceptions of persons from Latin America as a separate, unwelcomed race."⁹² A year after the act's enactment, Mexicans' classification in the U.S. Census was changed from White to "a distinct race."⁹³ Federal law had made Mexicans legally White, and decades later, federal law made them not White.

The Supreme Court has never addressed the effect of immigration and naturalization laws on interracial intimacy. The Court, however, did attempt to define who was White in two decisions holding that Asians were not White and were therefore ineligible for naturalization.⁹⁴ By categorizing persons of Asian ancestry as not White, the Court decided who could enter the United States and be part of the pool of potential marriage partners, thereby limiting opportunities for interracial intimacy.

In *Ozawa v. U.S.*, decided in 1922, Takao Ozawa, a man of Japanese ancestry, pointed to his light skin tone and that of many other persons of Japanese ancestry as evidence that he was White and thus eligible for naturalization.⁹⁵ The Supreme Court disagreed. Citing more than a half dozen federal and state cases, the Court concluded that a person of Japanese ancestry is not White because "the words 'white person' are synonymous with the words 'a person of the Caucasian race.'"⁹⁶ The Court rejected skin color as a determinant of race because it "differs greatly among persons of the same race" and relying on skin color "alone would result in a confused overlapping of races and a gradual merging of one into the other, without any practical line of separation."⁹⁷ Without explanation, the Court assumed that racial classifications are necessary—that "a practical line of separation" is needed—even as it acknowledged the difficulty of assigning race in some cases. The Court explained:

> The effect of the conclusion that the words "white person" means a Caucasian is not to establish a sharp line of demarcation between those who are entitled and those who are not entitled to naturalization, but rather a zone of more or less debatable ground outside of which, upon the one hand, are those clearly eligible, and outside of which, upon the other hand, are those clearly ineligible for citizenship. Individual cases falling within this zone must be determined as they arise from time to time by . . . "the gradual process of judicial inclusion and exclusion."⁹⁸

For the Court, *Ozawa* was not one of those cases falling within the zone of debate because in its view, a person of Japanese ancestry "is clearly of a race which is not Caucasian." The Court did not explain how it would determine whether a person is White in cases falling within the zone of debate or why a gradual merging of the races would be problematic. Its decision in *U.S. v. Thind* the following year suggests that it believed there are inherent differences between groups that have been classified into different races.

In *U.S. v. Thind*, decided in 1923, the Supreme Court was again confronted again with the question of who is White. Bhagat Singh Thind, a "high-caste Hindu," claimed that he was White and therefore eligible for naturalization.[99] A decade earlier, a federal court had held that because Asian Indians are part of the "race or family known to ethnologists as the Aryan, Indo-European, or Caucasian," they were therefore eligible for U.S. citizenship.[100] Mr. Thind argued that under this racial classification system, Hindus were Caucasian and thus eligible for U.S. citizenship. The Supreme Court disagreed and held that a "high-caste Hindu, of full Indian blood," is not White.[101]

The Court's decision in *U.S. v. Thind* highlights the arbitrary nature of racial classifications. In *Ozawa v. U.S.*, the Court held that "the words 'white person' are synonymous with the words 'a person of the Caucasian race'" and concluded that Mr. Ozawa was "clearly of a race which is not Caucasian."[102] In making this determination, the Court adopted a scientific approach to racial categories. It approvingly referenced the briefs that discussed the term "white person" from the standpoint "of the science of ethnology."[103] Moreover, when noting the "large number" of federal and state courts that had held that persons of Japanese ancestry are not Caucasian and therefore are not White, it observed that "these decisions are sustained by numerous *scientific authorities*."[104] Thus, the Court in *Ozawa* accepted and relied upon a scientific definition of race.

Yet, the following year in *U.S. v. Thind*, the Court rejected this "scientific" approach, noting that "various authorities are in irreconcilable disagreement as to what constitutes a proper racial division" and that there was no need "to pursue the matter of scientific classification further."[105] It adopted instead a "common understanding"[106] approach to determine who is White and explained that "it is a matter of familiar observation and knowledge that the physical group characteristics of the Hindus render them readily distinguishable from the various groups of persons in this country commonly recognized as white."[107] In the Court's view, the term "white person" "as so understood and used ... does not include [Hindus],"[108] and thus, irrespective of "the speculations of the ethnologist," Hindus could not be White.[109]

The contrast between the deference shown to "scientific authorities" and the "science of ethnology" in *Ozawa v. U.S.*, and the Court's rejection of these authorities and adoption of a common understanding or common knowledge approach to race only a year later in *U.S. v. Thind* illustrates the law's role in racial formation. It also demonstrates the arbitrariness of racial categories. Moreover, while the Court asserts in both *Ozawa* and *Thind* that it is not suggesting that any race is superior or inferior, its focus on a group's ability to assimilate—to become White— signals otherwise. The Court relied on what it perceived as Hindus' inability to assimilate into the U.S. population when it concluded that Hindus are not White. The Court explained:

> The children of English, French, German, Italian, Scandinavian, and other European parentage, quickly merge into the mass of our population and lose the distinctive hallmarks of their European origin. On the other hand, it cannot be doubted that the children born in this country of Hindu parents would retain indefinitely the clear evidence of their ancestry. It is very far from our thought to suggest the slightest question of racial superiority or inferiority. What we suggest is merely racial difference, and it is of such character and extent that the great body of our people instinctively recognize it and reject the thought of assimilation.[110]

It is not clear how a group's ability to assimilate into the population is relevant to racial classifications. But even if it were relevant, the ability of the children of immigrants to "merge into the mass" of the U.S. population depends on both the makeup of the population and the ability of the immigrant parents to procreate with certain members of the population. The majority of the U.S. population in 1923, when the Court decided that Mr. Thind was not White, was White as a result of federal laws that excluded non-White immigrants and state anti-miscegenation laws that prohibited Whites from marrying members of certain non-White groups.[111] The law deprived non-White immigrants, who were disproportionately single men, of the opportunity to marry and have children and thereby alter the racial makeup of the country. Indeed, it was the fear that non-White immigrant men would marry White women, have children, and change the racial makeup of the country that led states to prohibit marriages between Asians and Whites. Thus, the law itself created the conditions that made assimilation of non-White groups into the U.S. population unlikely.

While Congress repealed its race-based immigration and naturalization laws in 1965,[112] the perception that non-White immigrants and their U.S.-born children are unassimilable continues to this day.[113] During the COVID pandemic in 2020, for example, Asian Americans were once again reminded that, in the eyes of some, they remain perpetual foreigners.[114] The law bears at least some responsibility for this perception.

Law Kept Racial Groups Apart

State Anti-miscegenation Laws

The law has historically segregated Whites and groups it classified as not White. By keeping Whites and non-White groups apart and limiting opportunities for both casual interactions and deeper relationships, anti-miscegenation, immigration, and segregation policies created the physical and psychological distance that shaped, and continue to shape, societal perceptions of who is a desirable romantic partner. These policies, along with lawmakers' messages of White supremacy, facilitated and reinforced misconceptions about the abilities and values of non-White groups.

Anti-miscegenation laws achieved their primary purpose: they prevented marriages between Whites and members of certain non-White groups. California law, for example, prohibited Whites from marrying African Americans and persons of Asian ancestry but did not prohibit Whites from marrying American Indians or Mexican Americans. Not surprisingly, a study of recorded marriages from 1924 to 1933 found that very few African Americans or Asian Americans had a White spouse. In contrast, more than a one-third of American Indians and Mexican Americans at the time had a White spouse.[115] Anti-miscegenation laws, however, did much more than just prevent marriages between Whites and certain groups. These laws also signaled that the prohibited groups were inferior and thus unsuitable marriage partners for Whites. They implicitly conveyed the message that state actors often made explicitly—that the law needed to "prevent . . . the Caucasian race from being contaminated by races whose members are by nature physically and mentally inferior to Caucasians."[116]

Federal Laws

While preventing interracial intimacy may not have been the primary purpose of federal immigration and naturalization laws, these laws, which targeted Asians, Mexicans, and Indigenous persons from Latin America, were driven, at least in part, by hostility to interracial intimacy. Moreover, irrespective of their intent, federal laws served, as Rose Villazor's research demonstrates, to prevent or strongly discourage interracial relationships.[117] The Immigration Act of 1924 (known as the Johnson-Reed Immigration Act), for example, prohibited immigration of any person ineligible for citizenship.[118] Since only Whites and persons of African descent were eligible for citizenship,[119] and the Supreme Court had declared that persons of Asian ancestry were not White,[120] federal law excluded most Asians from the pool of marriage partners that Americans, the majority of whom were White, could consider.[121] Thus, immigration and naturalizations laws ensured that most Whites, even those who lived in states that did not prohibit marriages between Whites and Asians, would not marry persons of Asian ancestry.

Federal citizenship laws also served to discourage interracial intimacy between American women and Asian men. Until 1931, federal law stripped American women of their citizenship when they married men "ineligible for citizenship"[122]—a group comprised primarily of Asian men.[123] Laws that made a married woman's citizenship dependent on her husband's status not only discriminated on the basis of gender and marital status, but also strongly discouraged American women (most of whom were White) from marrying men of Asian ancestry.

Military Policies

Although U.S. servicemembers stationed abroad developed intimate relationships with foreign nationals of Asian ancestry, race-based immigration laws and military policies disrupted these relationships when servicemembers returned to the United States as their partners could not join them. After World War II, U.S. military regulations prohibited military personnel from marrying a person who was ineligible to become a U.S. citizen.[124] Thousands of U.S. servicemembers who had married and had children with women deemed ineligible for U.S. citizenship could not bring their families to live with them in the United States.[125] The ineligible spouses were usually women of Japanese ancestry married to White men, although some were married to African American men.[126] Congress enacted the War Brides Act of 1945 to facilitate the expedited admission of foreign spouses and children of U.S. servicemembers.[127] Yet, immigration officials and judges continued to deny admission to foreign spouses and their mixed-race children on the ground that they were ineligible for citizenship and were thus inadmissible under the 1924 Immigration Act.[128]

Arguably, the military's policies sought to prevent marriages in which spouses would likely be forced to live apart because the foreign spouse was ineligible for entry into the United States. In fact, military officials justified their denial of White servicemembers' requests to marry a Japanese national as protecting the state's interest in prohibiting marriages that were likely to end in divorce.[129] Yet, when servicemembers of Japanese ancestry sought permission to marry a Japanese national, their requests were generally granted. Those same-race marriages were presumably just as unlikely to succeed as marriages between White servicemembers and Japanese partners since the Japanese national, who was ineligible for citizenship, would not be allowed entry into the United States. As Rose Villazor's work demonstrates, "These laws tended to be selectively enforced to prevent interracial marriages and they impacted primarily White men and Japanese women.[130]

Military officials also sought to prevent interracial marriages between African American servicemembers and White European women. While military officials granted White servicemembers' requests to marry White European women (including women from Germany—a country that, like Japan, was at war with the United States), they denied African American soldiers' request to marry White European women.[131] Military officials claimed to be concerned that these marriages would be illegal in states with anti-miscegenation laws, even though a number of states had no such laws.[132] The military routinely denied African American servicemembers permission to marry White European women irrespective of whether the marriage would be prohibited by the state where the couple intended to reside.

In sum, although no federal laws expressly prohibited interracial relationships, federal immigration and naturalization laws, along with military policies, hindered the formation of interracial marriages. These restrictions eased when Congress amended the War Brides Act in 1947 to allow entry of racially inadmissible spouses but were not completely eliminated until 1952, when Congress passed the McCarran-Walter Act abolishing all race-based exclusions.[133]

Jim Crow

When people think about the civil rights movement, they often think about segregated neighborhoods, schools, and buses. They recall Rosa Parks's refusal to give up her seat on the bus[134] and the Court's pronouncement in *Brown v. Board of Education* that separate schools can never be equal.[135] *Loving v. Virginia* may not come to mind as many people do not associate it with the civil rights movement. However, preventing interracial marriage and mixed-race children was a driving force behind segregation. Lawmakers feared that if White and non-White individuals lived near each other, went to school together, and shared public spaces, they would develop friendships and eventually intimate relationships.[136] One segregationist's statement that "until we take the active steps necessary to adopt the program of physical separation of the races, we are on the road to amalgamation"[137] illustrates the role of Jim Crow laws in preventing interracial intimacy. Segregation was a tool to enforce racial categories and reinforce the message of White supremacy. As such, it served to limit opportunities for interracial intimacy even in states without antimiscegenation laws.

Residential Segregation

Preventing interracial intimacy was a primary purpose of laws mandating segregated housing. Indeed, lawmakers expressly defended residential segregation on this ground. In *Buchanan v. Warley*, the city of Louisville, Kentucky, passed a housing ordinance prohibiting a person of color from living on a block where the majority of homes were occupied by White persons and vice versa.[138] A White man who sold his property on a predominantly White block to an African American man challenged the ordinance. In its defense, the city argued that the ordinance was "essential to the maintenance of the purity of the races."[139] The Supreme Court rejected the city's argument and noted that the ordinance allowed White families to hire live-in servants and employees who were not White. In the Court's view, an ordinance that allowed individuals who were not White to live on the same property as their White employers did not serve to prevent interracial intimacy. The Court, however, did not reject the city's assertion that preventing "amalgamation of the races" was a valid justification for residential segregation.[140]

Other cities enacted similar housing ordinances to prevent interracial intimacy. The city of Richmond, Virginia, for example, enacted an ordinance that prohibited a person from living on "any street between intersecting streets where the majority of residences on such street are occupied by those whom said person is forbidden to intermarry."[141] Given that, apart from the Pocahontas exception discussed earlier, Virginia law prohibited Whites from marrying anyone who was not White,[142] Richmond's ordinance ensured that the vast majority of Whites would live on streets inhabited by Whites only. As Robin Lenhardt has argued, these ordinances reduced the possibility that interracial relationships could ever develop.[143]

Public Accommodations

While one might not expect to meet one's future spouse on a train in the late 1800s, lawmakers justified segregation in public spaces by reference to the state's interest in preventing interracial intimacy. In *Plessy v. Ferguson*, the Supreme Court upheld state-mandated segregation on railroads by reasoning that "laws permitting, and even requiring . . . separation [of Blacks and Whites], in places where they are liable to be brought into contact . . . have been generally, if not universally, recognized as within the competency of the state legislatures in the exercise of their police power."[144] To bolster its conclusion that the Constitution permitted racial segregation, the Court noted that anti-miscegenation laws were "universally recognized as within the police power of the state."[145] It also cited approvingly *State v. Gibson*, a case from the Indiana Supreme Court that upheld anti-miscegenation laws and which reasoned that "from social amalgamation it is but a step to illicit intercourse, and but another to intermarriage."[146] As Reginald Oh has argued, "The segregation of public accommodations, transportation, restaurants, beaches, and swimming pools can all be viewed as tools for eliminating sites of potential development of intimate interracial relations."[147]

Educational Segregation

Virtually all Americans are familiar with *Brown v. Board of Education*, the watershed decision that abolished de jure segregation in schools. They are equally familiar with segregationists' strong resistance to the Court's mandate to desegregate schools. During Black History Month each year, the media features images of six-year-old Ruby Bridges, the first African American child to integrate an all-white school in the South, as federal marshals escorted her and her mother to school past a crowd of Whites shouting racial slurs.[148] The first time I saw these images, when I was a child myself, I wondered why White parents were so resistant to having a Black little girl go to school with their children. Years later I understood that those White parents feared that if their White children attended schools with Black children, they might become more than classmates. They might become close friends and romantic partners.

Lawmakers recognized White parents' fears that "the key to the schoolroom door is the key to the bedroom door" and sought to reduce opportunities for White children to befriend and form intimate relationships with children from other racial groups.[149] While most of the discussion of de jure segregation in schools has focused on African American children in the racially segregated South, states across the United States, including New York and California, assigned American Indian, Asian, and Latino children to segregated schools.[150] Courts, including the U.S. Supreme Court, upheld such laws.[151] As Reginald Oh has observed, these laws were intended "to prevent the formation of interracial relationships in public schools and so prevent interracial marriages."[152] The Mississippi Supreme Court's 1925 decision in *Rice v. Gong* illustrates lawmakers' concerns that integrated schools would lead to interracial intimacy.[153]

In *Rice v. Gong*, nine-year-old Martha Lum attended the first day of school at the Rosedale School attended by White children. Later that day, a school official told her she could not return the next day because she was of Chinese descent and the Rosedale School was for White children only. Martha's father sued the school district arguing that the law violated Martha's right to equal treatment under the U.S. Constitution. The Supreme Court of Mississippi disagreed. In reaching its conclusion, the court looked at its state constitution, which required separate schools for White and "colored" students, and its prohibition of marriages between Whites and members of the "Mongolian race." The court explained that the purpose of both provisions was to preserve the "integrity and purity of the white race"[154] and held that "taking all of the provisions of the law together, it is manifest that it is the policy of this state to have and maintain separate schools and other places of association for the races so as to prevent race amalgamation."[155]

In the court's view, as Reginald Oh has observed, "racially segregating public schools was a legitimate way to preserve white racial purity" and "prevent... the development of intimate sexual and romantic relationships between whites and nonwhites."[156] As Oh notes, the court recognized Southern Whites' fears that in the absence of segregation, White and non-White students "would have continuous and regular social contact... [which] would erode notions of racial pride and racial consciousness among whites" and that "inevitably, intimate interracial relations would develop, inexorably leading to interracial marriage and the production of racially mixed children."[157] The U.S. Supreme Court unanimously affirmed the Mississippi Supreme Court's decision.[158]

Segregated schools also made it less likely that White children would see children of other races as their equals. Schools are where children are socialized and taught the beliefs and values of their community. This is clear from recent efforts to ban any discussion of race or gender identity in public schools and from the increase in the number of parents who have decided to home school.[159] Parents hold strong views about the school curriculum, the values their children absorb, and how they are socialized through peer interactions in the classroom. Lawmakers relied on Whites-only schools to facilitate White children's development of a White racial consciousness and teach them that children of other races were not their intellectual or social equals. Segregationists feared that integrated schools would challenge these ideas and lead White children to reject White supremacy and develop friendships and later romantic relationships with peers of other races.

Segregated schools prevented interracial relationships in yet another way. As the Court recognized in *Brown*, segregation inflicted psychic harm on Black children and thus interfered with their academic performance.[160] By impeding Black children's ability to learn and take advantage of opportunities available to Whites, segregation reinforced the beliefs that many Whites held about other racial groups and that some members of these groups had internalized about themselves—that they were less capable than Whites.[161] In this way, segregated schools gave meaning to the racial categories the law had created and minimized the likelihood that White children and children of other races would become friends and potential intimate partners as they entered adolescence and adulthood.

Law and the Creation of Racial Hierarchy

Not only did the law create racial categories and segregate on the basis of these categories; it also created a racial hierarchy that conveyed that Whites were a superior race. As the Court recognized in *Loving*, antimiscegenation laws expressly promoted White supremacy and did so for more than three hundred years.[162] African Americans were generally at the bottom of the racial hierarchy while the status of other non-White groups shifted depending on economic and political expediency. For example, as discussed above, lawmakers facilitated marriages between White men and American Indian and Mexican women during westward expansion, but support for these relationships waned once they no longer furthered White men's economic interests. Some courts began denying recognition to custom marriages between American Indians and Whites and treating Mexicans as a separate (and inferior) race despite their legally White status.[163] Legislators sought to restrict immigration from Latin America to reduce the likelihood that Whites would end up "mixing with 'inferior races,'"[164] and marriage clerks began denying marriage licenses to White and Mexican couples if the Mexican partner did not appear phenotypically White.[165]

Although a minority of states prohibited Whites from marrying American Indians,[166] some placed American Indians above Asians and African Americans.[167] As noted earlier, Virginia prohibited Whites from marrying a person with any trace of non-White ancestry but made an exception for American Indian ancestry so long as it was one-sixteenth or less. While the purpose of this exception was to recognize the descendants of John Rolfe and Pocahontas as White, it also signaled that any amount of non-White ancestry, except for American Indian ancestry, tainted Whiteness. Lawmakers' willingness to recognize persons with some American Indian ancestry as White further suggests that they placed American Indians higher on the racial hierarchy than other groups.

Oregon law conveyed a similar message. As noted earlier, Oregon prohibited Whites from marrying persons "with *one fourth* or more negro, Chinese, or kanaka [Native Hawaiian] blood" or "more than *one half* Indian blood."[168] This distinction between American Indians and other groups signaled that the law placed persons with American Indian ancestry higher on the racial hierarchy. Indeed, one legislator who opposed applying Oregon's anti-miscegenation law "to persons of light Indian blood" explained that "there are a great many people in the State of this class, who are persons of talent and respectability—some of them educated and highly accomplished."[169] Presumably, this legislator did not believe that persons with African American, Chinese, or kanaka ancestry were as talented or respectable as persons with American Indian ancestry.

Some states placed both Asians and American Indians above African Americans. In 1880, a federal court in Oregon lamented that Congress had extended the right to become a naturalized U.S. citizen to African Americans while denying it to "the intermediate and much-better-qualified red and yellow races."[170] In the majority of states, African Americans or persons with African ancestry were the only group that Whites were prohibited from marrying.[171] Anti-miscegenation laws that applied only to African Americans signaled that persons with African ancestry were inferior to all other groups. As Rachel Moran has concluded, "By identifying those who could not be loved, [anti-miscegenation laws] marked some races as inferior and undesirable."[172] In Oklahoma, for example, African Americans could not marry a person of any other race because anyone who was not African American was considered White for purposes of the state's anti-miscegenation law. In *Stevens v. United States*, a federal court interpreting Oklahoma law held that a person of African descent could not marry a full-blood Creek Indian because American Indians were members of the "white race."[173] While a few states enacted anti-miscegenation laws prohibiting Whites from marrying anyone who was not White, in practice, courts perpetuated a racial hierarchy between non-White groups. Courts in Arizona, Missouri, Oregon, and Washington, for example, recognized marriages between White men and American Indian women as valid despite laws prohibiting these marriages.[174] These courts, however, did not recognize marriages between Whites and African Americans.

Immigration Law and the Creation of a Gendered Racial Hierarchy

Federal immigration law also created a racial hierarchy. In 1952, Congress enacted the McCarran-Walter Act, which ended the exclusion of Asian immigrants,[175] and in 1965, it enacted the Hart-Celler Act, which granted priority to professionals and workers with specialized skills—which in turn served the United States' need for scientists and engineers during the Cold War.[176] As a result of the Hart-Celler act, many highly educated and skilled professionals from Asian countries were able to immigrate to the United States, and they and their children have excelled professionally and academically, becoming what commentators often refer to as a "model minority."[177] As historian Erika Lee has observed, "No group has benefitted more from the [Hart-Celler] Act than Asian Americans."[178]

As a result of federal immigration policies, many Asian immigrants who came to the United States after 1965 have had opportunities that African Americans, American Indians, and Latinos often lack. As Vinay Harpalani has explained, although highly skilled Asian immigrants experienced discrimination, they "were also structurally situated for upward mobility and achievement."[179] Consequently, they were "able to assimilate socially and economically into predominantly white communities."[180] In contrast, African Americans and Latinos, who tend to have lower levels of formal education and thus fewer opportunities for economic mobility, remain in racially isolated neighborhoods and schools.

Federal immigration policy also created a *gendered* racial hierarchy. While race-based exclusion and national-origin quotas restricted immigration from Asian countries until 1965, Congress carved out exceptions for spouses of U.S. citizens, the majority of whom were women. The War Brides Act as amended in 1947, for example, allowed the Asian spouses of U.S. servicemembers and their children to enter the United States despite the 1924 Immigration Act's exclusion of individuals from Asia. The majority of Asian nationals married to U.S. servicemembers were women, and their American spouses were White men. About 80 percent of Japanese immigrants in the 1950s and 40 percent of Korean immigrants from 1950 to 1964 were admitted as wives of U.S. servicemembers and almost all of the women who immigrated to the United States from the Philippines after World War II entered as the wives of U.S. servicemembers.[181] Marriage to American men, most of whom were White, allowed Asian women to bypass restrictive immigration laws. Thus, as a result of U.S. immigration policy, Whites are more likely to view Asian immigrants and their children as desirable co-workers and neighbors and potential marriage partners.[182] Furthermore, the exceptions to restrictive immigration laws for spouses of U.S. citizens made marriages between White men and Asian women visible and normative.[183]

How Groups See Each Other

The racial hierarchy that the law facilitated shaped interactions not only between Whites and racial minorities but also between different minority groups. American Indians, Asians, and Latinos have historically sought to distance themselves from African Americans in an effort to secure some of the privileges available to Whites. Several tribes, for example, adopted their own anti-miscegenation policies that prohibited tribal members from marrying African Americans and denied tribal membership to individuals with African-American ancestry.[184] During the Jim Crow era, Mexican Americans asserted that they were White and thus should not be subjected to the segregation and discrimination imposed on African Americans.[185] Puerto Ricans and Asian Americans have similarly claimed White status and argued that they should not be forced to attend segregated schools with African Americans.[186]

As a result of the racial hierarchy the law perpetuated, racial minorities often reject members of other minority groups as romantic partners. As noted in chapter 1, Asian Americans and Latinos express similar preferences as Whites when selecting a romantic partner of a different race: they tend to prefer White partners and reject African Americans. Immigrants from Asia, Latin America, and the Middle-East are taught that African Americans are at the bottom of the economic and social hierarchy and to distance themselves from them.[187] In fact, as Tanya Hernandez and Laura Gomez have shown, even Latinos with African ancestry often reject a Black identity and attempt to distance themselves from African Americans.[188]

How Law Continues to Shape Desire

The majority of Americans today expressly repudiate White supremacy.[189] Yet, ideas about racial difference and hierarchy are embedded in our subconscious. As Ian Haney Lopez has argued, the law translates "ideas about race into the material societal conditions that confirm and entrench those ideas."[190] As a result of state-sanctioned discrimination, racial minorities experienced, and continue to experience, conditions that reinforce societal beliefs about their intelligence, work ethic, and character. For example, some Americans presume that African Americans and Latinos are less intelligent than other groups.[191] The law shaped these beliefs by labeling Latinos "Greasers,"[192] an "undesirable but exploitable race,"[193] and by denying African American and Latino children equal access to education, thereby limiting their opportunities to pursue higher education and lucrative careers, own a home, reside in neighborhoods with desirable services, and acquire the resources that most people consider important when choosing a life partner. These conditions serve to legitimize societal beliefs that African Americans and Latinos are not as motivated or hardworking as other groups.

Americans often associate African Americans and Latinos with criminal behavior.[194] The law was instrumental in creating this association.[195] As Jeremi Duru has argued, slaveholders lived in constant fear of slave rebellions, and thus "the very existence of blacks as slaves reinforced the perception" that they were "sexually potent animalistic criminals."[196] States enacted Slave Codes and then, after Reconstruction, Black Codes, that criminalized routine activities when engaged in by African Americans. These laws conveyed that African Americans were predisposed to criminal activity and must be controlled.[197] The perception of Black and Latino criminality persists and is perpetuated when legal actors rely on racial stereotypes in criminal cases.[198] The disproportionately high percentage of Latinos and African Americans residing in high-crime neighborhoods—the result of decades of government-sanctioned segregation—further reinforces societal beliefs about Latino and Black criminality.[199]

Politicians are aware of the power of these stereotypes and exploit them to stoke racial fears. When discussing welfare reform during his presidential campaign, Ronald Reagan talked about "welfare queens" and "strapping young bucks buying T-bone steaks with food stamps."[200] Although Reagan did not mention race, he was eliciting stereotypes about African Americans' poor work ethic.[201] When Donald Trump asserted during his presidential campaign that Mexico was sending "bad hombres," rapists, and criminals to the United States, he was reminding potential supporters that African Americans and Latinos were "super predators" and undesirable immigrants[202]—stereotypes that affect not only immigrants but all racial minorities.[203] George H. W. Bush was similarly banking on societal beliefs about Black criminality when he aired an ad featuring Willie Horton, an African American man who committed a vicious crime while on furlough, to bolster his 1988 presidential campaign.[204]

The law also shaped societal beliefs about Asian Americans that persist today. Asian Americans are perceived as smart and hardworking but also conniving and disloyal—traits that lawmakers ascribed to members of Asian groups starting in the mid-1800s.[205] The effects of the law's depiction of Asians as "unassimilable" is evident today as Asian Americans are often perceived as perpetual foreigners. Asian Americans (and Latinos) who are repeatedly asked, "Where are you *really* from?"—after they name a U.S. city or state as their birthplace—are reminded that they are not seen as real Americans.[206] The COVID-19 pandemic demonstrated that Asian Americans' status as the "model minority" is quite precarious as they have been blamed for the global pandemic, told to go back to where they came from, and been the victims of thousands of racially motivated attacks and crimes.[207] Societal beliefs about Asian Americans in 2020 are eerily reminiscent of the racist beliefs cited by lawmakers to justify excluding Asians from the United States for seven decades and denying them the right to marry, testify in court,[208] or become U.S. citizens.[209]

As we saw in chapter 1, stereotypes influence our perception of who is a desirable partner. The law was instrumental in the creation of these societal beliefs, which are passed down from generation to generation even if unconsciously. By prohibiting African Americans, Asians, and American Indians from testifying against Whites in court, the law signaled that these groups were dishonest, conniving, and untrustworthy. By holding that persons of Asian ancestry would never be able to assimilate into the United States, the Supreme Court signaled that they could never be true Americans and would always be perpetual foreigners, a perception that persists today.

We do not need to look far back to be reminded of how the law regulates our intimate choices. In 2019, several couples who applied for a marriage license in Virginia discovered that state law required them to declare their race on the marriage license application. Seven other states had similar laws.[210] Virginia immediately revised its application to make the declaration of race optional. Yet, as a federal court concluded, the law, which included among its more than 200 racial classifications, terms such as "Quadroon," "Octoroon," "Nubian," "Moor," and "Aryan," was "born originally out of racial animus" and was used to enforce the state's prohibition against interracial marriage. This law, and others like it, are "a vestige of the nation's . . . codified racialization."[211]

3

Freedom of Association versus Discrimination in Intimate Spheres

Americans grapple with what might appear to be competing values. On the one hand, we value liberty. The First Amendment of the U.S. Constitution guarantees the freedom of intimate association, which suggests that the government may not interfere with our decisions to avoid associating with certain individuals. On the other hand, most Americans are committed to racial equality. We believe that discrimination on the basis of race is wrong and should be prohibited. Federal and state laws prohibiting discrimination in employment, housing, and public accommodations reflect our belief in equality.[1] Lawmakers have attempted to balance equality and liberty principles by permitting discrimination in certain cases. For example, although federal and state laws prohibit employers from discriminating on the basis of race,[2] no laws prohibit individuals from discriminating when hiring a nanny to work in their home. Similarly, although the law prohibits housing discrimination, it allows owners of owner-occupied properties with few units or guests rooms for rent to discriminate against potential tenants or guests on the basis of race.[3] The law also permits private clubs to exclude individuals on the basis of race even though it prohibits discrimination in establishments open to the public.[4]

As we saw in earlier chapters, many individuals take race into account when seeking a romantic partner—what some scholars have labeled "sexual racism."[5] There are no laws prohibiting discrimination in the dating market, but that does not mean that it does not cause harm or that the law should not attempt to address it. What messages does the law convey when it allows online dating platforms to facilitate discrimination? Should the law prohibit these platforms from facilitating such discrimination? How do the law's efforts to address discrimination in employment, housing, and public accommodations inform these questions? This chapter explores these issues.

Racial Preferences and Dating Platforms

Americans have always considered race when seeking a romantic partner, but online dating platforms allow individuals to publicize their preferences in ways that were unimaginable a few decades ago. These platforms ask users to indicate their race and racial preferences and allow them to filter their searches by race. Although several platforms have eliminated their race filters in recent years,[6] more than 75 percent of the top twenty-five grossing dating apps requested users' race at one point, and more than two-thirds allowed users to filter daters by race or ethnic background.[7] At least one site allowed users to filter by how light or dark a person's skin tone was.[8] Once a user selects the racial groups that they would consider dating, these platforms generally hide the profiles of members of the excluded groups. For example, if a user excludes Latino males, they will not see profiles of users who identify as Latino men. By making race salient, these platforms elicit preferences that at least some date-seekers might not have considered important, or considered at all, and signal that a romantic partner's racial or ethnic background is an important consideration when seeking a partner.

In 2018, in order to examine how online dating platforms elicit racial preferences and facilitate the exclusion of certain groups, my research assistants created fake profiles on six of the most popular dating platforms at the time: Zoosk, Match, Plenty of Fish, Elite Singles, OkCupid, and eHarmony. They learned that each of these platforms asked users to indicate their race or racial preferences. Zoosk, for example, asked users to indicate their race by selecting one of the following categories: Asian, Black/African, Indian, Latino/Hispanic, Middle Eastern, White/Caucasian, and Mixed/Other. The user's race then appeared on their profile, which other date-seekers would see. Zoosk also offered a "behavioral matching engine" called "Smartpick," which learned about a user's preferences by asking questions and using that information to introduce the user to potential matches. One of Smartpick's questions at the time was: "Would you like to restrict your matches to certain ethnicities?" A user then had two options: "(1) Open to dating people of all ethnicities or (2) Please restrict the ethnicity of my matches to the following choices." The second option provided a drop-down menu with the same racial categories listed when users were asked to indicate their race.

Created in 1995, Match.com is one of the oldest online dating platforms.[9] Like Zoosk, Match asked users to indicate their race, but allowed users to skip this question. My research assistants learned that once they created a profile, they could filter other date-seekers' profiles by race—even if they skipped the race question and did not indicate their own race—and exclude members of any group listed on the site—Asian, Black/African descent, East Indian, Latino/Hispanic, Native American, Pacific Islander, or White/Caucasian.

Plenty of Fish and Elite Singles similarly asked users to identify their race when creating an account. Like Match, Plenty of Fish allowed users to filter their search by race. Elite Singles offered a "preferences" section in which a user could indicate their racial preferences.

OkCupid elicited considerable attention when its co-founder Christian Rudder revealed the racial preferences of OkCupid's users on a blog post in 2009 and later published these results in his book *Dataclysm: Love, Sex, Race, and Identity—What Our Online Lives Tell Us about Our Offline Selves*.[10] As a result, I was particularly interested in OkCupid's design. Like the other dating platforms, OkCupid asked users about their racial preferences, but its questions were rather puzzling. First, it asked users: "Would you strongly prefer to date someone of your own skin color/racial background?" It then asked whether the user's perfect match would also have such a preference. These questions not only make race salient but suggest that same-race preferences are normative while preferences for partners of a different race, or the lack of a racial preference, are unusual and possibly aberrant. The first question assumes that users would always be willing to date individuals of their same race but might not be willing to date people of other races. As Elizabeth Emens has argued, why not ask, "Would you consider dating someone of your own race"?[11]

The second question—whether the user's perfect match would have the same racial preferences—was confusing because it did not ask about the user's own preferences but rather the user's feelings about the racial preferences of others. Imagine a White woman who expresses a strong preference for a White partner. If she indicates that she wants her perfect match to also have strong preferences for Whites, the site would not match her with a White user who is open to dating people of all races. Why would it matter whether another White date-seeker shares her preferences for Whites so long as that person likes Whites, too (and likes her in particular)? The question seemed to be asking, "If you are racist, would you prefer someone who is similarly racist?" A better question might be, "Would you date someone who has expressed racial preferences?," as such a question would include users who are willing to date someone who has expressed racial preferences as well as users who are not interested in dating someone who has expressed racial preferences. As a White colleague told me, she would not be interested in dating someone who would only date Whites because, in her view, that preference suggests that the person is close-minded and possibly racist.

eHarmony's site was also somewhat puzzling. It's Frequently Asked Questions page stated that race was not a factor in its "Compatibility Matching System."[12] However, when creating an account, my research assistants found that they had to identify their race. There was no option to skip this question. Moreover, the site required users to state whether they have a racial preference and if so, to select that preference. The choices were: "No Preference, White, Hispanic/Latino, Black/African Descent, Asian/Pacific Islander, Indian, Chinese, Native American, Arabic/Middle Eastern, Korean, Japanese, Other." Interestingly, on its main page, eHarmony included links to its "ethnic" dating sites: Asian Dating, Black Dating, Latin Dating. Clicking the link for "Asian Dating," for example, brought the user to another page indicating that "if you would like to date Asian women or Asian men specifically, make sure to adjust your criteria to reflect this preference." The links for "Latin Dating" and "Black-Dating" had similar language.

If race is not a factor in eHarmony's Compatibility Matching System, as eHarmony indicated, why require users to identify their race and racial preferences, especially when users who only wished to date individuals of a particular racial background could use eHarmony's ethnic dating sites? By requiring users to state their racial preferences, eHarmony strongly signaled that an intimate partner's racial background was an important consideration when seeking a partner, despite its statement to the contrary.

Dating platforms make race salient in ways that are not only prohibited in other contexts, such as housing or employment, as described below, but are also socially unacceptable outside the dating context. By asking users to indicate their race and the races they would not date, these platforms signal that a person's race is a legitimate and important consideration when searching for a romantic partner. A friend shared that she had never consciously held any racial preferences when dating offline and had dated individuals of all races before she tried online dating. However, when she created an account on an online dating platform and was confronted with the list of racial groups that she could exclude, she began to think that her likelihood of finding a compatible partner would be higher if she excluded daters of certain races. After all, why else would the platform highlight race and allow her to exclude certain groups? Given the stereotypes about certain groups (described in chapter 1), she excluded men of Asian descent, as most heterosexual female online daters do.

Anti-Discrimination Laws and Their Exceptions

While lawmakers have ignored discrimination in the dating market, federal and state laws prohibit race discrimination in virtually all other areas of our lives, including housing, employment, and public accommodations. These laws have, however, carved out exceptions to accommodate individuals' associational interests.

Housing and Lodging

In 1968 Congress enacted the Fair Housing Act, which, as amended, prohibits discrimination on the basis of race, color, religion, sex, national origin, or familial status in the sale or rental of housing.[13] Many states have enacted similar laws. These laws do not prohibit all housing discrimination, however. Fair housing laws generally do not apply to roommates,[14] and the federal Fair Housing Act carves out an exception, known as the Mrs. Murphy exception, for owners of owner-occupied dwellings with four or fewer units. Such owners may discriminate against potential tenants, for any reason, including race.[15]

Discrimination impacts the ability of racial minorities to find housing.[16] It also limits their ability to secure short-term accommodations. A 2015 study found that individuals with distinctly African American names who sought accommodations on the home sharing platform Airbnb were 16 percent less likely than identical users with White names to be accepted as guests.[17] These findings are supported by numerous stories posted by racial minorities who experienced blatant discrimination by hosts on

Airbnb.[18] Even so, the law does allow some hosts to discriminate. Title II of the federal Civil Rights Act of 1964 prohibits discrimination in public accommodations, including lodging, but makes an exception for owners who reside on the property and have five or fewer rooms for rent.[19]

While scholars have criticized these exceptions to anti-discrimination laws,[20] these exceptions recognize the associational rights of property owners not to associate with individuals they find objectionable for whatever reason, including race.[21]

Employment

Title VII of the federal Civil Rights Act of 1964 prohibits discrimination in employment on the basis of race, color, religion, sex, or national origin.[22] Title VII, however, applies only to employers with fifteen or more employees.[23] Thus, the millions of Americans who work for small employers, including the vast majority of domestic workers, are not protected by Title VII. States and municipalities have adopted their own anti-discrimination laws, and some prohibit all employers, even those with only one employee, from discriminating.[24] But these laws often do not apply to individuals hiring persons to work in their homes. For example, while New Jersey law prohibits all employers from discriminating, it provides that an "individual employed in the domestic service of any person" is not an employee.[25] Washington, DC, similarly excludes "domestic servants, engaged in work in and about the employer's household" from the protections of its laws prohibiting employment discrimination.[26] Thus, in these jurisdictions a person may refuse, on the basis of race, to hire a babysitter, housekeeper, or health care aide to work in their home. And individuals do discriminate. Employment agencies report that clients seeking a babysitter or housekeeper make comments such as "Colombians and Dominicans need not apply" or "No black" or "No Jamaican."[27]

Private Clubs

Title II of the Civil Rights Act of 1964 prohibits places of public accommodation from "discrimination or segregation on the ground of race, color, religion, or national origin."[28] Many states have adopted similar laws prohibiting establishments and institutions open to the public, such as restaurants, stores, sports and recreation facilities, from discriminating.[29] These laws, however, exempt private clubs and establishments, even those with hundreds of members, from anti-discrimination laws, so long as they are "not in fact open to the public."[30] Private clubs, including country clubs, fraternal lodges, and swim clubs have historically excluded African Americans, Jews, and all non-White groups.[31] In 2018, the all-White, eight-hundred-member Charleston Rifle Club in South Carolina denied membership to an African American doctor while all of the White applicants were approved.[32]

Why Does the Law Allow Discrimination?

The Supreme Court has recognized that individuals have a constitutionally protected freedom of intimate association—a right "to enter into and maintain certain intimate human relationships" without "undue intrusion by the State."[33] Lawmakers' protection of the freedom of intimate association, which "presupposes a freedom *not* to associate,"[34] helps explain the justification for the exceptions to anti-discrimination laws in the employment, housing, and public accommodations contexts.[35] For example, in his concurrence in *Runyon v. McCrary*, a 1976 case in which the Supreme Court rejected a private school's assertion that requiring it to admit Black students violated associational rights, Justice Lewis Powell observed that discrimination cases involving "close association (such as, for example, that between an employer and a private tutor, babysitter, or housekeeper) . . . would invoke associational rights long respected."[36]

More than twenty years later in *Thomas v. Dosberg*, the New York Appellate Division rejected a discrimination claim brought by a home health aide, because the law prohibiting employment discrimination did not protect individuals working in a private home. Citing the legislative history, the court found that "the Legislature did not intend to extend its reach into private homes and to subject private employment relationships of the most personal kind to governmental control." It explained that exempting personal relationships in homes from the anti-discrimination law "avoids intrusions which would stimulate resentment, stultify enforcement and risk various constitutional inhibitions."[37] Thus, in addition to concerns that individuals would resist the law's efforts to regulate employment relationships in a private home and that enforcement would be difficult, lawmakers feared that applying anti-discrimination laws to personal relationships would impinge on associational freedoms.

Similarly in *Fair Housing Council v. Roommate.com*, the U.S. Court of Appeals for the Ninth Circuit relied on the freedom of intimate association to conclude that federal and state anti-discrimination laws do not apply to individuals selecting a roommate or housemate.[38] The court reasoned that interpreting anti-discrimination law to apply to roommate selection would raise serious constitutional concerns, given the Supreme Court's recognition of a constitutional freedom of intimate association.

The Limits of the Freedom of Intimate Association: No Discriminatory Advertisements

Given the law's solicitude for associational freedom in intimate associations, one might conclude that it cannot address discrimination in the dating market. After all, romantic relationships are the epitome of intimate associations. The freedom of intimate association is not absolute, however. The law places restrictions on *who* may exercise it and *how* it may be exercised. It also prohibits the *facilitation* of discrimination by another person.

Although federal law allows Mrs. Murphy—the owner of a dwelling with four or fewer units who lives in one of those units—to reject prospective tenants or guests for any reason, including race, it prohibits Mrs. Murphy or anyone else from *publicizing* discriminatory preferences.[39] The federal Fair Housing Act prohibits printing or publishing of "any notice, statement, or advertisement, with respect to the sale or rental of a dwelling that indicates any preference, limitation, or discrimination based on race, color, religion, sex, handicap, familial status, or national origin."[40] Thus, the owners of a two-family home in which they reside may not post an ad in a newspaper, Craigslist, Reddit, or Facebook stating "Apartment for rent. White applicants preferred." They also may not post such an ad on their lawn or verbally express such preferences when attempting to rent the property.[41] The prohibition on discriminatory advertising applies not only to the owner of the property but to publishers as well. A newspaper or website that posts a discriminatory ad may be held liable if the ad expresses prohibited preferences.[42]

In *Fair Housing Council v. Roommate.com*, a non-profit organization alleged that Roommate.com, a roommate matching platform, violated the federal Fair Housing Act and California state law by (1) requiring users to indicate their sex, sexual orientation, and whether any children would be living with them, (2) asking users to list their preferences for a roommate, including sex, sexual orientation, and familial status, (3) matching users based on these preferences, and (4) allowing users to filter their searches based on sex, sexual orientation, and familial status. Although both federal and California state law prohibit discrimination on the basis of these categories, the court rejected the claim against Roommate.com because it concluded that neither the Fair Housing Act nor California law applied to shared units or the selection of roommates.[43] However, had Roommate.com posted an ad for an apartment in an owner-occupied three-family home that expressed a preference based on sex, sexual orientation, race, national origin, or other protected category, both the owner (Mrs. Murphy) and Roommate.com would have been in violation of the law even though the owner (Mrs. Murphy) had a legal right to discriminate. Furthermore, Craigslist and fair housing organizations have interpreted the prohibition on discriminatory advertisements to apply to advertisements for roommates, even though individuals may legally discriminate when deciding with whom to share their home.[44]

One might find it puzzling to prohibit individuals from advertising their intentions to engage in discrimination when they can legally discriminate. Why does the law allow Mrs. Murphy property owners to discriminate but prohibit them from *publicizing* discrimination? While the Fair Housing Act's "legislative history is frustratingly silent about the reasons for [its] ban on discriminatory statements," as Robert Schwemm has observed,[45] courts have offered a few rationales.

First, lawmakers are concerned about the psychic injury that members of protected groups may experience when confronted with discriminatory advertisements.[46] Courts have recognized that the psychic harm may be particularly widespread because advertisements are usually posted on media that is likely to be viewed by many individuals. Indeed, widespread dissemination is the goal of advertisements and may cause emotional distress to any member of the targeted group who sees the ad, including individuals who are not seeking a home. Fair housing laws seek to protect against this psychic injury by prohibiting all discriminatory statements and recognizing a claim for damages by individuals who suffer psychic harm as a result of viewing a discriminatory ad.[47]

In fact, a person who is not seeking a home, and thus is not a direct target of such discriminatory ads, may recover damages if they suffered psychic harm caused by a discriminatory ad.[48] As Robert Schwemm has observed, § 3604(c) seeks "to protect minorities from the insult of discrimination."[49]

Second, lawmakers fear that discriminatory advertisements will deter members of protected groups from seeking homes that are not exempt from fair housing laws' anti-discrimination provisions. A person seeking a home who sees a discriminatory advertisement in a newspaper, on a website, or on the lawn of a Mrs. Murphy property owner may be deterred from seeking housing on that block even if Mrs. Murphy's neighbors cannot legally discriminate or might welcome members of groups that Mrs. Murphy can legally reject.[50] The person seeking a home might not know that the owners of other homes on that block cannot legally discriminate or that some or many would welcome neighbors of different races.[51]

Third, lawmakers fear that discriminatory advertisements or statements will signal that housing discrimination is legally permissible and lead to even more discriminatory advertisements.[52] As the fair housing organization, Housing Opportunities Made Equal of Virginia, Inc., explains:

> Such discriminatory advertisements also have an impact through affirming to the reader, whether a home seeker or fellow housing provider, that such language is lawful and thereby allowing or encouraging its continued use. People often copy language they see in other advertisements believing it to be lawful. Because the general public most often believes that such language they view is lawful, if action is not immediately taken on discriminatory advertisements the result is a continued use of the language and an increase of more discriminatory advertisements.[53]

In short, the law prohibits discriminatory advertisements, even if the underlying housing discrimination is legal, because these statements (1) cause psychic harm, (2) deter individuals from seeking housing that is open to them, and (3) signal that discrimination is legally permissible and leads to even more discriminatory advertisements. Discriminatory advertisements have widespread effects that extend far beyond the targets of the discriminatory activity.

The Limits of the Freedom of Intimate Association: No Facilitation of Discrimination

Realtors

Although the law allows individuals to discriminate in certain cases, it prohibits another person or entity from facilitating such discrimination. For example, the federal Fair Housing Act's prohibition on discrimination in the sale or rental of property does not apply to an owner of a single-family house, "provided, That such private individual owner does not own more than three such single-family houses at any one time."[54] Thus, the owner of three or fewer single-family houses can legally discriminate on any basis when selling or renting a house—subject to some restrictions as to the timing of a sale.[55] But the exemption from the antidiscrimination provision does not apply if the owner of a single-family house uses the services of a real estate broker or any person in the business of selling or renting homes.[56] A private homeowner—who is not in the business of selling houses—may discriminate when selling or renting a house but is prohibited from using a broker to facilitate the transaction.

Fair housing laws prohibit facilitation of discrimination in yet another way. Although some, maybe most, individuals consider the racial demographics of a neighborhood when searching for a home, realtors may not provide prospective renters and buyers with information about the racial composition of a neighborhood as it may *steer* home seekers toward or away from certain neighborhoods based on race.[57] Indeed, in 2009, the National Fair Housing Alliance, a prominent civil rights organization, alleged that the realty site Movoto violated fair housing laws when it posted a neighborhood's racial composition alongside its property listings.[58] Racial steering, discussed in the next chapter, is a violation of fair housing laws.[59]

Employment Agencies

In many states, a person may discriminate on any basis when hiring someone to work in their home. They may not, however, use an employment agency to help them hire a nanny, housekeeper, or home care attendant of their preferred race. Although Title VII—the federal law prohibiting employment discrimination—applies only to employers with fifteen or more employees, it applies to any employment or recruitment agency—regardless of whether it has only one employee—that "regularly refers employees to employers . . . *even if the employment agency doesn't receive payment for this service.*"⁶⁰ The U.S. Equal Employment Opportunity Commission (EEOC), the agency responsible for enforcing federal laws prohibiting discrimination in the workplace, explains: "An employment agency may not honor discriminatory employer preferences. For example, it is unlawful to accept a job order specifying the race, color, religion, sex, national origin, age (over 40) or disability status of the candidate. An employment agency may not categorize, group or classify job applicants, jobs, or employers based on race, color, religion, sex, national origin, age (over 40) or disability status and make referrals based on the categorizations."⁶¹

State courts have interpreted state anti-discrimination laws to similarly prohibit employment agencies from accommodating clients' racial preferences. In 2005, an investigation by the New York Attorney General's Office revealed that ten domestic employment agencies in New York City routinely solicited and accommodated clients' racial preferences when screening and referring applicants for positions as housekeepers and nannies.⁶² Some agencies openly noted in their records "No Blacks," "No Islanders," and "Prefers Europeans" and used this information to determine an applicant's eligibility for certain positions.⁶³ In its civil rights case against several agencies, the state alleged violations of New York's anti-discrimination law.⁶⁴ At the time, New York's anti-discrimination law excluded domestic employees from its protection.⁶⁵ One agency challenged the claims against it on this ground.⁶⁶ The court agreed that "an individual may choose to hire a domestic servant using whatever criteria he or she may desire" but held that "the privilege does not extend to an agent acting on behalf of a prospective employer, the privilege is personal to the employer."⁶⁷ In short, an individual may discriminate on any basis when hiring someone to work in their home, but they may not use an employment agency to help them facilitate a racially discriminatory hiring search.

Adoption Agencies

The law prohibits adoption agencies that receive federal funding from accommodating a prospective adoptive parent's racial preferences even though adoption of a child undisputedly implicates an individual's freedom of intimate association. Racial preferences are prevalent in the adoption market, and some private adoption agencies charge different fees for their placement services depending on the child's race—as much as 50 percent less for placement of an African American child as compared to placement of a White child.[68] Private agencies have historically elicited and accommodated the preferences of prospective adoptive parents.[69] While scholars such as Richard Banks have argued that the law should prohibit these practices,[70] and some private agencies now refuse to accommodate prospective adoptive parents' racial preferences,[71] such accommodation is legal so long as the agency does not receive federal funding.

Foster care and adoption agencies that receive federal funding, however, may not elicit or accommodate the racial preferences of prospective adoptive parents. Title VI of the federal Civil Rights Act of 1964 prohibits agencies receiving federal funds from discriminating on the basis of race.[72] The federal Multi-Ethnic Placement Act (MEPA), as amended in 1996, prohibits agencies receiving federal funds from denying or delaying a child's adoption because of the race, color, or national origin of the child or the person seeking to adopt the child.[73] A violation of MEPA constitutes a violation of Title VI.[74] In a 2005 case often discussed by family law and race scholars, the U.S. Department of Health and Human Services (USDHHS) concluded that the South Carolina Department of Social Services (SCDSS) violated MEPA and Title VI by asking prospective adoptive parents about their racial preferences.

Like some of the dating platforms discussed above, SCDSS used a computer database to match children and prospective adoptive parents based on the prospective adoptive parents' racial preferences. SCDSS required individuals seeking to adopt a child to complete a "Child Factor Checklist" that asked applicants whether they would accept a child who is "Black, White, Black/White or Other."[75] Applicants who indicated that they preferred to adopt a White child were not considered when the agency was seeking to place an African American child.

In its attempt to accommodate prospective adoptive parents' racial preferences, SCDSS effectively excluded entire groups of children from consideration on the basis of race. In its findings, USDHHS reminded SCDSS that, under MEPA, an adoption agency "may not honor the request of birth parents to place their child with parents of a specific race, national origin, or ethnic group" and "may not use race to differentiate between otherwise acceptable placements."[76]

Thus, while prospective adoptive parents themselves may reject a child on the basis of race, an agency receiving federal funding may not facilitate such discrimination by asking the prospective adoptive parents about their racial preferences or making placement matches based on such preferences. Although MEPA's restrictions apply only to agencies that receive federal funding, they demonstrate that even as individuals may freely exercise their right of intimate association, the government can place limits on who can facilitate the exercise of such freedom if it discriminates on the basis of race.

Should the Law Regulate Discrimination on Dating Platforms?

Race discrimination in the romantic marketplace, and especially online dating platforms, is common. While personal ads in newspapers and magazines expressing racial preferences were common long before dating platforms, sexual racism on online platforms is of a different kind and magnitude.[77] First, only a small percentage of people posted personal ads in magazines and newspapers and even fewer met through such ads. In contrast, dating platforms are now the most common way to meet a romantic partner. Second, dating platforms facilitate the exclusion of entire racial groups by making them invisible to many users. Newspapers and magazines, in contrast, do not have the ability to facilitate such exclusion— they cannot provide readers with a drop-down menu and prompt them to exclude racial groups, and they do not match readers based on race or have filters that allow readers to see only the profiles of the racial groups they have selected. Third, unlike newspapers and magazines that merely publish date-seekers' ads, dating platforms elicit racial preferences, normalize those preferences, and, in some cases, create preferences that the user may not have considered when they first tried online dating.

While the law has not yet addressed discrimination on dating platforms, the reasons for regulating discrimination in the housing, employment, and adoption settings may warrant legal intervention in the dating market. As we saw, fair housing laws prohibit advertising of racial preferences because it (1) causes psychic harm, (2) deters individuals from seeking housing that is open to them, and (3) signals that discrimination is legally permissible and leads to even more discriminatory advertisements. As shown below, racial filters and advertising of racial preferences on dating platforms have similar effects. Moreover, the policies underlying the prohibition on facilitating discrimination in the housing, employment, and adoption settings warrant prohibiting online dating platforms from facilitating sexual racism.

Advertising of Racial Preferences and Psychic Harm

The psychic harm resulting from advertising of racial preferences in the romantic marketplace is just as, and possibly more, severe than that experienced in connection with the sale or rental of property.[78] Although I have not been in the market for a romantic partner in decades, a few years ago I learned that an acquaintance who was seeking a romantic partner said he would not date dark-skinned women like myself. I vividly remember how unattractive I felt at that moment and for days afterward. I felt rejected and undesirable even though I was not in the dating market, and nor did I want to be. The psychological harm I experienced was just as strong, and possibly stronger, than the emotional harm I would have experienced had a homeowner told me that she would not sell her home to me because I was too dark. Online daters have recounted similar experiences. One person explains:

> I remember the first time I experienced sexual racism masked as "preference." It was after sending a picture of my face to another person on the internet. He immediately told me, "I don't like black guys, sorry," and then signed off. And ever since, I have received a version of those words more times than I'd care to count.
>
> From my own experience, being told my skin color disqualifies me from being attractive is sometimes the most hurtful rejection—or it's at least the one that I can't seem to shake. . . . It leaves me stunned that my skin can so quickly repel a person who didn't even get to know me at all. My mind quickly translates race-based rejection into *Your body isn't worth loving.*[79]

Another dater received the following messages on different dating websites: "I don't date Asians—sorry, not sorry." "You're cute . . . for an Asian." "I usually like 'bears,' but no 'panda bears.'"[80] As another user noted,

"You run across these profiles that say 'no Asians' or 'I'm not attracted to Asians.' Seeing that all the time is grating; it affects your self-esteem."[81]

Virtually every person in the dating market experiences rejection. Rejection is often hurtful, regardless of the reason. However, rejection on the basis of race, especially when expressed in a public setting, may be qualitatively different. For racial minorities who experience discrimination in all aspects of daily life, pervasive rejection "whether on- or offline—can cultivate deep feelings of personal shame and lead subjects of discrimination to view themselves as less attractive or desirable."[82] One African American woman who recalled the pain of rejection because of her race described it as ache that "always starts in the throat, hums in the chest, drops to the lowest point of the belly. Sharp, thick, burning."[83] After describing her first experience with racial discrimination in second grade, she writes:

> The ache reappeared in high school when a friend told me I would be pretty if my skin were lighter. I tried to avoid the sun that summer and summers after. Needless to say, it didn't change anything. Far too many Black women are taught that romantic fantasies do not belong to us, that we are never someone's first choice or second or even third, and that we should feel lucky if we are wanted. . . .
>
> Nearly every Black girl I know has a story about being blatantly rejected for her Blackness—if not rejected outright, then fetishized or dismissed in some other racially charged way. . . .
>
> My friends and crushes openly told me that they didn't date Black women, confessing this stinging truth as easily as if they were stating a preference for pizza.
>
> Even when I dated my first boyfriend, I spent most of our relationship doubting the authenticity of his affection. I didn't know how to be desired because I didn't believe I was.[84]

A young African American female participant in a study examining skin tone discrimination described the long-term effects of rejection. She recalled her experience playing with other children as a child. "None of the boys wanted to marry me because I was too dark, and they were already asking me 'You know your children are going to come out really dark and that's not good.' But my light skinned friend got married to a different boy every day. But, I didn't because I wasn't light enough, and that really hurt my feelings, and to this day, it still brings me back to the idea that I'm not good enough."[85]

Due to the widespread visibility and accessibility of online dating profiles, sexual racism on online platforms may cause deeper psychic harm to a greater number of individuals than sexual racism offline. An online dater may experience psychic harm each time they log in to a dating platform and see the profiles of other daters who expressly exclude members of their group or when they receive few or no matches because the site considers racial preferences. Dating platforms are aware of the potential harm and some are attempting to address it. The platform Grindr, for example, created a video to raise awareness of the impact of sexual racism and later eliminated its racial filters.[86]

Race Filters Discourage Interracial Contact

Fair housing laws prohibit advertising of racial preferences because it may lead racial minorities to believe that most property owners on that block or neighborhood share those preferences and thus discourage them from seeking housing that is available to them. Similarly, race filters and advertising of racial preferences on dating platforms lead racial minorities to believe that many, if not most, date-seekers have similar preferences. Racial minorities have expressed reluctance to initiate contact with or reply to communications from White users because they assume that most White users will reject them. Not all date-seekers, however, have strong racial preferences, and many would consider dating (and many actually have dated) a person of a different race. Although relatively few date-seekers initiate contact with a person of a different race, a greater number respond to communications from a user of another race. Someone has to make the first move and initiate contact, but race filters and race matching on dating platforms, which signal that racial preferences are widespread, discourage interracial contact.

Race Filters Signal That Discrimination Is Permissible

Fair housing laws prohibit advertising of racial preferences because they may signal that housing discrimination is generally permissible and thereby lead to more widespread discrimination. Similarly, race filters implicitly convey that users' racial preferences are "normal and acceptable"[87] and may lead users to believe that the law supports racial discrimination on digital platforms. It may also lead users to assume that discrimination in other areas is legal. Studies suggest that individuals who exclude potential romantic partners of the basis of race often hold those same preferences in other settings, even when discrimination in those settings is prohibited.[88] The correlation between sexual racism and racial discrimination in other contexts is not surprising. As we saw in Chapter 1, individuals' reasons for rejecting members of certain groups as romantic partners are often based on racial stereotypes. Those same stereotypes affect perceptions of whether a person is a desirable tenant or employee; thus, race filters on dating platforms may inadvertently encourage discrimination in housing and employment.

Race Filters Facilitate Discrimination

Anti-discrimination laws allow certain individuals to discriminate when selling or renting a home or when hiring a nanny or housekeeper. The law also allows prospective adoptive parents to discriminate on any basis when adopting a child. Third parties, however, may not facilitate such discrimination in most cases. Yet, dating platforms that ask users to indicate their race, allow filtering by race, or match users based on race or racial preferences are engaging in the same type of behavior that the law prohibits in the housing, employment, and public adoption contexts. These platforms facilitate discrimination, or what Sonu Bedi calls "digital steering,"[89] by encouraging users, or making it easy for them, to discriminate. I agree with scholars who have argued that the law should prohibit dating platforms from facilitating discrimination.[90]

I am not suggesting that the law should push individuals to choose an intimate partner that they do not want. Just as the law allows prospective adoptive parents to reject a child on the basis of race and allows individuals to refuse to hire a nanny on the basis of race, the law should not interfere with an individual's choice of romantic partner. However, similar to real estate brokers, employment agencies, and public adoption agencies, dating platforms should be prohibited from categorizing users by race, eliciting or accommodating users' discriminatory preferences, and providing features that allow users to filter by race.

The law has the power to prohibit third-party commercial actors such as dating platforms from facilitating discrimination in the same way it prohibits employment agencies and real estate brokers from facilitating race discrimination even when the individual client may legally discriminate. Dating platforms are businesses similar to employment agencies and real estate brokers. Many dating platforms charge for their services, but even if they do not, the law could nonetheless prohibit them from facilitating discrimination by their users in the same way it prohibits employment agencies and real estate brokers that do not charge for their services from facilitating discrimination.

Section 1981

The law prohibits both public and private entities from discriminating when making and enforcing contracts. Section 1981 of the Civil Rights Act of 1866 provides that all persons "have the same right . . . to make and enforce contracts . . . as is enjoyed by white citizens"; this right includes the right to "enjoyment of all benefits, privileges, terms, and conditions of the contractual relationship."[91] Nancy Leong and Aaron Belzer have argued that "when a user signs up with a given [platform economy business], the user and the [platform economy business] become parties to a contract. A secondary or subsidiary contract is formed between the user and provider when the user engages with the application to take advantage of the service being offered. If a non-white user suffers inferior service or even a total denial of service on the basis of her race, her ability to contract with the [platform economy business] is impaired and section 1981 should apply."[92]

When a dating platform allows its users to filter by race or matches individuals based on race or racial preferences, it denies racial minorities the same opportunity as Whites to find an intimate partner. The dating platform has arguably denied them the "benefits, privileges, terms, and conditions of the contractual relationship" that White users enjoy, and therefore, violates Section 1981.

Public Accommodations Laws and Sexual Racism Offline

Although the law does not explicitly prohibit facilitation of sexual racism *offline*, public accommodations laws, discussed above, make such facilitation unlikely. A local bar that serves predominantly White customers may not exclude Latinos, for example, from entering the premises even if the bar's mostly White clientele requests it. The bar may not exclude Latinos even if it is holding a speed-dating event and the other participants have expressly stated that they will not date Latinos. Although the bar's customers may choose to ignore any Latino customers, they cannot be shielded from their presence. A person who goes to a bar in the hopes of finding a romantic partner of their preferred race cannot ask the bar to exclude customers of other races or to seat those persons in a separate area so that they never have to see them. Yet, this is precisely what online dating platforms do when they categorize users by race, design their platforms to facilitate filtering by race, or use algorithms that consider race when matching users. Dating platforms "hide" entire groups from the view of other users even though a bar could not legally exclude individuals on the basis of race or relegate them to the back room to be hidden from customers who do not wish to see members of that race. As Jevan Hutson, Jessie Taft, Solon Barocas, and Karen Levy have noted, these platforms "cause the users excluded from a search to become invisible: they are screened out of the 'dating pool' before they are even recognized as potential participants."[93]

Nancy Leong and Aaron Belzer have argued that websites and platforms are the new public accommodations and that the law should therefore prohibit them from facilitating discriminating just as it does in the case of establishments with physical locations.[94] They write: "Like the public accommodations traditionally covered by Title II of the Civil Rights Act, PEBs [platform economy businesses] are held out as open to the public, so ensuring that such entities do not engage in race discrimination comports with the purpose of that legislation. Moreover, if the traditional economy business that a [platform economy businesses] is replacing is a public accommodation, then it makes sense to categorize the two in the same way. To act differently would move an increasingly large number of businesses outside the scope of our civil rights enforcement mechanisms."[95]

Until recently, individuals seeking an intimate partner frequented bars and night clubs in the hopes of meeting someone, but dating platforms have replaced these establishments as places to meet intimate partners.[96] It is estimated that one-third of partners in recent marriages and 60 percent of same-sex couples met online.[97] Thus, dating platforms should not be permitted to discriminate to any greater extent than bars, nightclubs, and other places of public accommodations.

If dating platforms did not elicit racial preferences and provide race filters, users would have to do what readers of personal ads did for decades. They would have to browse each user's photo and profile before deciding to accept or reject them. Although users with strong racial preferences might reject an individual of their nonpreferred race based on the photo alone, racial or ethnic background is not always discernible from a photo. (For example, I am Latina but different people have assumed that I am Middle-Eastern, Indian, Pakistani, African American, Italian (specifically Sicilian), or Portuguese.) A date-seeker might contact another user based on their photo and profile without knowing their race and not learn their race until after they have met and discovered a mutual attraction. At this point, the date-seeker who thought they had strong racial preferences may find that those preferences were actually not as important as other traits. They might also discover that the person they are attracted to does not fit their racial stereotype. As studies have found, people often do not know what they want in an intimate partner; their "intimate preferences are somewhat fluid, and are shaped both by the options presented to them and through encounters with things they don't expect."[98]

This is what often happens in the offline world. When a person sees someone they find attractive at school, at the gym, or in a club and decides to approach them, they may not know the person's racial identity. They may not learn the person's racial identity until after several dates as it might seem like an odd question to ask on a first date (or before the first date). At that point they might realize that their racial preferences were not as strong as they thought. Platforms that elicit racial preferences and enable searches that exclude profiles on the basis of race eliminate these opportunities for individuals of different racial backgrounds to even see each other. These filtering tools not only deny racial minorities equal access to the platform's services, but also impoverish the experience for all daters, including Whites.

Freedom of Intimate Association

Online daters might argue that requiring platforms to eliminate race filters or algorithms that match users based on racial preferences infringes on their constitutional freedom of intimate association. Specifically, they might assert that because the underlying activity—discrimination when seeking a romantic partner—is constitutionally protected, the law may not prohibit dating sites from facilitating the protected activity. As shown, however, the law currently prevents third parties from facilitating discrimination in several different settings. Employment agencies and real estate brokers are prohibited from accommodating their clients' racial preferences, but no court has found that these restrictions violate the client's freedom of intimate association.

Furthermore, requiring dating platforms to eliminate race-based filters and race-based algorithms would not deprive users of the ability to express racial preferences on their profiles and to exclude other users on any basis, including race. Some users state their race and racial preferences on their profile, along with a description of other characteristics, preferences, and interests. When creating a profile on Zoosk, for example, date-seekers may describe their "perfect match." Zoosk does not place any restrictions on what a user may write in this section, and platforms are not required to monitor what information users include in their profiles. Indeed, section 230 of the federal Communications Decency Act of 1996 protects websites from liability based on users' discriminatory statements so long as the website did not facilitate discrimination.[99] Like Zoosk, Plenty of Fish offers users the option of writing a summary about their interests and preferences, and while it prohibits "sexual language" in this section, it does not prohibit users from expressing racial or ethnic preferences.

Given the harms caused by advertising of racial preferences, it is worth exploring whether the law should prohibit users from making discriminatory statements in their profiles in the same way that the Fair Housing Act prohibits a Mrs. Murphy owner from advertising racially discriminatory preferences even though she may legally discriminate. While the government may not interfere with an individual's choice of an intimate partner, it can arguably prohibit users from advertising discriminatory preferences on online platforms. Advertising discriminatory preferences on online platforms where they may be seen by thousands of users is not an intimate activity protected by the freedom of intimate association. As David Bernstein has argued, although the government may not restrict a person's choice of roommate, "It is *not* unconstitutional for the government to prohibit someone from advertising discriminatory preferences" when seeking a roommate.[100] As he explains, "While who one chooses to live with involves intimate association rights, publicly advertising one's discriminatory preferences in an advertisement for a roommate is not only not an 'intimate' activity, it's a very public one." Similarly, while one's choice of a romantic partner involves intimate association rights, advertising for a partner on a dating platform that millions of people may see is a very public activity and one that might suggest that the platform and the law condone discrimination.

Platforms' Voluntary Efforts to Address Sexual Racism

Dating sites are not the only platforms in which racial discrimination occurs. In recent years, Craigslist, Airbnb, and Uber have faced allegations that their platforms enabled users to discriminate against racial minorities.[101] Craigslist, Airbnb, and Uber's role in facilitating discrimination is significantly smaller than that of most dating platforms. They never asked users to indicate their race, they never elicited racial preferences, and they never provided drop-down menus allowing users to exclude other users on the basis of race or any other protected category. Craigslist and Airbnb provided a forum for users to include any information they deemed relevant when posting a room or home for rent, and Uber provided a tool for individuals seeking a ride to connect with drivers in the area. Yet, although online platforms are generally not liable for the discriminatory content posted by their users unless the site encouraged discrimination,[102] amidst pressure from social media such as #AirbnbWhileBlack, these platforms have chosen to expressly prohibit users from posting discriminatory statements or discriminating.[103] Airbnb, for example, adopted the following nondiscrimination policy:

> Airbnb hosts may not
> - Decline a guest based on race, color, ethnicity, national origin, religion, sexual orientation, gender identity, or marital status.
> - Impose any different terms or conditions based on race, color, ethnicity, national origin, religion, sexual orientation, gender identity, or marital status.

- Post any listing or make any statement that discourages or indicates a preference for or against any guest on account of race, color, ethnicity, national origin, religion, sexual orientation, gender identity, or marital status.[104]

Uber similarly prohibits discrimination "against users based on race, religion, national origin, disability, sexual orientation, sex, marital status, gender identity, age or any other characteristic protected under applicable law" and explains that "such discrimination includes ... any user refusing to provide or accept services based on any of these characteristics."[105] Craigslist has also taken steps to curtail discrimination on its platform by interpreting fair housing laws to prohibit racially discriminatory advertisements for roommates or housemates,[106] even though the U.S. Court of Appeals for the Ninth Circuit has held that fair housing laws do not apply to roommates or housemates. Users who discriminate in violation of these platforms' policies may be banned from the platforms.

Some dating platforms have attempted to address sexual racism. Chappy, for example, prohibits users from stating any racial preferences in their profiles,[107] and Hornet prohibits users from posting any discriminatory content.[108] While some platforms, such as Tinder, Bumble, and HER, have never had racial preference filters,[109] others made changes to their policies in response to complaints. Grindr, for example, launched its Kindr campaign in 2018 after the Asian American actor Sinakhone Keodara came across a user's profile bio that read "Not interested in Asians" and announced plans to bring a class action suit against Grindr for perpetuating "blatant sexual racism by not monitoring or censoring anti-Asian and anti-black profiles."[110] The Kindr campaign includes videos that seek to raise awareness of the harms caused by sexual racism and discriminatory postings.[111] As part of its campaign, Grindr also announced that it would remove discriminatory statements from users' profiles.[112] Two years later, after protests over the murders of Black men by police officers, Grindr and Hornet (which have more than 34 million users combined) went a step further and announced that they would remove race and ethnicity filters from their platforms.[113]

The decisions of these platforms to address sexual racism might suggest that legal intervention is unnecessary as social norms will push platforms to stop facilitating discrimination or prohibit it altogether as Uber and Airbnb did. Not all platforms, however, will stop facilitating discrimination in the absence of legal action.[114] Even if they do, the law's signal that such conduct is undesirable is powerful. There is a difference between when an entity *voluntarily* decides not to discriminate and when the law expressly prohibits discrimination. By prohibiting platforms from facilitating race discrimination, the law *signals* that it condemns discrimination in the intimate context. As Matt Zwolinski has argued, "Legal regulations can serve an important role, even if they are very difficult to enforce, by sending a message to the public that they ought not engage in a certain behavior. . . . By regulating private discrimination, the law could effectively send a message of disapproval regarding such behavior, regardless of whether its regulations could be effectively enforced."[115]

Platforms that facilitate sexual racism cause psychic harm and signal that sexual racism is acceptable. They may also limit the ability of members of some racial groups to find romantic partners with whom to form intimate connections. These reasons are sufficient to warrant legal intervention. But sexual racism has even broader long-term economic and social consequences. These are discussed in subsequent chapters.

4

How Law Shapes Opportunity for Interracial Intimacy

In our segregated society, many Americans do not have opportunities to interact with people of different backgrounds. Most Whites live in neighborhoods with few African Americans or Latinos even though these groups comprise one-third of the U.S. population.[1] African American and Latino children often attend K–12 schools with few White students,[2] and, with the exception of historically Black colleges and universities (HBCUs), the majority of selective institutions are predominantly White.[3] Workplaces are more racially diverse, but Whites and racial minorities often hold vastly different jobs, with the latter disproportionately represented in positions wrongly labelled as "low-skilled/unskilled labor."[4] As a result, even in integrated workplaces, Whites and racial minorities may find that they rarely cross paths.[5] Dining areas in workplaces and schools are often segregated, with Whites sitting with Whites and racial minorities sitting with other racial minorities.[6] The majority of White individuals do not have any African American friends, and neither do most Latinos.[7] It is no surprise then that the rate of interracial marriage is significantly lower than it would be if race did not play a role in our choice of romantic partners.[8]

This chapter builds on the work of legal scholars who have examined the structural barriers to interracial relationships.[9] As we saw in prior chapters, legally sanctioned discrimination limited interactions between people of different races and thereby influenced our romantic preferences for centuries. Although the law now prohibits discrimination in housing,[10] education,[11] and employment,[12] racial segregation in neighborhoods, schools, and workplaces is ubiquitous. One reason is that the consequences of discriminatory practices in effect throughout most of the twentieth century, such as redlining, racial steering, and racially restrictive covenants, continue to be felt today. The disadvantages experienced by (and perpetrated on) African Americans, Latinos, and other groups who were denied access to desirable neighborhoods, government programs that made home ownership possible, quality schools, and educational and employment opportunities did not disappear with the enactment of civil rights laws. These disadvantages were passed on to future generations and continue to reproduce racial inequality.

Current practices further serve to facilitate and maintain racial segregation and isolation. Exclusionary zoning laws and legally permitted discrimination by owners of owner-occupied multi-family dwellings arguably facilitate racial segregation as effectively as the explicitly racially discriminatory policies of the past. The school assignment system in most districts ensures that the majority of children who live in segregated neighborhoods will attend similarly segregated K–12 schools. The inadequate education provided by schools that Gary Orfield and Danielle Jarvie have referred to as "apartheid schools, comprised of 99 to 100 percent non-White students,"[13] keep all but a small percentage of African American and Latino students out of selective colleges and universities. In the workplace, racial minorities tend to be clustered in low-wage positions and sectors, which makes interactions with the predominantly White managerial and professional staff unlikely. The opportunities for meaningful interaction that are a prerequisite to interracial partnering across races are limited.

These limited opportunities for individuals of different races to interact at work, school, or in their neighborhood are the result of historically discriminatory practices and current practices sanctioned by law. These structural barriers not only make interracial partnering challenging but also reinforce racial stereotypes and the perception that members of certain groups are not suitable long-term partners.

Residential Segregation before 1968

Consider the places where people are likely to find a romantic partner. While many couples who began dating relatively recently met online, many (and certainly those who have been together for many years) met through school, work, the gym, the local coffee shop, or family and friends. A surprising number of couples meet at weddings.[14] While no one can predict where they will meet the person who will become their long-term partner, whom one meets is largely determined by past and present legally sanctioned practices that brought (and still bring) some people together and kept (and still keep) those of different races apart.

From Race-Based Zoning to Exclusionary Zoning

I live in New Jersey, one of the most racially and ethnically diverse states in the country, where 36.6 percent of the population identify as African American, Asian American, or Latino.[15] I work in Newark, the largest city in New Jersey and the third most residentially segregated city in the United States.[16] How did a large city in a racially diverse state become so segregated?

While many factors contribute to residential segregation, the role of federal, state, and local government actors in segregating our neighborhoods is well-documented.[17] Indeed, the U.S. Department of Housing and Urban Development has acknowledged the active role of federal, state, and local actors "in creating segregated living patterns and inequalities of opportunity."[18] The government created segregated living patterns through zoning laws such as that passed by the city of Louisville, Kentucky, requiring "separate blocks, for residences, places of abode, and places of assembly by white and colored people respectively."[19] As discussed in prior chapters, one of the primary goals of these zoning laws was to prevent interracial intimacy.[20]

Race-based zoning laws have been illegal for more than a century since the U.S. Supreme Court held in 1917 in *Buchanan v. Warley* that these laws violated the U.S. Constitution.[21] As historian Richard Rothstein has noted, after the Court's decision, lawmakers enacted race-neutral single-family zoning (also known as exclusionary zoning) laws that prohibited the construction of apartments and multi-family dwellings "as a way to circumvent the ruling."[22] Although single-family zoning was a direct response to the Court's ruling in *Buchanan*, the Supreme Court has upheld single-family zoning laws, reasoning that apartments are a "mere parasite" on single-family neighborhoods.[23] Today, 75 percent of residential land in most large cities and suburbs is zoned for detached single family homes only.[24] Single-family zoning disproportionately excludes African Americans and Latinos from majority White neighborhoods and ensures that neighborhoods remain segregated.

Redlining

While zoning is local, the federal government's policies created racially segregated neighborhoods throughout the entire country. In the 1930s, the federal government, through the Home Owners' Loan Corporation and later through its successor, the Federal Housing Administration (FHA), began offering federally insured mortgages to qualified homebuyers. The federal government, however, refused to insure properties in neighborhoods with mostly African American residents. Using color-coded maps, it outlined the neighborhoods it determined were most likely to decrease in value, and thus too risky to insure, in red.[25] These "redlined" neighborhoods all had significant numbers of African American residents. In contrast, areas that were virtually 100 percent White were outlined in green, which indicated minimal risk and thus insurable properties.[26] In some cases, mere proximity to an African American neighborhood was sufficient to disqualify homes in White neighborhoods from federal support. For example, the FHA refused to insure a development for White families because it determined that it was too close to an African American community. It was only after the developer agreed to build a six-foot high, half-mile long concrete wall separating the White development from the African American neighborhood that the FHA agreed to insure the project.[27] *Ninety-eight percent* (98 percent) of the homes built with federal financing in the 1940s and 1950s were sold to Whites.[28]

Following the federal government's lead, private banks also denied mortgages for properties in areas that the federal government would not insure.[29] In short, the federal government's actions not only led to the devaluation of properties in redlined areas but also deprived these neighborhoods of the resources needed to provide essential services such as quality schools. While some African Americans sought to purchase homes in neighborhoods that were not redlined,[30] other policies, such as racially restrictive covenants and racially motivated violence (both discussed below), prevented such purchases. Thus, African Americans could neither purchase homes in White neighborhoods nor secure loans to purchase homes in Black neighborhoods.

Racially Restrictive Covenants

In 1950, the population of Newark, New Jersey, was more than 80 percent non-Hispanic White.[31] By 2020 that figure had shrunk to less than 10 percent.[32] Government actors in New Jersey and across the county adopted a number of policies that encouraged White families to leave the cities for the suburbs but precluded racial minorities from doing the same. While redlining deprived minority neighborhoods of resources, racially restrictive language in housing deeds kept racial, and in some cases, religious minorities out of White neighborhoods. Although the language in these deeds varied, they typically provided that "no persons other than members of the Caucasian or White race shall be permitted to occupy any portion of said property, other than as domestics in the employ of the occupants of the premises."[33] These racial restrictions were common as private developers, homeowners' associations, and homeowners across the country included these clauses in residential deeds. In fact, in 1948, when the Supreme Court declared in *Shelley v. Kramer* that racially restrictive clauses violate the U.S. Constitution, three of the nine sitting justices had such clauses in the deeds of their homes.[34]

The law made it possible for private developers and homeowners to keep racial minorities from purchasing homes in White neighborhoods. Courts routinely enforced racially restrictive covenants until 1948,[35] when the Supreme Court in *Shelley v. Kramer* reversed its prior decision upholding these covenants and held that their enforcement violated the Constitution's guarantee of equal treatment.[36] At times, government actors even required developers to include racially restrictive covenants in their properties as a condition of federal support.[37] For example, when the developer William Levitt sought to build 17,000 homes in Long Island for veterans after World War II, the federal government agreed to insure the loans only if African Americans were barred from purchasing the new homes and the deeds prohibited selling or renting to African Americans in the future.[38] In other cases, state actors facilitated discrimination by developers. For example, New York amended its laws in 1938 to permit the Metropolitan Life Insurance Company to build a development "for white people only" in Parkchester in the Bronx and later Stuyvesant Town in Manhattan.[39] My parents (who are Latino) bought a condo in Parkchester in 1989, decades after the Whites-only restriction had been rendered illegal by the Fair Housing Act's prohibition on housing discrimination and the vast majority of Whites had moved out.[40] Stuyvesant Town in Manhattan, however, remains predominantly White.[41]

Seventy-five years after the Court's decision in *Shelley v. Kramer* and more than five decades after the enactment of the Fair Housing Act, one can still find these racially restrictive clauses in many deeds.[42] They are, of course, no longer enforceable, but their legacy is evident in the many neighborhoods that remain predominantly White. Although the law no longer requires nor facilitates any racial restrictions on the purchase of property, racial minorities continue to be excluded from these neighborhoods as a result of single-family zoning laws and the lost opportunity to purchase these homes when they were affordable. As a result, these neighborhoods remain predominantly White.

State-Sanctioned Harassment and Violence

While zoning restrictions, redlining, and racially restrictive covenants kept the majority of racial minorities out of White neighborhoods, a small percentage of minority families managed to purchase properties in White neighborhoods, especially after the Court's decision in *Shelley v. Kramer*. These families often faced harassment and racially motivated violence perpetrated by White neighbors determined to keep racial minorities out.[43] The police rarely protected them.[44] To the contrary, the police often harassed and detained racial minorities as they moved about the neighborhood.[45] These tactics discouraged all but the bravest racial minorities from moving into White neighborhoods and ensured that communities would remain predominantly White even after formal barriers to entry were removed.

Racial Steering

While federal, state, and local government policies engineered residential segregation, professional organizations adopted and enforced these policies. The 1924 National Association of Realtors' Code of Ethics, for example, provided that a realtor should never introduce "into a neighborhood ... members of any race or nationality, or any individuals whose presence will clearly be detrimental to property values in that neighborhood."[46] Given the belief, as reflected by the federal government's practices, that racial minorities would drive down property values, real estate agents steered racial minorities away from White neighborhoods and toward minority neighborhoods only. They also steered Whites toward White neighborhoods and away from minority neighborhoods.[47]

The Past Affects the Present

Adults tend to dine, exercise, and volunteer in their neighborhood while children and adolescents go to school and play with their peers who live near them. These interactions sometimes lead to friendships and romantic relationships, but residential segregation limits opportunities for interactions and meaningful relationships across racial lines. Not surprisingly, rates of interracial marriage are significantly lower in cities with highly segregated neighborhoods as compared to cities with integrated communities, which strongly suggests, as Rose Villazor has argued, that residential segregation is a barrier to interracial partnering.[48]

The government's direct role in segregating our neighborhoods ended in 1968 when Congress passed the Fair Housing Act banning racial discrimination by government or private actors in connection with the sale or rental of housing.[49] Yet, despite the Fair Housing Act[50] and state laws[51] prohibiting racial discrimination in the sale and rental of housing, residential segregation persists as a result of decades of federal, state, and local practices that excluded racial minorities from White neighborhoods.[52] Today, the neighborhoods that previously excluded racial minorities are out of reach for the majority of racial minorities as real estate prices have skyrocketed and affordable housing is concentrated in predominantly low-income minority neighborhoods.[53] Thus, the law continues to shape our intimate desires and choices based on race through both the continuing effects of historic practices and new policies that have race-based effects.

The explicitly racially discriminatory policies that officially ended in 1968 shaped our neighborhoods, opportunities, and desires in ways that continue to be felt by later generations. Whites had opportunities to accumulate wealth as the value of the properties they purchased with government assistance multiplied and provided resources that could fund college educations and down payments on homes for their children. The government denied racial minorities similar opportunities to build wealth.[54] For example, some of the homes that only Whites were permitted to purchase in the 1940s for $5,450 (the equivalent of about $100,000 today) are currently worth about $1.5 million,[55] but redlining and racially restrictive covenants prevented racial minorities from acquiring these properties. This is a main reason the median net worth of African

American households today is less than 15 percent of that of White households[56] and that only 45 percent of African American families as compared to 75 percent of White families own their own home.[57] Marcia Fudge, secretary of the Department of Housing and Urban Development, has remarked that "homeownership is the principal source of wealth creation for most American households,"[58] but as Richard Rothstein has explained, "The enormous black-white wealth gap . . . is in large part a product of black exclusion from homes whose appreciation generated substantial equity for white working-class families with [federally insured] mortgages that propelled them into the middle class."[59]

Individuals today can purchase any home they can afford without regard to race. Yet, as a result of past government policies, many African Americans lack the down payment to purchase a home at all, and they often cannot afford homes in neighborhoods with quality schools and desirable amenities—neighborhoods that tend to be disproportionately White. African American parents and grandparents are less likely than their White counterparts to be able to provide a child with assistance for a down payment because their homes, which tend to be located in predominantly African American and formerly redlined neighborhoods,[60] are valued much lower than comparable homes in predominantly White neighborhoods.[61]

Some predominantly African American and Latino neighborhoods experience overcrowding, underperforming schools, and higher crime rates. Whites point to these conditions to explain why they flock to predominantly White neighborhoods. Government policies created these conditions. The government denied racial minorities access to White neighborhoods—forcing them to remain in cities even as they experienced an increase in residents. It also denied these families access to mortgages to purchase properties in redlined minority neighborhoods and deprived these neighborhoods of the resources needed to fund quality schools and secure the concomitant opportunities that peers in White areas enjoy. As economists have demonstrated and the federal government has acknowledged, redlining created and exacerbated residential segregation and poverty.[62] The redlined "maps became self-fulfilling prophesies" as redlined neighborhoods "were starved of investment."[63] Not surprisingly, neighborhoods that were redlined in the 1930s and 1940s remain racially segregated and extremely poor today.[64] Moreover, private lenders today continue to deprive residents of these communities of services, leading the U.S. Department of Justice in 2021 to create a Combating Redlining Initiative to "combat discriminatory race and national origin-based lending practices."[65]

While the government now prohibits racial steering, its prior policies contributed to current residential segregation. The majority of racial minorities who were steered away from White neighborhoods cannot afford to purchase homes in these neighborhoods today. Thus, historically White neighborhoods remain White even if realtors no longer engage in racial steering. In addition, some realtors continue to engage in racial steering. Although the National Association of Realtors has apologized for its past discriminatory policies,[66] it acknowledged in 2020 that racial "steering continues to be pervasive."[67] A groundbreaking investigation conducted by *Newsday* in 2019 found that in 24 percent of cases, realtors showed different properties to White testers as compared to minority testers.[68]

The effects of prior discriminatory practices are likely to be felt for generations. As Richard Rothstein has asserted, the policies adopted by the government "to create, enforce and sustain residential segregation ... were so powerful that, as a result, even today blacks and whites rarely live in the same communities and have little interracial contact or friendships outside the workplace."[69] When Whites and racial minorities do interact, the potential for meaningful friendships and romantic relationships is hampered by policies that ensured that their childhood neighborhoods and schools were so different that they might as well have been separate nations.[70]

Current Policies Perpetuate Segregation

While the effects of practices that are now illegal affect the present, current policies and practices—such as single-family zoning, the Mrs. Murphy exception, the school assignment system, and spatial segregation—perpetuate physical and psychological distance between racial groups and limit opportunities for interracial relationships.

Residential Segregation

SINGLE-FAMILY ZONING
Single-family zoning disproportionately excludes African Americans and Latinos from predominantly White neighborhoods. The substantial

down payment that single-family homes require places those homes out of reach for most African Americans and Latinos whose median wealth is a fraction of median White wealth, as a result, at least in part, of government policies that helped Whites accumulate wealth.[71] Thus, single-family zoning serves to maintain much of the segregation created by the explicitly discriminatory past practices. Single-family zoning further exacerbates segregation by requiring developers to place multi-family dwellings—including moderate- and low-income units that disproportionately house African Americans and Latinos—in predominantly African American and Latino neighborhoods, since predominantly White areas tend to be zoned for single-family homes only.[72] Single-family zoning also perpetuates the racial wealth gap by pushing African Americans and Latinos into predominantly minority neighborhoods, where property values do not appreciate as rapidly as in White neighborhoods.[73] This wealth gap makes racial minorities less desirable intimate partners and decreases the likelihood of interracial partnering.

As Richard Kahlenberg has observed, single-family zoning creates "barriers that exclude millions of low-income African Americans and Latinos from wealthier white communities."[74] This is not accidental. Single-family zoning, which has been labeled "the new redlining,"[75] is often motivated by a desire to keep racial minorities out of White neighborhoods.[76]

THE MRS. MURPHY EXCEPTION

When Congress enacted the Fair Housing Act in 1968, making racial and other types of discrimination in the sale or rental of housing illegal, it carved out an exception for property owners of certain multi-family dwellings. This exception, known as the Mrs. Murphy exception, allows the owner of a multi-family dwelling with four or fewer units who lives in one of those units to reject a potential tenant for any reason, including race.[77] The exemption sought to protect the First Amendment rights of owners who live in close proximity to their tenants not to associate with members of groups they find objectionable.[78]

The Mrs. Murphy exception might seem inconsequential in cities in which the majority of rental housing is in buildings with more than four units. However, the exception perpetuates the exclusion of racial minorities from predominantly White suburbs where rental housing is often in a two-family or three-family owner-occupied house. These suburbs typically offer better-resourced schools than predominantly minority neighborhoods. With many companies moving to the suburbs, these areas also provide access to jobs. Moreover, as Tanya Hernandez has demonstrated, Mrs. Murphy lessors are not an insignificant source of housing for African Americans and Latinos, even in cities, where renters sublease bedrooms in their apartments.[79] Thus, the law perpetuates residential segregation when it allows property owners to discriminate on the basis of race.

Segregated K–12 Public Schools

The law permitted (and in some states, mandated) segregated schools until 1954 when the U.S. Supreme Court held in *Brown v. Board of Education* (*Brown I*) that segregated schools violated the U.S. Constitution.[80] A year later, the Court ordered schools to desegregate "with all deliberate speed."[81] Yet, public schools in many states are as segregated today as they were in 1954. Approximately 75 percent of African American children attend schools where the majority of students are not White, and 15 percent attend what Gary Orfield and Danielle Jarvie have labeled "apartheid schools, comprised of 99 to 100 percent non-White students."[82] The majority of Latino students also attend schools with mostly racial minorities while most White children attend schools with few Black and Latino students.[83]

Educational segregation today is a direct result of housing segregation. Most students attend schools in their neighborhood, and since most neighborhoods are segregated, the neighborhood school is likely to be segregated as well. In addition, after World War II many White families moved to the suburbs–to those new homes for Whites only discussed above. Given the exclusion of racial minorities from the suburbs, schools in the suburbs were almost exclusively White while the schools in the cities that Whites had fled for the suburbs were predominantly Black or Brown. In an effort to desegregate schools as the Supreme Court had ordered, lower courts imposed desegregation plans that required busing students between predominantly African American cities and their neighboring White suburbs. Legislators, in turn, redrew school district lines to allow children from predominantly African American cities to attend schools in the predominantly White suburbs. Despite many parents' opposition to busing,[84] in 1971 the Supreme Court upheld the redrawing of school district attendance zones and busing as mechanisms to integrate schools.[85]

Three years later, however, in *Milliken v. Bradley*, the Supreme Court invalidated a busing plan between the predominantly African American city of Detroit and its surrounding suburbs, which were predominantly White.[86] The Court reasoned that an inter-district desegregation plan was inappropriate absent evidence of intentional segregation by government actors.[87] Although the lower court found that Detroit's segregated school system was the result of government policies adopted "to establish and maintain the pattern of residential segregation,"[88] on appeal, the Supreme Court disagreed. The Supreme Court rejected the evidence of state-created segregation even though, as shown above, local, state, and federal policies had created the segregated cities and suburbs that led to segregated neighborhood schools. Matthew Lassiter has noted that after the Court's decision in *Milliken*, "White parents in most cities knew that if they moved to the suburbs, their children would be beyond the reach of any busing plan."[89] This is only true, however, because of our school assignment system.

Segregated schools are a direct result of residential segregation, but they are not an inevitable consequence. The school assignment system, not residential segregation per se, places students from segregated neighborhoods in segregated schools. In most states, students are assigned to schools within their school district and cannot attend a public school outside that district. More than 70 percent of public school students attend schools in their district even if their zoned school is underperforming and there is a superior school in the neighboring district.[90] In fact, it is a crime to falsely represent that a student lives in a particular district—for example, by using another family member's address—for the purpose of attending school in that district.[91] Despite the risks, some parents violate these laws in an effort to provide their children with access to quality schools.[92]

School zones are generally drawn along the boundaries of residentially segregated municipalities. Although these municipalities may be next to each other geographically, in many cases, their schools could not be farther apart. To illustrate, I focus on school districts in Union County, New Jersey, where I reside. Approximately 90 percent of the students in four of the poorest school districts in the county—Elizabeth, Hillside,

Plainfield, and Roselle—are predominantly Black and Latino. The poverty rate in these districts is at least 65 percent.[93] In contrast, only 2 percent of the student body in three predominantly White and wealthy school districts in the same county—Cranford, Mountainside, and Westfield—is African American.[94] The same racial and economic disparity exists in two neighboring school districts in Westchester County, New York—the Bronxville Union Free School District and the Mount Vernon School District. Only 1 percent of the students in the Bronxville Union Free School District are African American as compared to 63 percent of the students in the Mount Vernon School District. The median household income of parents with children in the Bronxville public schools is more than four times that of parents with children in Mount Vernon public schools.[95] Although schools in majority-minority districts are typically under-resourced and under-performing, students from predominantly African American and Latino neighborhoods are zoned out of schools in predominantly White and wealthy school districts, even when these schools are in close proximity to their homes. Resistance to changing the current school assignment system continues today, even in the most progressive communities that claim to be committed to racial equality.[96]

Children who attend segregated schools have few opportunities to develop friendships with peers of other races or to date interracially in high school. As noted in earlier chapters, opponents of integration were well aware of this. They feared that if schools were integrated, White children would become friends with racial minorities and that White adolescents—especially their White daughters—would date interracially.[97] Much of the opposition to busing in both southern and northern cities was based on fear that integrated schools would lead to interracial relationships.[98]

The Effects of Segregation in K–12 Schools and Beyond

Equal educational opportunity is a prerequisite to achieving racial equality in our Nation.
—*Students for Fair Admissions, Inc. v. President & Fellows of Harvard College* (Sotomayor, J., dissenting)[99]

Segregated schools not only limit opportunities for interracial friendships and romantic relationships; they also deprive racial minorities of the educational resources and opportunities enjoyed by students in better-resourced predominantly White schools. By fostering educational inequality, segregated schools contribute to racial isolation in higher education and the workplace, and the effects may persist in the next generation. In short, segregated public schools limit opportunities for interracial relationships far beyond their temporal and geographical boundaries.

THE ACHIEVEMENT GAP

Schools with mostly White students are typically better resourced than schools with mostly African American and Latino students and offer superior curricula, facilities, and more experienced teachers and counselors.[100] As such, segregated schools deprive racial minorities of equal opportunities for academic and professional success.[101] This is evident from the achievement gap. In 2019, only 18 and 23 percent of African American and Latino fourth grade students, respectively, were proficient in reading as compared with 45 and 57 percent of White and Asian American students, respectively.[102] There is a similar gap in math proficiency.[103] Attending a school with predominantly African American and Latino students or students from low-income families is correlated with poorer academic performance by students of all races.[104] Only 40 percent of high school students at predominantly African American and Latino schools graduate on time, regardless of race.[105]

To be clear, I am not suggesting that racial minorities must attend schools with White children in order to learn. Proximity to White students per se does not lead to better educational outcomes. But schools with mostly African American and Latino students tend to be high-poverty schools and typically lack the resources of majority White schools. As David Troutt has observed, "No variable is as important to creating a strong learning environment and reducing racial achievement gaps than the presence of a middle-class majority of kids in the classroom."[106]

HIGHER EDUCATION

Segregated K–12 schools limit African American and Latino students' access to higher education and thereby limit opportunities for interracial relationships. Students who attend predominantly African American and Latino K–12 schools are typically not as well-prepared for college as their peers who attended better-resourced, predominantly White schools. They are thus less likely to attend, or even apply to, college and in particular, elite universities.[107] Those who do attend often experience racial isolation at predominantly White institutions as racial segregation is common in dormitory life, dining halls, and social activities.[108]

White students who attended predominantly White K–12 schools often experience racial anxiety—"they worry that they will be perceived as racist"[109]—when interacting with African-American and Latino students in college for the first time. African-American and Latino students also find interactions with White peers awkward at times. As a result of this racial anxiety on both sides, many White students graduate from college without having had a close African-American or Latino friend.[110] This is not surprising. In the absence of opportunities to interact with peers of different racial backgrounds while growing up, our beliefs about members of these groups are likely to be shaped by stereotypes, media representations, and the ideas that parents, other family members, and friends convey explicitly or unintentionally. As we saw in earlier chapters, college students hold many of the same implicit racial biases as the rest of the population.[111] Young adults who did not have opportunities as children to develop interracial friendships are less likely to have interracial relationships in college. Segregated K–12 schools create psychological distance between groups that may continue even when a college or university is racially diverse and makes it difficult for college students to see their peers of different races as potential romantic partners.

Although dating apps are now the most common way to meet a long-term partner, a 2019 study of 10,000 recently married or engaged couples found that 17 percent met in college and another 13 percent met through work.[112] Given that the rate of intermarriage is higher among college-educated individuals, interracial couples may be even more likely to have met in college. Justice Ketanji Brown Jackson, the first African American woman on the U.S. Supreme Court, for example, met her husband, who is White, when they were students at Harvard University.[113]

Universities have long been known as a place to meet a potential spouse. This led to the now antiquated term "Mrs. Degree," used sarcastically to describe the course of study undertaken by a woman who attends college for the primary purpose of finding a successful husband.[114] In fact, a quick Google search pulls up articles listing the best colleges for finding a spouse; these include well-known institutions such as Vanderbilt,

Cornell, Princeton, Middlebury, and Washington and Lee.[115] While some college students might be reluctant to admit that they are searching for a life partner while in college, their participation in The Marriage Pact, a matching service for students at their institution, suggests otherwise. The Marriage Pact, which was available in 78 selective colleges and universities as of June 2023, markets itself as a "back-up plan" because "college is the best place to find The One."[116] Participants complete a detailed questionnaire that claims to uses an algorithm to "analyze every single one of the thousands of participants on your campus to find your perfect match."[117] The program even provides participants with the name of their perfect match, presumably so they can find that person on campus. While colleges provide opportunities to meet a potential long-term romantic partner, the underrepresentation of African Americans and Latinos in these institutions limits opportunities to find a romantic partner of a different race.

Opportunities for interracial interactions on some college campuses are likely to decrease even as the percentage of college-age racial minorities is increasing. While selective colleges and universities used race-conscious policies for many decades in an effort to admit a diverse student body, the number of African-American and Latino students at these institutions will likely decrease as a result of the Supreme Court's decision in *Students for Fair Admissions Inc. v. President & Fellows of Harvard College* in 2023.[118] In that case, the Court held that the use of affirmative action in college admissions violates the U.S. Constitution's Equal Protection Clause and barred public and private institutions receiving any federal funding from considering an applicant's race. As a result of the Court's decision, selective institutions are likely to experience a significant reduction in the representation of African-American and Latino students.[119] Indeed, a 2020 study conducted more than twenty years after California banned affirmative action in public universities found that enrollment of African-American and Latino students across the entire state university system had declined.[120] Thus, college students in the coming years may have even fewer opportunities to date interracially than students today.

THE WORKPLACE

Segregated K–12 schools may also contribute to segregation and stratification in the workplace. Since segregated schools deny African American and Latino students equal educational opportunities and since these groups are less likely to attend or complete college as a result, they are significantly more likely to be employed in low-wage positions. While they may work in the same organizations as the White professionals who likely had greater access to educational opportunities growing up, the opportunities to interact with those from other backgrounds and to develop friendships and romantic relationships across class and racial lines are quite limited. A law firm might employ people of all races and ethnic backgrounds, for example, but African Americans and Latinos are more likely to work in the mail room, photocopying department, dining services, janitorial services, and other support positions while those in professional and managerial positions are disproportionately White. Thus, while approximately 13 percent of recently married or engaged couples met through work,[121] the opportunities for meaningful cross-racial interactions necessary for intimate relationships are limited.

FUTURE GENERATIONS

Groups that are denied access to educational opportunities are unlikely to hold the higher salary positions that might enable them to rent or purchase homes in wealthier neighborhoods. As a result, African Americans and Latinos will likely continue to live in segregated neighborhoods and send their children to segregated schools similar to those that they themselves attended, thereby ensuring that opportunities for interracial friendships and romantic relationships will be far between and few.

Spatial Segregation

Our neighborhoods and schools are not the only spaces that are segregated by race. As Elise Boddie has observed, "Places can also have a racial identity and meaning based on socially engrained racial biases regarding the people who inhabit, frequent, or are associated with particular places and racialized cultural norms of spatial belonging and exclusion."[122] The places where we shop, dine, and play have a racial identity. Many public spaces—shopping centers, restaurants, and parks—are what sociologist Elijah Anderson describes as "white spaces" that "reinforce . . . a normative sensibility in settings in which black people are typically absent, not expected, or marginalized when present."[123] Other spaces serve mostly racial minorities and are recognized as "Black spaces" or "Latino spaces", for example, but relatively few spaces outside of large cities are racially integrated. Even places of worship have a racial identity, leading church leaders to remark that "eleven o'clock on Sundays is still the most segregated hour in America," as Martin Luther King Jr. lamented in 1963.[124] In the most heinous exploitation of spatial segregation, White supremacists have targeted public spaces that they knew to be Black, Latino, or Asian and murdered dozens of people in these racialized spaces.[125]

As Elise Boddie has shown, when spaces are racialized, racial minorities often find that they "are excluded from public spaces that are identified as 'white' and treated as being only for white people."[126] Although racial minorities are no longer explicitly excluded from public spaces such as restaurants, hotels, and public swimming pools as they were in the past,[127] their freedom to enter spaces reserved for Whites is limited by the racial profiling they encounter when they enter a store or drive or walk through a White neighborhood, experiences described as "driving while Black" or "driving while Brown."[128] In New Jersey, where I reside, African American friends have refused to dine at restaurants in certain predominantly White neighborhoods because the police are known to stop African Americans driving or walking in these neighborhoods.[129] Mark Denbeaux, a professor of law at Seton Hall, and his students conducted a study that demonstrated that African Americans and Latinos driving through Bloomfield, a predominantly White suburb in New Jersey, were disproportionately targeted by the police and ticketed for traffic and other minor offenses.[130] The majority of those ticketed were residents of Newark and East Orange, two predominantly African American and Latino cities.

Racial minorities in predominantly White neighborhoods continue to experience racial harassment from neighbors and the police.[131] In 2009 Henry Louis Gates, an African American professor at Harvard University, was arrested in his home after a White neighbor called the police alleging that two Black men were trying to break into a house. Unbeknownst to the caller, the object of the alleged break-in was Gates's own home.[132] Gates had just returned home from a trip to China and found that his front door was jammed so he forced it open with the help of his cab driver, who was also Black. The police officer who responded to the White neighbor's call did not believe Gates when he explained that he was trying to enter his own home even after he provided identification.

Fortunately, Gates was not harmed during his encounter with the police, but other African Americans whom neighbors have deemed to be suspicious have lost their lives. In 2012, seventeen-year-old Trayvon Martin, who was African American, was killed when a member of a neighborhood watch decided that he did not belong in a White neighborhood.[133] Similarly in 2020, three White men chased Ahmaud Arbery, an African American man who was running through their predominantly White neighborhood, and fatally shot him.[134] Harassment by neighbors and the police is so prevalent that scholars have coined the terms—"driving while Black,"[135] "walking while Black,"[136] or "running while Black"[137] to describe it. These experiences or the expectation thereof leads racial minorities to avoid White neighborhoods.

Police stops of racial minorities in White neighborhoods are the most obvious example of how state actors perpetuate spatial segregation. Legislative decisions, while more subtle, have similar effects. Lawmakers have rejected proposals to expand public transportation that would allow racial minorities without automobiles to access White spaces.[138] Constituents in wealthy White suburbs in Atlanta, San Francisco, and Washington, DC, for example, have urged legislators to oppose transit stops in their neighborhoods because they would otherwise allow low-income racial minorities to access their spaces and, as Sarah Schindler has argued, "elected local officials . . . often act at the behest of their constituents."[139]

In upstate New York, the owners of a mall in Cheektowaga, a predominantly White suburb of Buffalo,[140] refused to allow buses from low-income African American neighborhoods to stop at the mall because, in the words of their executives, those were not "the type of people they want to come to the mall."[141] Instead the buses had to stop across the highway, and so anyone who wanted to go to the mall from there would have to cross seven lanes of traffic. After Cynthia Wiggins, a seventeen-year-old African American resident of Buffalo, was killed when she was hit by a dump truck as she crossed the highway, African Americans accused the mall of using "the highway as a moat" to deny low-income African Americans access.[142] Although the mall was private property, town officials could have required it to allow buses from these neighborhoods to stop at the mall, especially since the mall allowed buses from other areas, including Canada, to stop there.[143] The mall ultimately did allow buses from inner-city Buffalo to stop on its grounds, but its action was too late for Cynthia Wiggins.

The failure of lawmakers to invest in public transportation denies racial minorities, who are more likely than Whites to rely on public transportation, access to jobs in the suburbs.[144] Cynthia Wiggins was crossing the seven-lane highway to get to her job at the mall when she was crushed by the dump truck. The lack of access to jobs in the suburbs not only deprives individuals of employment opportunities but also limits opportunities for people of different races to work together or interact. As noted, even today some people meet their romantic partners at work. However, this is not possible if some workplaces remain predominantly White because racial minorities cannot access them.

The majority of racial minorities are not poor, and some can afford to live in wealthy and predominantly White neighborhoods and to shop, dine, and play in White spaces. But many chose not to because they sense that they are not welcome.[145] When a Black or Brown person walks into a White space, Whites notice and, in some cases, look at the person with suspicion, even though they might be unaware that they are doing so.[146] The absence of Black and Brown people in White spaces—the result of decades of government-sanctioned (and government-mandated) segregation—signals to racial minorities who venture into these spaces, whether for work or leisure, that they do not belong. Thus, spatial segregation limits opportunities for interracial interactions and intimate relationships in two ways. First, it limits propinquity. Second, it creates discomfort for individuals whose racial identity is different from that of the space, which in turn can make them avoid that space and thus make interracial interactions less likely.

Assume that an Afro-Latina woman, who attended schools with few White students and who lives in a predominantly Latino neighborhood, works at an upscale clothing store in a White suburb. Most of the shoppers are White. When the woman takes her lunch break, she notices that all of the customers at the local deli are White. She purchases her lunch to go and decides to eat it in a nearby park. Most of the people in the park are White. She spots a bench with an attractive White man sitting on one end. Although all of the other benches are occupied, she is hesitant to ask the man if he would mind sharing the bench with her because she feels that she does not belong in that park. Had the park not been a White space, she would have felt more comfortable asking to share the bench.

As it turns out, the White man on the bench is attracted to women of all racial backgrounds but he lives and works in White spaces and has few opportunities to interact with people who are not White. Although he spots the Afro-Latina woman as she is clearly looking around for a place to sit, given his limited interactions with racial minorities, he is hesitant to invite her to sit. Had he had more interactions with people of color in the past, or had the park not been a White space, he might have felt comfortable inviting her to sit and share the park bench.

We are unlikely to partner interracially if we do not have the opportunity to meet and develop relationships with people of different races where we live, work, go to school, or play. This was true before the internet and dating apps. It is still true today. Our geographic location no longer limits whom we see as dating sites allow us to browse profiles of people across the state, country, and world. Yet, the people we see (or saw growing up) in our neighborhoods, at school, at work, at the gym, or at restaurants influence our comfort around people of other races, our cross-racial interactions, and whether we will see those people as potential partners. At the same time, the lack of interracial partnering perpetuates segregation, as same-race couples are more likely to live in neighborhoods with people of their own race and to only have friends of that race.

5

Perpetuating Inequality

The Psychological, Economic, and Social Consequences of Racial Preferences

Love markets that are limiting mean that we are limiting some people's access to all the benefits that flow from romantic partnership—status, income, health, education, social and professional networks, community impact, and more.
—Orly Lobel, *The Equality Machine: Harnessing Digital Technology for a Brighter, More Inclusive Future*

Thus far this book has focused on describing the gendered racial hierarchy in the dating market, demonstrating how the law has shaped our romantic preferences, and illustrating how legal institutions continue to influence and facilitate racial preferences. This chapter, in turn, examines the psychological, economic, and social consequences of racial preferences in the dating market. It concludes that the law and society should be troubled by these preferences, and more importantly, by racial hierarchy, because they cause harm to individuals and contribute to economic and social inequality.

For many individuals, marriage provides myriad psychological, economic, and societal benefits. Racial preferences in the dating market may limit a person's opportunity to secure these benefits for themselves and their children. These preferences exact significant psychic harm on individuals rejected as intimate partners. Furthermore, by labeling an entire group as less desirable, racial preferences stigmatize and potentially harm all members of these groups, including individuals who are not seeking intimate partners. Racial preferences also limit opportunities for long-term romantic relationships—a social good that scholars have identified as "the single most important source of life satisfaction."[1] While the opportunity for intimacy is a matter of social justice and consequently we ought to care about how this opportunity is distributed,[2] this chapter uncovers other harms caused by racial exclusion in the dating market, including limited access to the economic security associated with marriage and the denial of "white privilege"[3]—or what sociologist Eduardo Bonilla-Silva has named "honorary white" status[4]—to less-preferred individuals and their children.

Marrying for Love (and Other Benefits)

My niece was seven years old when a cousin announced that she was getting married. My niece was particularly excited about the wedding and the dress that she would wear as the flower girl. Her excitement about the wedding is not uncommon. In 2022, weddings were a $61 billion-dollar industry in the United States,[5] and couples invest significant time and resources planning their weddings. Yet, as anyone who is or has been married can attest, marriages and weddings have very little in common. Marriage and marriage-like relationships are hard work. They require compromise and, in many cases, living with a person who has different habits, schedules, and expectations. Married and cohabitating couples argue about virtually every issue ranging from money to children, housework, sex, religion, technology (the iPhone in the bedroom), and where and with whom to spend holidays. Committed relationships have high points—periods of joy marked by frequent expressions of affection—but they have many lows as well—periods marked by pain, resentment, and even betrayal. Marriage also brings the risk and turmoil of divorce. As divorce lawyer Raoul Lionel Felder has quipped, "Marriage is the first step on the road to divorce."[6]

Yet, despite the sacrifices and risks that accompany marriage, most Americans report that they would like to marry someday.[7] Although the marriage rate in the United States is at a historic low,[8] about 70 percent of Americans believe that being married is either important or essential for a fulfilling life.[9] Ironically, the decrease in the marriage rate may be evidence of the high value Americans place on marriage. Marriage is seen as a last step—a capstone—that one takes only after completing an education, advancing sufficiently in one's career, paying off debt, saving for a down payment, and attaining financial security.[10] Men, in particular, may feel pressure to forego marriage until they have checked these boxes.

While wages for men without college degrees have declined since the 1970s and home ownership is financially out of reach for most Millennials and Gen Z's,[11] more than two-thirds of Americans believe it is very important for a man to be able to support a family financially to be a good husband or partner.[12]

Why is marriage so significant? Why do most Americans want to marry? While the most prevalent answer is love and companionship,[13] individuals and lawmakers recognize that marriage may bring many other benefits.

The U.S. Supreme Court attempted to explain the meaning of marriage in *Obergefell v. Hodges*, the 2015 decision recognizing the right of same-sex couples to marry.[14] Describing "the transcendent importance of marriage,"[15] the majority wrote that "no union is more profound than marriage, for it embodies the highest ideals of love, fidelity, devotion, sacrifice, and family"[16] and "always has promised nobility and dignity to all persons."[17] It continued its glorification of marriage, declaring that "rising from the most basic human needs, marriage is essential to our most profound hopes and aspirations" and that "through its enduring bond, two persons together can find other freedoms, such as expression, intimacy, and spirituality."[18] The majority stressed that marriage is a "union unlike any other in its importance to the committed individuals,"[19] which "offers the hope of companionship and understanding and assurance that while both still live there will be someone to care for the other."[20] While many commentators, including myself, are skeptical about these mystical powers of marriage,[21] there is no denying that marriage is important to many people.

The Supreme Court also recognized the importance of marriage to communities and society generally. Quoting its 1888 decision in *Maynard v. Hill*, the majority in *Obergefell* reiterated that "marriage is 'the foundation of the family and of society, without which there would be neither civilization nor progress'" and noted that it is the reason that "society pledge[s] to support the couple, offering symbolic recognition and material benefits to protect and nourish the union."[22] The "symbolic recognition and material benefits"[23] the state provides to married individuals are, in the words of the Supreme Court of Massachusetts, "enormous, touching nearly every aspect of life and death."[24] They include tax benefits, inheritance rights, the right to a share of a deceased spouse's estate irrespective of the deceased spouse's will, the right to be covered under a health care policy provided by a spouse's employer, and the right to sue a person or entity who wrongly causes a spouse's death. The law also provides certain protections in the event of divorce, such as the right to seek spousal support and the right to an equitable share of property acquired during the marriage, including a share of a spouse's retirement benefits or pension.[25]

In addition to these extensive property rights for spouses, the state provides many noneconomic rights that reflect the state's interest in protecting marital families. The presumption that a child born to a married couple is the child of both spouses, for example, eliminates the need to establish legal parentage and grants both spouses presumptive custodial and visitation rights. The marital communications privilege prohibits a spouse from testifying against the other about their private conversations. Other noneconomic benefits of marriage include the right to make health care decisions for an incompetent spouse who does not have a contrary advance directive or health care proxy, the right to donate a deceased spouse's organs if the deceased spouse did not leave instructions specifying their wishes, and the right to be buried in the lot or tomb owned by a deceased spouse.[26]

The U.S. Supreme Court has similarly recognized the extensive legal benefits of marriage. Noting that the "State itself makes marriage all the more precious by the significance it attaches to it," the *Obergefell* majority explained that "marriage [is] the basis for an expanding list of governmental rights, benefits, and responsibilities" under state law and "is also a significant status for over a thousand provisions of federal law."[27] These include the right to transfer unlimited wealth to a spouse without gift or estate tax liability,[28] Social Security Benefits for a surviving spouse caring for the married couple's child, and veterans spousal benefits, to name a few.[29] Individuals are aware of these legal benefits. Almost half of LGBT individuals, who until recently were denied the right to marry, point to the "legal rights and benefits" of marriage as a "very important" reason to get married.[30]

The U.S. Supreme Court has recognized that the "profound benefits" of marriage extend not only to married individuals, but also to their children.[31] In affirming that the right to marry is protected by the Constitution, the majority in *Obergefell* explained that marriage "safeguards children and families" and "affords the permanency and stability important to children's best interests."³² It concluded that "by giving recognition and legal structure to their parents' relationship, marriage allows children 'to understand the integrity and closeness of their own family and its concord with other families in their community and in their daily lives.'"³³ Other courts have similarly noted that children of married couples benefit from "the special legal and economic protections obtained by civil marriage."³⁴ Indeed the Supreme Court of Massachusetts acknowledged that "marital children reap a measure of family stability and economic security based on their parents' legally privileged status that is largely inaccessible, or not as readily accessible, to nonmarital children" including "the greater ease of access to family-based State and Federal benefits that attend the presumptions of one's parentage."³⁵

As the Supreme Court of Massachusetts noted in *Goodridge v. Dep't of Pub. Health*, children of married parents also enjoy societal benefits "such as the enhanced approval that still attends the status of being a marital child."³⁶ *Goodridge* was decided in 2003, but recent studies suggest that the court's observation then is still true today. While most Americans do not object to cohabitation, the majority (53 percent) believe that society is better off if individuals who plan to stay together get married.³⁷ Americans have even stronger views about unmarried parenthood. Two-thirds of participants (and 83 percent of Republicans) in a 2018 Pew research survey said that the increase in single women having children was bad for society, and almost half (48 percent) said the same about cohabitating parents.³⁸ In short, Americans value marriage not only for themselves but for society as well.

I agree with commentators who have criticized the Supreme Court's elevation of marriage above other relationships, especially the Court's suggestion that individuals who do not marry are "condemned to live in loneliness" and its statement that "marriage responds to the universal fear that a lonely person might call out only to find no one there."³⁹ That said, while correlation is not causation, the *Obergefell* majority's belief that marriage is associated with positive outcomes for spouses and children is supported by social science. In addition to the expected intimacy, companionship, and security of a caring partner highlighted by the *Obergefell* majority, studies have found that married individuals and those in committed long-term relationships enjoy other benefits. They are happier and report greater life satisfaction and better sex lives than their single counterparts.[40] They also experience lower levels of psychological distress and depression,[41] better overall health,[42] and longer lives.[43] Married couples also tend to have higher incomes and accumulate greater wealth,[44] including intergenerational wealth,[45] than their never-married or divorced counterparts.[46] These tendencies have led researchers to conclude that marriage is a wealth-enhancing institution.[47]

While these benefits are, at least in part, the result of selection, not causation—happier, healthier, and wealthier people are more likely to marry in the first place[48]—Americans are well aware of the association between marriage and financial stability. Financial security is one of the most attractive traits in a romantic partner.[49] Indeed, African Americans, Latinos, and individuals with low incomes or a high school education or less—the groups with the lowest rates of marriage—are significantly more likely than college-educated Whites to cite financial stability as a "very important reason" to get married.[50]

Marriage is also associated with myriad benefits to children. As the *Obergefell* majority observed, children living with married parents enjoy greater stability and permanence than children with single, cohabitating, or divorced parents.[51] They are also more likely to grow up in a safe environment,[52] attend high-quality schools, and graduate from college,[53] and they are less likely to experience poverty,[54] poor academic performance,[55] substance abuse,[56] teen pregnancy,[57] behavioral problems,[58] or delinquent behavior.[59]

Most of these benefits to children are not the result of marriage per se but of who enters into marriage. In recent decades, marriage has become an institution inhabited primarily by college-educated Whites and Asian Americans who marry partners with similarly high levels of formal education, income, and wealth—a practice known as assortative mating, as discussed in Chapter 1.[60] Whites, Asian Americans, and individuals with at least a bachelor's degree are more likely to be married than African Americans, Latinos, or persons without a bachelor's degree.[61] As a result of assortative mating—which has exacerbated income inequality[62]—and the postponement of marriage, but not childbearing, by African Americans, Latinos, and individuals without a college degree,[63] married parents are more likely to be White or Asian American[64] and to have higher levels of formal education,[65] higher incomes,[66] and greater financial resources than single or cohabitating parents.[67] Married parents are also more likely than nonmarital families to own a home, which is associated with more and better public services such as libraries, parks, public safety, and higher quality public schools.[68] Married parents are also more likely to live in higher income neighborhoods, and thus their children may have greater access to opportunities such as prestigious internships and enrichment camps, as well as to the social capital that wealthier parents bring.[69] Thus, nonmarital children's poorer outcomes likely stem primarily from fewer financial resources and the concomitant lack of access to safe neighborhoods, high-quality schools, and opportunity networks, as well as the legal benefits the law grants to married couples,[70] rather than their parents' marital status.[71]

Given the emotional, economic, and social benefits associated with marriage, it is no surprise that the majority of Americans wish to marry someday. However, an individual's access to marriage may be dependent on their race. As a result of the racial hierarchy in the romantic market, individuals of nonpreferred races have fewer opportunities for marriage or marriage-like commitments than individuals of preferred races.

The Harmful Effects of Racial Preferences

While scholars disagree about whether the state should continue to privilege marriage or extend the legal benefits of marriage to nonmarital relationships, most people would agree that an individual's opportunity to marry or enter marriage-like commitments should not be influenced by race. Yet, as Elizabeth Emens has observed, "Social stigma and structural constraints exclude some people from meaningful participation in the dating, sex, and marriage markets."[72] Racial preferences limit opportunities to enter into committed long-term romantic relationships and as a result, create and exacerbate disparities in the emotional well-being, economic security, and life opportunities of different groups and their children.

Psychological

Racial preferences have many negative consequences, including limited access to desirable sex partners and the emotional security (or promise of emotional security) associated with marriage-like commitments as well as psychic injury inflicted on individuals of nonpreferred races. The latter includes both direct harm to individuals who experience rejection because of their race and stigmatic harm to all members of groups labeled as less desirable romantic partners because of race.

Access to Committed Relationships and the Promise of Emotional Security

Marriage and marriage-like relationships are associated with numerous benefits but racial preferences reduce some individuals' opportunities to find intimate partners. For example, as a result of mass incarceration and early death,[73] "the pool of 'marriageable' (i.e., employed)" African American men is significantly smaller than the number of African American women seeking marriage or marriage-like commitments.[74] The pool of college-educated African American men is even smaller. Thus, African American women seeking a committed relationship may find that they have basically three options: share an African American man with other individuals (nonmonogamy), partner with a woman, or partner with a man of a different race. The first two options might not be viable choices for most heterosexual women. First, although some women are open to polyamorous relationships,[75] many strongly prefer a monogamous union. Second, while recent studies suggest that sexual orientation is more fluid than once believed,[76] most heterosexual women are unlikely to consider a female partner.

Scholars such as Richard Banks have argued that given the small pool of eligible African American men, heterosexual African American women should consider men of other races, as Asian American and Latina women have done for decades.[77] As shown in Chapter 1, however, Asian, Latino, and White men reject African American women at disproportionately high rates.[78] Consequently, heterosexual African American women seeking committed relationships have fewer opportunities to find a partner than other women who have a larger pool of eligible men from which to choose—they "face more difficult 'marriage markets.'"[79] Thus, racial preferences not only reduce the likelihood of interracial partnering; they may also reduce the opportunities of members of less preferred groups to enter into a committed relationship *at all*.

Some individuals would prefer to remain single rather than partner with a person of a different race. As discussed in Chapter 1, although most studies suggest that African American women are more willing to date interracially than other groups are to dating them,[80] some African American women have strong preferences for African American men—in contrast to Asian American women and Latinas who often prefer White men. There are, however, some African American women who would consider partnering with a person of a different race especially if that was their best opportunity to find a partner and reap the benefits of a long-term committed relationship. This is not surprising given how highly African Americans value committed relationships. A Pew Research Survey found that more than 85 percent of African Americans believe that being in a committed romantic relationship is important or essential for a fulfilling life. In contrast, only 52 percent of Whites and 50 percent of Latinos said the same.[81] But given the scarcity of eligible African American men and the racial hierarchy in the dating market, African American women may have fewer opportunities to enter into committed relationships.

Racial preferences negatively impact other groups—especially men of Asian descent and dark-complexioned women (regardless of race)—as well. Sexual racism is also apparent in the LGBTQ dating market, as noted in chapter 1. Education and money, however, may lessen sexual racism's effects on men's opportunities to find a partner. Highly educated and financially secure men of all races have access to the benefits of committed relationships. Indeed, given the scarcity of college-educated African American men, these men often find themselves with a large pool of potential partners of all races to choose from.[82] In contrast, high educational attainment and financial resources do not raise the position of African American or dark-complexioned women in the dating market. College-educated Black women, for example, receive significantly less attention on dating platforms than women of other races with a high school diploma. Thus, regardless of education and financial resources, racial preferences deprive dark-complexioned women of opportunities to enjoy the emotional benefits of committed relationships.

Individual Rejection and Psychic Injury

Dating and rejection often go hand in hand. Virtually everyone who has been in the dating market has been attracted to someone who is not attracted to them and has experienced the hurt of rejection. Rejection because of one's race is different, however. Race was the basis for the legal subordination of racial minorities for multiple generations. The law stamped African Americans, American Indians, Asians/Asian Americans, and Latinos as inferior on the basis of race or race markers—skin tone, facial features, and hair texture. Race marked a person as less than fully human, one who could be enslaved and had to be kept away from Whites to "prevent . . . the Caucasian race from being contaminated by [inferior races]."[83] Thus, rejection on the basis of race may be experienced and internalized as evidence of one's inferiority. As one woman writes:

> We always blamed ourselves because we did not want to grapple with the morose reality that we could be denied the most fundamental of human experiences—love—because of the color of our skin.[84]

Racial minorities often experience discrimination in other areas of their lives—at school, at work, when walking or driving, for example. Each racial microaggression—the subtle and pervasive (but often unconscious) indignities directed at racial minorities—sends a denigrating message that signals racial inferiority.[85] The cumulative effect of discrimination, including microaggressions, causes significant psychological (and often physical) harm.[86] Thus, while rejection in the dating market, by itself, might not cause significant or long-lasting harm to most individuals, for racial minorities, each instance of sexual racism contributes to the psychic harm caused by the constant stress of racism.

Racial Stigma and Group Harm

Racial preferences not only affect individuals seeking an intimate partner but may also harm other members of a group that has been stigmatized as less desirable. Members of these groups experience "stigmatic harm."[87] Several years before the Supreme Court held that laws prohibiting interracial marriage were unconstitutional, the sociologist Erving Goffman identified three types of stigmatizing traits, including "tribal stigma of race, nation, and religion . . . stigma than can be transmitted through lineages."[88] Members of devalued racial groups are stigmatized in our society. While individuals are stigmatized for a wide variety of reasons, social scientists agree that all "stigmatized persons possess an attribute that is deeply discrediting and ... are viewed as less than fully human because of it."[89] For racial minorities, that attribute is, as Robin Lenhardt has argued, dark skin or specifically African, American Indian, Asian, or Latino ancestry. Such ancestry is a disfavored feature and a basis for discrimination.[90] In addition, as Lenhardt has shown, as a result of their ancestry, racial minorities are viewed as inferior to Whites and less than fully human. As demonstrated in Chapter 2, the state contributed to the stigmatization of racial minorities through laws and practices that branded them as inferior, including slavery, anti-miscegenation laws, discriminatory immigration and naturalization laws, segregation, and laws prohibiting racial minorities from testifying against a White person.[91]

Stigmatized groups may experience psychological harm as a result of the constant anticipation of discrimination in every aspect of their lives—when seeking employment or performing their job, when shopping (they fear that they will be followed around and suspected of shoplifting), when seeking to rent or purchase a home, when driving or walking down the street, when encountering law enforcement, and when seeking a romantic partner.[92] The anticipation of discrimination may require members of racially stigmatized groups to expend substantial cognitive resources attempting to avoid situations and environments in which they might be targets of racial bias, discrimination, or racial microaggressions.[93] It also requires them to expend mental energy deciphering ambiguous actions or statements by others that may or may not have been motivated by racial bias. An Asian American man who posts a profile and photo on a dating site but receives little interest may wonder whether his profile wasn't very interesting or the photo did not capture his good side. He may also wonder whether the low response rate was the result of his race and negative stereotypes about Asian American men. The anticipation of discrimination leaves members of stigmatized groups "feeling somewhat insecure or uncertain in their social interactions with others" and may make it "difficult [for the stigmatized individual] to determine whether, in a given context, a comment or behavior is reflective of racial bias or prejudice."[94]

Racial preferences may also negatively impact the self-esteem of members of groups that society has deemed unappealing. Members of groups at the bottom of the racial hierarchy, including individuals not in the dating market, are aware that society does not value them as highly as members of other racial groups. As shown in chapter 1, racial minorities are well aware of their reduced value in the intimate market, and some attempt to increase their value by emphasizing physical traits, such as a lighter complexion or straight hair, or altering their appearance (for example, through skin-lightening products). Others attempt to distance themselves from racial stereotypes by highlighting their educational pedigree; distancing themselves from non-White immigrants and not speaking Spanish or other stigmatized languages;[95] and denying the existence of dark-skinned relatives or their own African ancestry.[96] Some racial minorities internalize society's perception of members of their group and believe that members of their group (including themselves) are less attractive and desirable.[97]

In short, the psychological consequences associated with racial preferences in the romantic marketplace are substantial. The economic harms and lack of equal access to opportunities for one's children may be just as significant.

Economic

Access to Financial Security

Marriage and marriage-like commitments are associated with greater financial security, especially for college-educated and higher-income individuals who increasingly choose partners with similar education and income. Racial preferences deny members of less-preferred groups equal opportunities to access the economic benefits associated with committed relationships. As noted, the pool of marriageable African American men is significantly smaller than the number of heterosexual African American women seeking to marry: "There are 51 employed young black men for every 100 young black women."[98] In addition, African American women are twice as likely as African American men to graduate from college and almost three times as likely to obtain a postgraduate degree. Moreover, college-educated African American men are more likely than African American women to marry women of other races. Consequently, many highly educated African American women will not have the opportunity to enter into committed relationships with similarly educated African American men.[99] They could partner with less-educated African American men—"marry down"—but this choice comes at a significant financial cost as college-educated women who marry less-educated men suffer a loss of household income of $25,000 a year.[100] Despite this economic loss, many African American women do make the choice to "marry down." More than 50 percent of college-educated African American women marry men who did not attend college. In contrast only 16 percent of college-educated White women do the same.[101]

Another option is to expand the pool of available mates by partnering with men of other races as Asian American and Latina women have done, and coincidentally or not, benefited financially in the process. Asian American and Latina women with White male partners have higher household incomes and greater wealth, including intergenerational transfers of wealth, than their counterparts with same-race partners.[102] As a result of the racial hierarchy in the dating and marriage market, however, college-educated African American and darker-complexioned women may not have as many opportunities to partner with men of other races.

College-educated Asian American and light-complexioned Latina women are often courted by White men, which means that they have a larger pool of potential partners. Moreover, their pool includes more college-educated, high-income individuals. In the United States, White men typically have higher incomes and wealth, including intergenerational wealth, than men of other races.[103] Consequently, women who have the opportunity to partner with White men have access to more financial resources. As a result of racial preferences, however, some women do not have the same access to these resources as women of other races.

Some (and possibly many) readers will find this discussion of marriage markets and "marrying down" off-putting. I share that sentiment. Yet, individuals do consider financial security when choosing an intimate partner and increasingly engage in assortative mating,[104] as we saw in prior chapters. Highly educated individuals tend to seek and partner with similarly highly educated individuals.[105] As one commentator has observed, "The best way to ensure a financially stable future is to get an education. Another way is to choose a partner who has one, too."[106] However, racial hierarchy in the dating market denies some groups this opportunity. While we should be concerned about the effects of assortative mating on class inequality,[107] we should also be concerned about the effects of racial preferences on the opportunities of less preferred groups to find a partner with similarly high education, income, wealth, and networks. We should be especially concerned about their effects on the children of African American women.

Effects on Children

As we saw earlier, children raised in financially stable two-parent households are more likely to flourish academically and attend college than children raised in single-parent households. While studies have focused on poor single-parent households, children raised by college-educated single parents do not enjoy the same opportunities as children raised by two college-educated parents. College-educated parents today invest more resources in their children than prior generations ever have. Most single parents, even those with college educations, do not have access to the same resources, financial or otherwise (in terms of time, for example), to invest in their children. Assortative mating has magnified the inequality of resources and opportunities between children raised in single-parent households and children raised by married parents.[108]

College-educated women are significantly less likely than women who did not attend college to have children outside of marriage. As a result of the limited pool of marriageable African American men, however, along with racial preferences, college-educated African American women are more likely than college-educated women of other races to be single when they become parents. When they are married, their spouses tend to have less formal education and lower incomes. "Marrying down" not only makes it more difficult to provide children with a middle-class standard of living but also increases the likelihood that their children will actually have a lower standard than their parents when they grow up.[109] Furthermore, African American women who marry men with less education are more likely to divorce,[110] thereby increasing the likelihood that their children will spend part of their childhood in a single-parent home with potentially even fewer resources.

The children of African American women may not have access to the same resources and opportunities as children of college-educated women of other races. As noted, college-educated Asian American and Latina women who partner with White men have significantly higher household incomes and wealth. They are also more likely to live in neighborhoods with high-quality schools and to have access to social capital. They use all of these resources to provide their children with advantages. A child who resides in a wealthy neighborhood with high-quality schools may have greater access to coveted internships and academic opportunities not available in less privileged, and often segregated neighborhoods and schools. Some of these opportunities are formal—the school in the wealthy neighborhood may have more guidance counselors who search for opportunities and help students secure them. Other opportunities are informal and are best described by an African American single mother who enrolled her children in a private, predominantly White school as "access to power."[111] These networks help individuals obtain internships and jobs, opportunities that are not available to individuals outside the network.[112]

Single parents choose to raise children without a partner for a variety of reasons, and society and the law should support single-parent families. However, although the children of college-educated single parents are unlikely to experience the increased risk of poor outcomes faced by children of low-income parents, they rarely have *all* of the advantages of children raised by two (or more) college-educated parents. First, many parents need two (or more) incomes to maintain a home in a neighborhood with high-quality schools and access to the extracurricular and cultural activities that are important when applying to selective colleges.[113] Many parents also need two incomes to pay for a child's college education and the post-college support that adult children increasingly depend on as they navigate their first job or graduate school. Single parents, even those who are financially secure, are less likely than two parents to be able to provide a child with these financial resources. Second, single parents may not have someone with whom to share the "logistical, or emotional burdens of being a parent."[114] Third, single parents, and by extension their children, may be excluded from networks that married parents inhabit, all the more so for African American single mothers and their children. As one woman observed, "As an African American woman—even with an Ivy League education and a middle-class income—I was still subject to the stereotypical perception of 'the black single mother.'"[115] Moreover, a high percentage of African American college-educated mothers are first-generation college graduates and thus lack access to other social networks.[116]

In sum, by limiting an individual's choices in the dating and marriage market, racial preferences deprive the children of less preferred racial groups of opportunities available to the children of preferred individuals.

Social

Racial preferences in the dating market allow some racial minorities to access privileges that historically were generally available only to Whites, including well-resourced neighborhoods and high-quality schools, as well as White spaces, as described in prior chapters. They also provide access to social networks that can lead to employment opportunities. As such, racial preferences create division and tensions between racial minorities who have access to what Eduardo Bonilla-Silva calls "honorary white" status as a result of their ability to partner with individuals with higher racial status and those that do not have access to privileges generally accessible to Whites only and those in their proximity.[117] They also serve to further isolate nonpreferred racial minorities and thereby contribute to residential, educational, economic, and social inequality.

In Latin America, there is a well-recognized preference for lighter skin tone and European phenotype. Family members encourage darker-complexioned individuals to whiten future generations by choosing partners with lighter complexions with whom to have children.[118] In her study of anti-Black racism in Mexico, Christina Sue interviewed a dark-complexioned woman who said she was not attracted to dark-complexioned men because given her own dark skin tone, they would have dark children, which in her view, was undesirable.[119] Another woman in Sue's study explained that if two dark-complexioned people had children together, their children would be unattractive—"They are going to have very flat noses, or in other words, be very unrefined."[120] As Tanya Hernandez has demonstrated, Latino families in the United States often share these views.[121] As Cynthia Feliciano, Rennie Lee, and Belinda Robnett have concluded, "The majority of Latinos accept racial hierarchies that privilege whites."[122]

Similar to families in Latin America, Latino families in the United States also encourage their children to partner with and have children with Whites or light-complexioned partners as a way to *mejorar la raza*—literally translated as "to improve the race." Scholars refer to this strategy for upward racial mobility as *blanqueamiento*, or "whitening the race," a practice that leaders (and dictators) in Latin America utilized and endorsed, along with facilitating immigration of European Whites, to whiten their populations.[123] The desire for upward racial mobility is a primary reason that Latino parents object to their children's romantic relationships with African Americans as they believe that these will lead to downward racial mobility.[124] Some Asian Americans similarly believe that partnering with African Americans is a step toward downward racial mobility.[125] Throughout history, some lighter-complexioned African Americans who were able to pass as White or secure access to White privileges as a result of their lighter complexions also rejected darker-complexioned partners. They feared a dark-complexioned romantic partner would jeopardize their higher social position, which included access to educational and professional opportunities. Although individuals who benefit from honorary White status do not generally claim to be White and thus are not attempting to pass as White, they distance themselves from individuals who do not have honorary White status at least some of the time.

Racial minorities with White partners are more likely to have access to White spaces and networks. They are more likely to live in predominantly White neighborhoods that offer superior schools (as measured by students' academic achievement) and desirable amenities. They are also more likely to have a social network of White friends and family members who can facilitate educational and professional opportunities. In my field—law—we impress upon our students the importance of attending events where they can network. These are undoubtedly important but might not be as valuable as having a family member or family friend who can facilitate connections and even make a call or send an email on one's behalf.

At least some individuals consider the potential for racial mobility when choosing a partner. Asian Americans and Latinos who wish to access the networks and privileges that Whites enjoy may find a White partner attractive, even if they are unaware that their attraction is the result of their internalization and acceptance (consciously or unconsciously) of the current racial hierarchy.[126] They may find White partners attractive in part because they recognize that if they have children together, their children might have honorary White status—lighter skin, acceptance by Whites, ability to blend in at a predominantly White school (the racial makeup of most high-quality schools) and in a predominantly White neighborhood. At least one study suggests that like other racial minorities, African Americans also seek upward racial and social mobility for their children and that those who want to have children are more likely to date Whites and Asian Americans, groups perceived to be of higher status, than those who do not plan to have children.[127] This result is consistent with sexual strategies theory,[128] which predicts that individuals who want to have children will seek to gain access to greater resources.[129]

Racial preferences foster division between racial minorities. Individuals who are higher on the racial hierarchy or who have the ability to climb it through interracial coupling may have competing interests and alliances. On the one hand, as racial minorities who have experienced discrimination, they have an interest in eradicating racism against anyone. On the other hand, as honorary Whites, they may have an interest in maintaining the current racial hierarchy as they benefit from their proximity to Whites. Thus, as Eduardo Bonilla-Silva has argued, racial minorities who attain or have the ability to attain honorary White status may align themselves with Whites, leaving African Americans, and other dark-complexioned and disproportionately poor minorities with few opportunities for mobility.[130]

* * *

Racial preferences in the dating market harm individuals and perpetuate racial, economic, and social inequality. They not only affect who has access to a partner but may impact who is hired or is able to live in a desirable neighborhood. As Elizabeth Emens has argued, "Whom I desire and date and marry, and whom my children desire and date and marry, shapes whom I know to hire. And further. Whom I hire shapes who has the social capital to be good enough to date my children. And whom my children marry shapes the people I want to hire, the people to whom I want to give opportunities for advancement and access to the good life."[131]

The law should not ignore these harms. The next chapter outlines possible steps forward.

6

Working toward Equality

If intimate preferences are so individualistic and mysterious, why are they so similar and predictable?
—Celeste Vaughan Curington, Jennifer Hickes Lundquist, and Ken-Hou Lin, *The Dating Divide: Race and Desire in the Era of Online Romance*

The law's influence on our intimate preferences has contributed to and continues to perpetuate racial and social inequality. Consequently, lawmakers should explore how the law can address racial preferences in the dating market.

Admittedly, this is not an easy task. Romantic attraction is multifaceted—one person may be attracted (or not attracted) to another for many reasons, some of which are unknowable. That mystery is part of what makes love magical. Thus, any efforts to reduce the law's influence on our intimate choices must take account of the limits of law and the influences outside of it. As shown in chapter 1, our racial preferences are shaped by family, friends, and societal norms. Moreover, individuals may want a partner who understands their family's culture, values, religion, and language (in some cases) and who can help pass these on to their children (if any).[1] As discussed in earlier chapters, racial minorities often grow up in different neighborhoods, attend different schools, and experience interactions with teachers, employers, and police officers differently from Whites, whose social networks are often overwhelmingly White.[2] A White partner, for example, may be less likely than a racial minority partner to recognize a remark or action as a racial microaggression or understand why it is hurtful or offensive.[3] Given these differences in perception, some racial minorities, and especially those who have experienced fetishization by daters of other races,[4] may prefer intimate partners who have experienced the challenges of navigating daily life in the United States as a minority.

The recognition that romantic preferences are complex and are shaped by extra-legal influences does not render the law's historic and current effects on our romantic choices any less disturbing or make legal interventions inappropriate. The law influences our preferences, and therefore it should, at minimum, remove any remaining barriers to interracial partnering. As we saw in chapter 2, as of 2019, at least eight states continued to ask marriage license applicants to declare their race, thereby reifying the salience of race. Legal actors continue to signal that racial minorities are undesirable partners, and segregated neighborhoods, schools, and spaces deny people of different races opportunities to interact. Even online, where individuals of all backgrounds can meet without the limitations of geography and segregated spaces, the law allows dating platforms to categorize and steer users on the basis of race.

Many individuals are not aware that the law has influenced their intimate preferences. Educating children and adults about the law's role in creating residential and educational segregation and psychological distance between racial groups may help reduce the barriers to interracial partnering. But the law must do more. This chapter explores several reforms that would promote the law's racial neutrality in the dating market.

Dating Platforms

As we saw in earlier chapters, some dating platforms allow users to filter the profiles they will be shown on the basis of race. Civil rights laws prohibit businesses with physical locations from categorizing individuals on the basis of race or from accommodating or facilitating discrimination by their customers. The law should prohibit digital platforms from doing the same.

Digital platforms did not exist when lawmakers enacted public accommodations laws prohibiting establishments that are open to the public from discriminating on the basis of race and other protected characteristics. Not surprisingly, these laws generally defined public accommodations by reference to physical spaces. Now that our lives are increasingly conducted on digital platforms, lawmakers should recognize that platforms that discriminate violate the spirit and intent of public accommodations laws. Nancy Leong and Aaron Belzer have argued that the law should treat platforms such as Airbnb and Uber as public accommodations,[5] and Sonu Bedi has argued that the law should treat dating platforms similarly.[6] I agree. Lawmakers should amend public accommodation laws to expressly include digital platforms. Alternatively, they should define public accommodations broadly to include any business that holds itself out as open to the public irrespective of whether it has a physical location. California's Unruh Civil Rights Act, for example, entitles every person in California "to the full and equal accommodations, advantages, facilities, privileges, or services *in all business establishments of every kind whatsoever.*"[7] Such language is sufficiently broad to encompass dating platforms and prohibit them from facilitating discrimination by their users in the same way it prohibits bars and nightclubs from facilitating discrimination by their customers.

A person's selection of an intimate partner is a deeply personal decision. Thus, I am not suggesting that the law should prohibit individual users from expressing or acting upon their racial preferences. Rather, I am arguing that the law should prohibit dating platforms from facilitating discriminatory conduct by its users. As several scholars have argued, dating platforms that classify users by race or provide racial filters encourage users to discriminate and thus are not neutral actors.[8] The law already prohibits public establishments with physical spaces from facilitating discrimination. It should prohibit digital spaces from engaging in similar conduct.

Some dating platforms have eliminated their racial filtering tools. Grindr, for example, removed its race filters after the police's murder of George Floyd in June 2020 forced the country to reckon with the persistence of racial discrimination.[9] Grindr's racial filter "was one of the most widely mocked—and, often, plainly condemned—features on Grindr,"[10] and its elimination was met with substantial support. Some racial minorities, however, expressed support for race-filtering tools that allow them to easily find profiles of other racial minorities.[11] Based on this feedback, some popular dating apps decided to retain their race filters.[12]

I am sympathetic to individuals, who, for myriad reasons discussed earlier, welcome tools that make it easier to find other users who share their racial background. But race filters reinforce sexual racism and racial hierarchy. They make it possible for Whites to exclude racial minorities from view in the same way that public spaces in the Jim Crow era excluded African Americans, Mexicans, and other groups. Race filters "reify—and tacitly validate—extant stereotypes related to race, ethnicity."[13] They "map onto historical notions of psychological and physical group difference, and promote these categories as both natural characterizations of other users as well as appropriate axes for determining romantic or sexual (dis)interest."[14] Moreover, despite dating platforms' assertions that race filters honor the preferences of racial minorities seeking same-race partners, African Americans on dating platforms are ten times more likely to message White users than White users are to message them.[15] In fact, 80 percent of White users send messages only to other Whites, and just 3 percent send messages to African Americans.[16] Thus, racial filters tend to serve the racial preferences of White users to a greater extent than the preferences of racial minorities. In addition, while race filters make it easier for racial minorities to find each other, they also make it easier for other users to fetishize them and reinforce the stereotypes that lead to fetishization.

Without race filtering tools, online date-seekers would be able to exercise their individual racial preferences to the same extent they are able to exercise those preferences offline. As illustrated in earlier chapters, when a person goes to a bar in the hopes of meeting a potential romantic partner, they cannot request that the "pool" of potential partners include only members of certain races. Of course, a person who is interested in dating only members of a particular race can choose to ignore everyone who is not a member of their preferred race (assuming they can identify them—a difficult task since race is not always apparent from a person's skin tone and phenotype), but they cannot exclude them from view. Users of dating platforms would similarly be able to ignore users on the basis of race, but the platform would not provide them with the tools—racial filters—to exclude them from view. The platform would not help them discriminate.

Moreover, individuals seeking a partner of a particular background could continue to use dating platforms that bring together date-seekers of certain racial, religious, educational, or professional backgrounds.[17] Just as people today still frequent particular bars and other public spaces because they expect that most of the people there will be of a certain background, so, too, can they use dating platforms such as Black People Meet (for people seeking Black partners)[18] and JDate (for people seeking

Jewish partners).[19] These platforms are open to everyone even though they attract users seeking partners of certain backgrounds. But just as a bar or nightclub with a primarily Asian American clientele, for example, cannot exclude members of another racial group or force them to sit in the back where customers who object to their presence do not have to see them, the law should not permit dating platforms to exclude users on the basis of race or hide them from users who have indicated their wish to categorically exclude members of those groups.

When dating platforms provide tools that allow other users to exclude entire groups on the basis of race, they reinforce racial stereotypes and exacerbate social distance. As Orly Lobel has observed, "Technology has an immense impact not only on what we see and whom we meet, but also on how we feel."[20] Dating platforms that provide race filtering tools signal to users that it is reasonable, acceptable, and even desirable to categorically exclude an entire group based on stereotypes and assumptions about its members.[21] As discussed in prior chapters, studies have found that racial preferences in the dating market are closely associated with racial discrimination in nonintimate settings.[22] By facilitating sexual racism, dating platforms signal that discrimination in other settings is also acceptable. Thus, if lawmakers wish to eliminate race discrimination in housing and employment, for example, they cannot simultaneously allow dating platforms to encourage and facilitate discrimination in the dating market.

Freedom of Speech and Expression

Although lawmakers can and should require dating platforms to eliminate race filtering tools that facilitate discrimination, any *legal* restrictions on individual users' ability to state their racial preferences on their profile could potentially infringe on their First Amendment right to freedom of speech and expression.[23] Just as important, strong policy reasons weigh against any *legal* attempts to prevent online daters from expressing their racial preferences on their profiles despite the psychic harms that such statements may inflict on other users. First, prohibiting users from describing their racial preferences on their profiles may lead to backlash from users who believe sexual racism is acceptable or even desirable. Second, any restrictions would have to apply to all users even though some individuals may have reasons for preferring certain groups that do not reinforce racial hierarchy. Racial minorities' preferences for other minorities may be based on a desire for a partner who shares a similar culture or experience as a racial minority in a race-conscious society. These preferences do not reinforce racial hierarchy and, as noted in the introduction to this book, Whites' same-race preferences do not always perpetuate racial hierarchy. A White immigrant, for example, who prefers a partner who shares their country of origin, immigrant experience, culture, and language, is not excluding individuals on the basis of race, and thus does not reinforce racial hierarchy. Third, we may want individuals with strong racial preferences to express them in their profile so that users who find such preferences repugnant can avoid them. A White user who finds racial preferences objectionable might not want to initiate contact with or respond to a user who has strong preferences for Whites and therefore would want to be aware of the user's racial preferences. Similarly, an African American user might want to see those preferences on a user's profile so as to save time and the rejection that would likely result if they contact a user with strong racial preferences against African Americans.

For these reasons, the law should not attempt to limit individual users' expression of their racial preferences. The elimination of racial filters would not prevent users from stating their racial background and racial preferences, if any, in their profiles; they could do so in the same way that a person in a bar or night club can express their racial preferences. Despite my personal objections to statements such as "Only here to talk to white boys"[24] on users' profiles, the First Amendment likely protects such speech. So long as the dating platform does not direct, encourage, or help its users express their racial preferences, the law probably cannot regulate their expression on users' profiles.

Although lawmakers cannot prevent users of dating platforms from expressing their racial preferences on their profiles, dating platforms can choose to do so. The First Amendment protects individuals' freedoms from restrictions placed by the government, but not from restrictions imposed by private businesses and institutions.[25] A private employer or university, for example, can restrict an employee's or student's speech, respectively. As discussed in earlier chapters, several platforms, such as Chappy, Bumble, and Grindr, prohibit users from stating racial preferences on their platforms.[26] The federal Communications Decency Act protects websites and platforms that choose to prohibit offensive language from civil liability. Accordingly, "No provider or user of an interactive computer service shall be held liable on account of . . . any action voluntarily taken in good faith to restrict access to or availability of material that the provider or user considers to be obscene, lewd, lascivious, filthy, excessively violent, harassing, or *otherwise objectionable, whether or not such material is constitutionally protected.*"[27]

When users express racial preferences on their profiles, they normalize sexual racism by signaling that it is acceptable. They also inflict psychic harm on members of the targeted groups, as we saw in earlier chapters. Although individuals have always expressed their racial preferences to friends and family members offline, the number of people who may see these preferences on a dating platform is exponentially larger, and thus their potential for harm is vast. Consequently, although lawmakers probably cannot restrict such statements without running afoul of the First Amendment, I would encourage dating platforms to educate their users about the harms of such statements and to follow the lead of platforms that prohibit users from stating racial preferences in their profiles.

Infrastructure

The structural barriers to interracial intimacy, including residential, educational, and spatial segregation, limit opportunities for individuals of different racial backgrounds to meet and develop friendships and romantic relationships. The law should eliminate these obstacles or reduce their effects by abolishing single-family zoning, the Mrs. Murphy exception, and the school assignment system used in most districts. It should further reduce structural barriers to interracial relationships by supporting policies that will enable colleges and universities to enroll a racially diverse student body and by investing in public transportation.

End Single-Family Zoning

As Sara Bronin has asserted, zoning may be the most effective tool available to facilitate interactions between different racial groups.[28] Racial minorities are more likely than White families to live in multi-family housing, but the majority of predominantly White suburbs restrict most residential blocks to single-family homes. Thus, single-family zoning keeps minority families who often cannot afford single-family homes out of predominantly White neighborhoods.

Scholars have focused on how exclusionary zoning has contributed to a shortage of affordable housing. They have also shown how it creates educational segregation and inequality as children are generally not permitted to attend a school in a district where they do not reside. In addition, exclusionary zoning limits opportunities for people of different races to meet and develop friendships and intimate relationships. It limits propinquity. If municipalities permitted multi-family dwellings in otherwise single-family zones, as several towns have done recently,[29] more African American and Latino families would be able to move into predominantly White neighborhoods. Their children would attend schools with White children, and both would have opportunities to develop interracial friendships and intimate relationships.

Lawmakers should explore the use of economic incentives to encourage homeowners to allow multi-family housing in their community. The government subsidizes home ownership by allowing homeowners to deduct the interest they pay on their mortgage—the mortgage-interest deduction. Thus, the law subsidizes and thereby facilitates exclusion of moderate and lower-income families, which are disproportionately racial minorities, from predominantly White neighborhoods.[30] As John Boger has suggested, the government should consider reducing or eliminating the mortgage-interest deduction in municipalities with exclusionary zoning.[31] It should also consider denying federal funding for infrastructure to municipalities that refuse to allow multi-family housing.[32]

Eliminate the Mrs. Murphy Exception

The government should reduce the barriers to interracial relationships resulting from residential segregation by prohibiting all housing discrimination, including the Mrs. Murphy exception (discussed in chapter 3). Admittedly, eliminating the Mrs. Murphy exception might not significantly reduce residential segregation for several reasons. First, lessors may have nondiscriminatory reasons for refusing to rent a unit to a particular person, and, in any case, it is difficult to prove that a lessor refused to rent to an applicant because of their race. Second, even if a potential tenant could prove that a lessor rejected them because of their race, most applicants are unlikely to file a complaint, given the time and cost involved. Individuals seeking to rent a home are focused on finding a place to live so they are likely to shift their attention to the next listing and direct their time and energy to finding something comparable to the unit they "lost." Third, even if the applicant did file a complaint, their remedy would likely be limited to monetary damages, possibly for the additional rental costs of the home they eventually secure and the dignitary harm of discrimination. They are unlikely to seek a specific action—such as to force the lessor to rent to them—as living in close proximity to a lessor who does not wish to rent to them but is being forced to do so by law is not an ideal environment.

Despite the challenges of enforcing laws prohibiting discrimination by lessors of owner-occupied dwellings, there is a symbolic value in eliminating the Mrs. Murphy exception. By permitting discrimination, the Mrs. Murphy exception signals that it may be reasonable to believe that some racial groups are undesirable neighbors and by extension, undesirable romantic partners. These messages are not only stigmatizing and cause psychic harm but are remnants of the messages conveyed by redlining, restrictive covenants, racially explicit zoning, and legally segregated schools. As such, they serve to create not only physical distance between racial groups but psychological distance as they reinforce perceptions that certain racial groups are inferior. Abolishing the Mrs. Murphy exception might help reduce the psychological distance that makes interracial partnering unlikely, in part, as a result of laws that kept racial groups apart and signaled that they should remain apart to avoid taint.

* * *

Property scholars have proposed other ways to integrate neighborhoods, including Section 8 vouchers that can only be used in low-poverty neighborhoods and financial incentives for Whites to move to predominantly minority neighborhoods.[33] While these policies may further integration, they have the potential to harm racial minorities by coercing them to live in predominantly White neighborhoods where they may feel isolated and not welcome and by pricing them out of their neighborhoods—the effects of gentrification—when Whites move in.[34] Thus, these proposals require further study. However, I urge scholars who are exploring reforms to reduce residential segregation and inequality to consider how those reforms could reduce the structural barriers to interracial relationships.

Abolish the Current K-12 School Assignment System

Schools are where children make friends and often develop their first crush. As a result of segregated schools, however, many children lack opportunities to meet peers of different races. While residential segregation leads to segregated schools and reducing residential segregation will likely lead to more integrated schools, the law can also reduce educational segregation by changing the current school assignment system in place in most states, even while neighborhoods remain segregated. The majority of children in the United States attend schools in their school district or zone, and it is a crime in some states to misrepresent a child's address in order to enroll them in a school in a different school district. The law should allow children to attend schools outside their district. Some African American and Latino parents would send their children to predominantly White schools outside their district even if they require traveling longer distances because these school districts tend to have superior resources and offer more opportunities. Few White parents, however, would want to send their children to predominantly African American and Latino schools as those schools tend to have significantly fewer resources and consequently are more likely to underperform. Since crowding all students into White schools with greater resources is not practical or conducive to learning, states should explore whether building interdistrict magnet schools and locating them in minority neighborhoods would reduce segregated schools as some advocates have proposed.[35] The curricular programs in magnet schools are likely to attract some White students (or their parents) who would otherwise attend a school in their predominantly White neighborhood. Minority students would also be attracted to these schools, thus providing opportunities for children of different races not only to learn together, but to participate in co- and extra-curricular activities together and develop friendships as well as dating relationships when they enter adolescence.

Building new schools requires substantial investment and will not happen overnight. State lawmakers could also consider a lottery system by which students are randomly assigned to a school within a certain radius of their home.[36] In densely populated states, such as New Jersey, such a system would result in integrated schools as students from neighboring, but racially segregated, towns would attend school together. Lawmakers might also consider consolidating school districts: for example, merging a district with predominantly non-White students with a district that has predominantly White students.[37]

Segregated schools are not the only obstacle to interracial friendships and relationships. Segregation within integrated schools is common as students gravitate toward other students whom they believe share their identity and will be welcoming.[38] The law should not interfere with these preferences. When the student body is integrated, students have opportunities to interact with peers of other backgrounds in the classroom and in co- and extra-curricular activities, if they so choose. The law's role is to remove the obstacles to interracial relationships that it created. Once it removes these obstacles, however, it should not attempt to engage in social engineering to bring people together as these have the potential to backfire and may infringe on individuals' associational freedoms. Even so, we should not underestimate the effects of removing the structural obstacles to interracial friendships and relationships. Adults who attended integrated schools as children are more likely to have close interracial friendships and to date and marry across racial lines.[39]

Create Racially Diverse College Campuses

Individuals may spot their first crush in elementary school or middle school but college may be the place where they find a long-term partner. College students know this as demonstrated by their participation in The Marriage Pact discussed in chapter 4. The Marriage Pact's participants recognize that college may provide the best opportunity to meet a long-term partner even when they will not be ready to commit for many years and wish to keep their romantic options open. Their likelihood of finding an African-American or Latino partner at these institutions, however, is rather slim.

The student body in the majority of selective colleges and universities in the United States does not represent the diversity of our nation.[40] African Americans and Latinos are underrepresented at these institutions even though they are no less interested in obtaining a college education than

Whites or Asian Americans. Yet, disproportionately high numbers of African Americans and Latinos are unprepared for college as a result of attending under-resourced and underperforming K–12 schools—the schools they were forced to attend under our current school assignment system. In addition, as a result of redlining, racial steering, racially restrictive covenants, and exclusionary zoning, African American and Latino families are significantly less likely than Whites to be able to afford to send their children to college. The barriers to higher education for African American and Latinos are also barriers to interracial intimacy. College is a time when young adults are open to relationships with people of different backgrounds, but those opportunities are not available on racially homogenous campuses.

For decades, proponents of race-conscious admissions policies have argued that they are a necessary tool to create a diverse learning environment that benefits all students.[41] A racially diverse student body also reduces the barriers to interracial friendships and romantic relationships that result from lack of propinquity and from the psychological distance that the law helped to create. Students who attend racially diverse colleges and universities are more likely to have friends of other races and to date and marry interracially.[42] Now that the Supreme Court has held that race-conscious admissions policies violate the Fourteenth Amendment's guarantee of equal treatment,[43] however, colleges and universities seeking to enroll a racially diverse student body will have to change the ways they recruit and evaluate applicants. They should actively recruit students from high-poverty schools, which, given the racial wealth gap, tend to have a student body that is disproportionately African-American and Latino. Colleges should also consider each applicant's circumstances, including their family's economic resources, the opportunities and support provided by their high schools, and how the applicant spent their time outside of school. Was the applicant working to help support their family or taking care of younger siblings, for example, and thus unable to devote more time to co-curricular activities? As Olufemi Ogundele, the associate vice chancellor of enrollment and the dean of undergraduate admissions at the University of California, Berkeley has observed:

> Having equitable college admissions requires an understanding of the broader context of students' applications, information about their neighborhoods . . . , their schools, the courses available, access to those

courses and their situations at home, because experiences vary greatly in K–12.

    It entails admissions leaders looking at their university's application review process and ensuring it is equitable: How does your understanding of the educational environment inform how excellence is defined? *Do your staff members receive regular bias training before they start to read applications, to ensure a fair review? How does your evaluation process humanize your applicants so different versions of excellence can emerge?*[44]

While students at high-poverty, predominantly Black and Latino K–12 schools lack access to the rigorous academic and co-curricular experiences available to students in wealthy, predominantly White schools, with adequate support they can succeed in college, and their experiences will enrich the educational environment for all students. Colleges and universities should work with high school admissions counselors so they can teach students to write admissions essays that highlight the qualities that will enable them to succeed and demonstrate how they will contribute to the campus. In some cases, these essays will address the applicant's racial background. Indeed, the Supreme Court expressly noted that its decision striking affirmative action should not "be construed as prohibiting universities from considering an applicant's discussion of how race affected his or her life, be it through discrimination, inspiration, or otherwise" so long as "a benefit to a student who overcame racial discrimination . . . [is] tied to *that student's* courage and determination."[45] The Court also recognized that a college could positively consider an applicant's discussion of how "heritage or culture motivated him or her to assume a leadership role or attain a particular goal" so long as it is "tied to *that student's* unique ability to contribute to the university."[46] Thus, universities can create racially diverse environments that provide opportunities for interracial friendships and romantic relationships, even without race-conscious policies.

Invest in Public Transportation

I grew up in Washington Heights, a predominantly Latino and low-income neighborhood in New York City and attended a racially diverse magnet high school in Brooklyn in a predominantly African American neighborhood. On weekends, my friends and I took the subway to movie theaters in the Upper East Side, a predominantly White and wealthy neighborhood, where the theaters had plush seats and featured foreign films that were not screened in low-income minority neighborhoods. Afterward, we went out for pizza or burgers or walked along Fifth Avenue and admired the fancy buildings with doormen. Although the *residents* of these neighborhoods—Washington Heights, downtown Brooklyn, and the Upper East Side—were predominantly Latino, African American, or White, respectively, the *spaces* where my friends and I ate and played were racially integrated. I did not experience spatial segregation until I moved to a predominantly White suburb in New Jersey as an adult and for the first time found that I was the only (or one of two or three) Black or Brown person dining at local restaurants, shopping at the neighborhood pharmacy, or attending the holiday concert at a local church.

Spatial segregation is a barrier to interracial relationships. Racial minorities are often "excluded from public spaces that are identified as 'white'"[47] as a result of harassment by public and private actors and limited access, specifically, transportation, to these spaces. Racial minorities are less likely than Whites to own cars.[48] Thus, the lack of public transportation in predominantly White neighborhoods keeps these groups out. This is not accidental. Lawmakers in predominantly White neighborhoods opposed public transportation in their towns because their constituents did not want low-income minorities in their towns.[49] As Deborah Archer has argued, the United States' "transportation system was planned[, funded]—and is operated—to provide unequal access along race and class lines."[50] Lawmakers should address how the failure to invest in public transportation perpetuates spatial segregation and is a barrier to interracial relationships.

Public transportation allowed me, as a sixteen-year-old in a predominantly Latino neighborhood, to go to a school in an African American neighborhood and to eat and play in White neighborhoods. Unfortunately, public transportation in most parts of the United States is limited or virtually nonexistent, and individuals who do not have reliable transportation lack access to spaces outside their immediate neighborhood. There are many reasons why the government should invest in public transportation.[51] Providing access to public spaces in different neighborhoods that may increase propinquity and reduce barriers to interracial interactions and intimate relationships is yet another reason.

The Limits of Law and Education's Promise

The proposals outlined in this book seek to reduce barriers to interracial relationships by removing physical and psychological barriers to contact. They rely on studies showing that when people share the same spaces, they are more likely to become friends or intimate partners. This is known as the "propinquity effect," which is "the tendency of individuals to form close relationships with people they repeatedly encounter" and which recognizes that "the more often one comes into contact with another person, the more likely it is that one will form a friendship or romantic relationship with that person."[52] Despite the prevalence of online dating, couples continue to meet at school, work, the gym, and church. In our segregated society, however, individuals of different races rarely benefit from the propinquity effect. Given assortative mating patterns, interracial friendships and intimate relationships between people with vastly different levels of education and socioeconomic status are unlikely to develop even if they share the same spaces. However, removing the barriers to propinquity that the law helped create and perpetuate might allow relationships between people of different races with similar levels of education and interests to naturally develop.

Our intimate preferences reinforce racial hierarchy and inequality in society. Accordingly, some readers might be disappointed by the "soft" proposals in this chapter, which focus on removing the barriers that the law created but do not suggest legal mechanisms to directly encourage interracial relationships. This is intentional. First, while our collective racial preferences reinforce racial hierarchy, individuals have many reasons for preferring partners of certain races. When Asian Americans and Latinos express same-race preferences, for example, these are often based on a desire for a partner who shares their culture, language, or experience as a racial minority. These preferences are unlikely to stigmatize other racial groups. In contrast, when Asian Americans and Latinos pursue White partners but reject African American partners, their preferences are likely to be rooted in anti-Black bias.[53] Likewise, a White date-seeker's romantic preferences may or may not be rooted in White supremacy. An Italian American date-seeker who expresses a preference for a partner with Italian heritage may be seeking commonality of culture, language, and religion, and such preference does not necessarily reinforce racial hierarchy. In contrast, when a date-seeker's preference for a White partner trumps other traits, it is likely rooted in White supremacy. Given the breadth of reasons for our racial preferences, the law should steer clear of the matchmaking business.

Second, heavy-handed state efforts to encourage interracial intimacy are likely to meet resistance. As many parents learn, opining on their adolescent or adult child's love life is likely to backfire. Americans value the freedom to select romantic partners without interference from the people who love them most, and certainly without interference from the government. Moreover, even if the law could push individuals toward partners of different races, no one wants to wonder whether their partner chose them because the government nudged them to make that choice.

Third, I am a pragmatist. Consequently, I favor reforms that lawmakers might seriously consider adopting. Given the tensions between liberty and equality principles, any proposals to limit an individual's freedom of expression, religion, or association would fall prey to accusations that legal academics are out-of-touch intellectuals whose scholarship does little to solve legal problems.[54] Moreover, in recent years the Supreme Court has placed liberty interests above equality in several cases. In 2018, in *Masterpiece Cakeshop v. Colorado Civil Rights Commission*, the Supreme Court ruled that the Colorado Civil Rights Commission had discriminated against a baker in a civil rights proceeding brought against him for refusing to sell a custom-made wedding cake to a same-sex couple. Although the Court reaffirmed its holding in *Obergefell v. Hodges* that same-sex married couples and those seeking to marry are entitled to exercise their "freedom on terms equal to others," it also reiterated that "religious and philosophical objections" may be protected forms of expression in some cases.[55] Three years later, in *Fulton v. City of Philadelphia*, the Court favored the religious liberty interests of a foster care agency that refused to certify same-sex married couples as foster parents based on the agency's religious objections to marriage equality.[56] In 2023, the Supreme Court was faced yet again with the question of whether a private entity could refuse to provide services to same-sex couples. In *303 Creative LLC v. Elenis*, a graphic designer who sought to expand her business to create wedding websites sought an injunction to prevent Colorado from enforcing its public accommodations law prohibiting any business from denying any customer goods or services on the basis of race, sexual orientation, disability and other protected traits.[57] The designer, who believes that marriages should be between one man and one woman, argued that requiring her to create a website for a same-sex couple would violate her First Amendment freedom of expression by compelling her to convey a message—support for same-sex marriage—that she does not believe. The Court agreed. In short, when freedom of expression and freedom from discrimination are pitted against each other, freedom of expression often prevails.

While these recent cases have all involved challenges to marriage equality based on sexual orientation, not race, the Court's attentiveness to individual liberty interests suggests that it would not entertain any restrictions on individuals' expression of racial preferences on their profiles. Moreover, although religious and philosophical objections to interracial relationships are no longer common, some individuals still hold such views. Indeed, Congress thought it prudent to include interracial marriages when it sought to protect same-sex marriages in the event the Supreme Court overrules *Obergefell v. Hodges*, as some feared it might after its 2022 decision in *Dobbs v. Jackson Women's Health*, holding that there is no federal constitutional right to abortion, cast doubt on the constitutional right to marry.[58] The 2022 bipartisan federal Respect for Marriage Act prohibits states from denying recognition to same-sex marriages and interracial marriages performed in other states.[59] New Jersey enacted similar legislation, explaining that "as our country faces an era of uncertainty regarding the basic principles of equality and personal freedom, it is critical that we protect interracial marriage in New Jersey statutory law."[60] Lawmakers are unlikely, however, to support legislation regulating individual freedom to express racial preferences.

This book is an attempt to uncover the role of law in our intimate lives. But this uncovering can and should begin in school. For decades, most schools have not adequately taught students our history of slavery, conquest, and segregation or the immigration and citizenship laws that excluded individuals on the basis of race. If they had, we might think differently about our intimate preferences. We might question the basis of our attraction toward individuals of a particular race or our lack of attraction toward others. We might discover that preferences that seemed "natural" were shaped by external influences, including the law, and start to see individuals of racial backgrounds whom we had never considered as appropriate long-term partners as potential mates. In the end, our romantic preferences might remain unchanged, but we would have a better understanding of how our intimate choices affect racial and economic inequality in society.

In August 2020, on the heels of our country's racial reckoning, Seton Hall Law School, in Newark, New Jersey, where I teach, asked incoming law students to read Richard Rothstein's *The Color of Law: A Forgotten History of How Our Government Segregated America*.[61] Since then, a group of faculty has led a discussion of the book at orientation each August. For many students, the book is eye-opening as they come to understand why their town (and most of New Jersey) is racially segregated despite being one of the most racially diverse states. Before reading this book, many White students thought that their neighborhoods were predominantly White because racial minorities could not afford to live there or preferred to live in predominantly minority neighborhoods. Once they discover that the federal, state, and local governments created their segregated neighborhoods, they are motivated to find solutions to remedy the governments' segregation of neighborhoods across the country.

My hope is that anyone who reads this book will have the same reaction that many Seton Hall Law students had when they first read *The Color of Law* and will be motivated to explore the solutions that I propose and to come up with others that will help dismantle the racial hierarchy in the intimate market. Education is the first step toward helping to ensure that the freedom to choose an intimate partner is not hindered by racial preferences that the law created or facilitated. But it is not the last. Our work will continue for decades.

ACKNOWLEDGMENTS

I began thinking about the ideas in this book more than a decade ago but never imagined I would publish them until Nancy Dowd convinced me that my ideas were book-worthy. I am deeply grateful for Nancy's guidance, wisdom, and support throughout this project. I am also indebted to Robin Lenhardt, who, together with Nancy, pushed me to the finish line.

I am grateful to Seton Hall University School of Law and especially Dean Patrick E. Hobbs and Dean Kathleen M. Boozang for providing research funding and a sabbatical to work on this book. I am indebted to Kendall Thomas and the Center for the Study of Law and Culture at Columbia Law School for providing me with an academic home during my sabbatical.

This work would not have been possible without the assistance of a uniquely dedicated group of research assistants: Rhyan Almonacy, Sonia Badyal, Nicole Chamberlain, Kerdesha Desir, Sandy De Sousa, Emily Fea, Logan A Forsey, Amy Gromek, Chané Jones, Rachel Forman, William Brad McConnell, Meghan McSkimming, Zannatual Mustafa, Estefania Pugliese-Saville, Christina Sloan, Jordan Stefanacci, Elisia Tadros, Bisola Taiwo, Chrishana White, and Jia Zhang. I am also grateful to my colleague Teresa Rizzo who assisted me with the technical aspects of putting the manuscript together and to the librarians at Seton Hall Law who went above and beyond to locate any sources I needed wherever they might be. Thanks to my former colleague Trang Nguyen for gathering and organizing sources when I first began the research for this book.

I have benefited greatly from the opportunity to present ideas and portions of this book to faculty and students at numerous workshops and conferences. These included presentations at Boston University School of Law, Cardozo Law School, Columbia Law School, Fordham Law School, Georgetown University Law Center, New York University Law School, Notre Dame Law School, Rutgers School of Law-Camden,

Seton Hall Law School, University of Houston Law Center, University of Iowa College of Law, University of Missouri-Kansas City School of Law, AALS Annual Meeting, AALS Midyear Meeting on Shifting Foundations in Family Law, Family Law Scholars and Teachers Conference, LatCrit Conference, Latina Law Scholars Workshop, New York Area Family Law Scholars Workshop, and the Northeast People of Color Legal Scholarship Conference. These exchanges provided a breadth of perspectives and immensely enriched the book.

I owe special thanks to Edward Stein who read and commented on the entire manuscript. I am also grateful to the many friends, colleagues, and family members who read drafts of different chapters and provided feedback and inspiration. I thank them in alphabetical order: R. Richard Banks, Steven Bender, Gaia Bernstein, Alexander A. Boni-Saenz, Naomi Cahn, Ann Cammett, Wilfredo Caraballo, June Carbone, Jennifer Chacon, Carl Coleman, John Kip Cornwell, Rose Cuison-Villazor, Doron Dorfman, Marie Amelie George, Timothy Glynn, Rachel Godsil, Tristin Green, Judge Joseph Anthony Greenaway, Yolanda Harrison, Thomas Healy, Tanya Katerí Hernández, Clare Huntington, Kristin Johnson, Suzanne Kim, Marina Lao, Anibal Rosario Lebrón, Linda McClain, Nerys Maldonado, Rachel Moran, Angela Onwuachi-Willig, Catherine Powell, Neoshia Roemer, Carol Sanger, Brian Sheppard, Marc Spindelman, Emily Stolzenberg, Charles Sullivan, David Dante Troutt, Philomila Tsoukala, and Sarah Waldeck. My sincerest apologies to anyone I may have inadvertently missed. Thank you for your assistance and support.

Parts of this book previously appeared in one of my law review articles, "Romantic Discrimination and Children," *Chicago Kent Law Review* 92, no. 1 (2017): 105–33, and are included here in edited form with the permission of the *Chicago Kent Law Review*.

Last but certainly not least, I am thankful for the love and encouragement of my huge and wonderful family. I dedicate this book to my daughter, Briela, and to Carlos Bellido, my soulmate and best friend. Thank you for believing in me and supporting me unconditionally.

NOTES

INTRODUCTION

1 Shawn Nottingham, "Louisiana Justice Who Refused Interracial Marriage Resigns," CNN, November 3, 2009, https://CNN.com. Bardwell was forced to resign shortly thereafter.
2 I use the term "White" to mean Caucasian, not of Latino origin, and the term "Black" to mean African American, not of Latino origin.
3 "Interracial Couple Banned from Kentucky Church," *Huff Post*, November 30, 2011, https://huffpost.com.
4 Jon Terbush, "Nearly Half of Mississippi Republicans Think Interracial Marriage Should Be Illegal," Talking Points Memo, April 7, 2011, https://talkingpointsmemo.com.
5 Karen Zraick, "Mississippi Event Hall Refused to Host Interracial Wedding, Then Apologizes," *New York Times*, September 3, 2019, https://nytimes.com.
6 Deniz Gevrek, "Interracial Marriage, Migration and *Loving*," *National Economic Association* 41, no. 1 (January 2014): table 1. Alaska, Connecticut, Hawaii, Minnesota, New Hampshire, New Jersey, New York, Vermont, Wisconsin, and the District of Columbia never had anti-miscegenation laws.
7 Peggy Pascoe, *What Comes Naturally: Miscegenation Law and the Making of Race in America* (New York: Oxford University Press, 2010), 99, 118. I use "American Indian" instead of "Native American" because, as Neoshia Roemer has explained, it more accurately describes "the legal status of federally recognized Indian tribes and tribal citizens." Neoshia R. Roemer, "Un-Erasing American Indians and the Indian Child Welfare Act from Family Law," *Family Law Quarterly* 56, no. 1 (December 2023): 75. The U.S. Census defines American Indian and Alaska Native as "[a] person having origins in any of the original peoples of North and South America (including Central America) and who maintains tribal affiliation or community attachment." U.S. Census Bureau, American Community Survey, https://census.gov.
8 Perez v. Sharp, 32 Cal.2d 711, 724–27 (1948).
9 *Perez*, 32 Cal.2d at 731–32.
10 Treaty of Peace, Friendship, Limits and Settlement, February 2, 1848, U.S.-Mex., art. VIII, 9 Stat. 922, 929.
11 Loving v. Virginia, 388 U.S. 1, 12 (1967).
12 Kristen Bialik, "Key Facts about Race and Marriage, 50 Years after Loving v. Virginia," Pew Research Center, June 12, 2017, https:// pewresearch.org.

13 Kim Parker and Amanda Barroso, "In Vice President Kamala Harris, We Can See How America Has Changed," Pew Research Center, February 25, 2021, https://pewresearch.org.

14 Renee Romano, *Race Mixing: Black-White Marriage in Postwar America* (Cambridge, MA: Harvard University Press, 2003), 45.

15 Justin McCarthy, "U.S. Approval of Interracial Marriage at a New High of 94%," Gallup, September 10, 2021, https://gallup.com.

16 Raymond Fisman, Sheena S. Iyengar, Emir Kamenica, and Itamar Simonson, "Racial Preferences in Dating," *Review of Economic Studies* 75 (May 2008): 117–32.

17 For excellent books analyzing the role of race and gender in the intimate sphere, see Angela Onwuachi-Willig, *According to Our Hearts: Rhinelander v. Rhinelander and the Law of the Multiracial Family* (New Haven, CT: Yale University Press, 2013); Randall Kennedy, *Interracial Intimacies: Sex, Marriage, Identity, and Adoption* (New York: Vintage Books, 2004); Rachel F. Moran, *Interracial Intimacy: The Regulation of Race and Romance* (Chicago: University of Chicago Press, 2001).

18 Bialik, "Key Facts about Race and Marriage."

19 Bialik, "Key Facts about Race and Marriage."

20 Bialik, "Key Facts about Race and Marriage."

21 Daniel T. Lichter and Zhenchao Qian, "Social Boundaries and Marital Assimilation: Interpreting Trends in Racial and Ethnic Intermarriage," *American Sociological Review* 72 (February 2007): 68.

22 Orlando Patterson, *Rituals of Blood: Consequences of Slavery in Two American Centuries* (Washington, D.C.: Civitas Counterpoint, 1998), 157–58 (arguing that African Americans' marital isolation is the result of "three and a half centuries of slavery, Jim Crow, lynching, racist caricature, minstrelsy, public dishonor, anti-miscegenation laws and sentiments, economic discrimination, and residential segregation").

23 Elizabeth F. Emens, "Intimate Discrimination: The State's Role in Accidents of Sex and Love," *Harvard Law Review* 122, no. 5 (March 2009): 1367.

24 Abby Budimen, Christine Tamir, Lauren Mora, and Luis Noe-Bustamante, "Facts on U.S. Immigrants, 2018," Pew Research Center, August 20, 2020, table 9, https://pewresearch.org.

25 Belinda Robnett and Cynthia Feliciano, "Patterns of Racial-Ethnic Exclusion by Internet Daters," *Social Forces* 89, no. 3 (March 2011): 807–28; Glenn T. Tsunokai, Allison R. McGrath, and Jillian K. Kavanagh, "Online Dating Preferences of Asian Americans," *Journal of Social and Personal Relationships* 31, no. 6 (September 2014): 798, https://doi.org/10.1177/0265407513505925; James H. Liu, Susan Miller Campbell, and Heather Condie, "Ethnocentrism in Dating Preferences for an American Sample: The Ingroup Bias in Social Context," *European Journal of Social Psychology* 25, no. 1 (1995): 95–115. https://doi.org.10.1002/ejsp.2420250108.

26 George Yancey, *Who Is White? Latinos, Asians, and the New Black/Non-Black Divide* (Boulder, CO: Lynne Rienner Publishers, 2003); Wendy Wang, "The Rise of Intermarriage," Pew Research Center, February 16, 2012; Erica Morales, "Parental

Messages Concerning Latino/Black Interracial Dating: An Exploratory Study among Latina/o Young Adults," *Latino Studies* 10, no. 3 (September 2012): 314–33; Eileen O'Brien, *The Racial Middle: Latinos and Asian Americans Living Beyond the Racial Divide* (New York: New York University Press, 2008), 120.

27 Cynthia Feliciano, Rennie Lee, and Belinda Robnett, "Racial Boundaries among Latinos: Evidence from Internet Daters' Racial Preferences," *Social Problems* 58, no. 2 (May 2011): 189–212; Kumiko Nemoto, *Racing Romance: Love, Power, and Desire among Asian American/White Couples* (New Brunswick, NJ: Rutgers University Press, 2009).

28 Morales, "Parental Messages."

29 Eduardo Bonilla-Silva, *Racism without Racists: Color-Blind Racism and the Persistence of Racial Inequality in America*, 6th ed. (Lanham, MD: Rowman & Littlefield, 2022), 1.

30 Dan Slater, *Love in the Time of Algorithms: What Technology Does to Meeting and Mating* (New York: Penguin, 2013).

31 Clare Huntington, "Familial Norms and Normality," *Emory Law Journal* 59 (October 2010): 1103; Elizabeth Scott, "Social Norms and the Legal Regulation of Marriage," *Virginia Law Review* 86 (November 2000): 1901; Margaret Brinig and Steven Nock, "'I Only Want Trust': Norms, Trust and Autonomy," *Journal of Socio-Economics* 32 (October 2003): 471; Solangel Maldonado, "Beyond Economic Fatherhood: Encouraging Divorced Fathers to Parent," *University of Pennsylvania Law Review* 153 (July 2005): 921.

32 Emens, "Intimate Discrimination."

33 Geeta Gandbhir and Perri Peltz, "A Conversation with Police on Race," *New York Times*, November 11, 2015 (statement of retired police officer Glenn Cunningham).

34 Sonu Bedi, *Private Racism: Intimacy as a Matter of Justice* (New York: Cambridge University Press, 2019).

35 Shawn Grover and John F. Helliwell, "How's Life at Home? New Evidence on Marriage and the Set Point for Happiness," *Journal of Happiness Studies* 20, no. 2 (2019): 373–90, https://doi.org/10.1007/s10902-017-9941-3.

36 Cheryl Harris, "Whiteness as Property," *Harvard Law Review* 106, no. 8 (June 1993): 1709; Stephanie M. Wildman and Adrienne D. Davis, "Language and Silence: Making Systems of Privilege Visible," *Santa Clara Law Review* 35, no. 3 (1995): 893 (defining White privilege as "an invisible package of unearned assets"); Eduardo Bonilla-Silva, "From Bi-Racial to Tri-Racial: Towards a New System of Racial Stratification in the USA," *Ethnic & Racial Studies* 27, no. 6 (November 2004): 931–50, https://doi.org/10.1080/0141987042000268530; Eduardo Bonilla-Silva and David R. Dietrich, "The Latin Americanization of U.S. Race Relations: A New Pigmentocracy," in *Shades of Difference: Why Skin Color Matters*, ed. Evelyn Glenn (Stanford, CA: Stanford University Press, 2009), 59–60.

37 Tanya Kateri Hernandez, *Racial Subordination in Latin America: The Role of the State, Customary Law and the New Civil Rights Response* (New York: Cambridge University Press, 2013) (discussing *blanqueamiento*, whitening or lightening the

race, and the use of marriage and reproduction as a tool to *mejorar la raza*, improve the race by lightening it).
38 Nemoto, *Racing Romance*, 5.
39 One study found that 46 percent of adult children of White and Asian American parents identified "White" as their "main" race. Yancey, *Who Is White?*, 131.
40 Richard Rothstein, *The Color of Law: A Forgotten History of How Our Government Segregated America* (New York: Norton, 2018).
41 Ben Mintz and Daniel H. Krymlowski, "The Ethnic, Race, and Gender Gaps in Workplace Authority: Changes over Time in the United States," *Sociological Quarterly* 51, no.1 (2010): 20. For further discussions on occupational segregation, see Judith K. Hellerstein and David Neumark, "Workplace Segregation in the United States: Race, Ethnicity, and Skill," *Review of Economics and Statistics* 90, no. 3 (August 2008): 459–77; Natalie J. Sokoloff, *Black Women and White Women in the Professions: Occupational Segregation by Race and Gender, 1960–1980*, Perspectives on Gender (Milton Park, UK: Routledge, 2014); Coral del Río and Olga Alonso-Villar, "The Evolution of Occupational Segregation in the United States, 1940–2010: Gains and Losses of Gender-Race Ethnicity Groups," *Demography* 52, no. 3 (2015): 967–88.
42 Suzann Pileggi Pawelski, "The Happy Couple," *Scientific American* 25 (March 2016): 48–53.
43 Sonu Bedi, "Sexual Racism: Intimacy as a Matter of Justice," *Journal of Politics* 77 (October 2015): 998.
44 Ralph Richard Banks, *Is Marriage for White People? How the African American Marriage Decline Affects Everyone* (New York: Plume, 2012).
45 Russell K. Robinson, "Racing the Closet," *Stanford Law Review* 61 (April 2009): 1463, 1503 (arguing that "Romantic Segregation Limits Romantic Possibilities for Black Women and Black MSM [men who have sex with men]").
46 Letter from Emily Dickinson to Mary Bowles, quoted in Richard Sewall, *The Life of Emily Dickinson* (Cambridge, MA: Harvard University Press, 1994), 493.
47 The law also influenced our preferences for partners of a different sex and without any physical or mental disabilities. For discussion, see Emens, "Intimate Discrimination," 1325–34.
48 Emens, "Intimate Discrimination," 1373, citing David Mura, "The Internment of Desire," in *Under Western Eyes: Personal Essays from Asian America*, ed. Garrett Hongo (Albany, NY: Anchor, 1995), 282.
49 Matthew Frye Jacobson, *Whiteness of a Different Color: European Immigrants and the Alchemy of Race* (Cambridge, MA: Harvard University Press, 1999); Karen Brodkin, *How Jews Became White Folks: And What That Says About Race in America* (New Brunswick, NJ: Rutgers University Press, 1998); Noel Ignatiev, *How the Irish Became White* (Milton Park, UK: Routledge, 1995).
50 Erica Pandey, "America the Single," Axios, February 25, 2023, https://axios.com.
51 Richard Thaler and Cass Sunstein, *Nudge: Improving Decisions about Health, Wealth, and Happiness* (New York: Penguin, 2009).

52 JDate, accessed September 2, 2023, https://jdate.com.
53 Latino People Meet, accessed September 2, 2023, https://latinopeoplemeet.com.
54 The dating site "Where White People Meet" has been removed, but see Zach Stafford, "That Dating Site for White People? It's Racist, No Matter How It's Justified," *Guardian*, January 8, 2016, https:// theguardian.com.
55 Krissah Thompson, "Segregated Clubs in Kentucky Raise Issues for Private Business, Civil Rights Law," *Washington Post*, June 2, 2010, https://washingpost.com.

CHAPTER 1. A GENDERED RACIAL HIERARCHY IN THE INTIMATE MARKET

1 Justin McCarthy, "U.S. Approval of Interracial Marriage at a New High of 94%," Gallup, September 10, 2021, https://gallup.com.
2 Debra Blackwell and Daniel Lichter, "Homogamy Among Dating, Cohabiting and Married Couples," *Sociological Quarterly* 45, no. 4 (Fall 2004): 719–37.
3 Melissa Herman and Mary Campbell, "I Wouldn't, but You Can: Attitudes Toward Interracial Relationships," *Social Science Research* 41, no. 2 (March 2012): 343–58.
4 Herman and Campbell, "I Wouldn't, but You Can," 356.
5 Andrew Daniller, "Majorities of Americans See at Least Some Discrimination against Black, Hispanic and Asian People in the U.S.," Pew Research Center, March 18, 2021, https://pewresearch.org.
6 Cristina Mora, *Making Hispanics: How Activists, Bureaucrats, and Media Created a New American* (Chicago: University of Chicago Press, 2014); Mark Hugo Lopez, Jens Manuel Krogstad, and Jeffrey S. Passel, "Who Is Hispanic?," Pew Research Center, September 15, 2022, https://pewresearch.org.
7 Justin McCarthy and Whitney Dupree, "No Preferred Racial Term among Most Black, Hispanic Adults," Gallup, August 4, 2021, https://gallup.com.
8 Almost one-third (20 million) of the 62.6 million Latinos in the United States. identified with "more than one race" on the 2020 Census, and almost 42 percent identified as "some other race." Lopez, Krogstad, and Passel, "Who Is Hispanic?" The majority of Latinos who identified as "some other race" indicated that their race was "Latino" even though the census form explicitly states that, for the purpose of the census, "Hispanic origins are not races." U.S. Census Bureau, "2020 Census Informational Questionnaire," U.S. Census Bureau, June 3, 2023, https://census.gov. Less than 2 percent (1.2 million) of Latinos who identified as single-race indicated their race as Black. Twenty percent (12.6 million) of Latinos who identified as single-race indicated their race as White. Lopez, Krogstad, and Passel, "Who Is Hispanic?"
9 According to the U.S. Census, "The concept of race is separate from the concept of Hispanic origin," and "people who identify their origin as Hispanic, Latino, or Spanish may be of any race." U.S. Census Bureau, "American Community Survey," May 15, 2023, https://census.gov.
10 Jennifer Lundquist and Ken-Hou Lin, "Is Love (Color) Blind? The Economy of Race among Gay and Straight Daters," *Social Forces* 93, no. 4 (June 2015): 1423, n14.

11 Lopez, Krogstad, and Passel, "Who Is Hispanic?"; "Majority of Latinos Say Skin Color Impacts Opportunity in America and Shapes Daily Life," Pew Research Center, November 4, 2021 (citing U.S. Census). Forty-one percent of Latinos in the 2020 U.S. Census stated their race as "some other race" and wrote in "Mexican," "Hispanic," or "Latin American" as their race. Lopez, Krogstad, and Passel, "Who Is Hispanic?"
12 Tanya K. Hernandez, *Racial Innocence: Unmasking Latino Anti-Black Bias and the Struggle for Equality* (Boston: Beacon Press, 2022), 8–9.
13 Jose A. Cobas, Jorge Duany, and Joe R. Feagin, *How the United States Racializes Latinos: White Hegemony and Its Consequences* (Boulder, CO: Paradigm, 2009), 1.
14 Vilma Ortiz and Edward Telles, "Racial Identity and Racial Treatment of Mexican Americans," *Race Social Problems* 4, no. 1 (April 2012): 41.
15 *In re Rodriguez*, 81 F. 337 (W.D. Tex. 1897).
16 See Chapter 2. William Carrigan and Clive Webb, "When America Lynched Mexicans," *New York Times*, February 20, 2015, https://nytimes.com.
17 "Bad Hombres: From Colonization to Criminalization," LatinoJustice PRLDEF Decolonize Justice Documentary Series, accessed September 9, 2023, https://decolonizejustice.org. See also Michele Stacey, Kristin Carbone-Lopez, and Richard Rosenfeld, "Demographic Change and Ethnically Motivated Crime: The Impact of Immigration on Anti-Hispanic Hate Crime in the United States," *Journal of Contemporary Criminal Justice* 27, no. 3 (July 2011): 278.
18 Eduardo Bonilla-Silva, "From Bi-racial to Tri-Racial: Towards a New System of Racial Stratification in the USA," *Ethnic & Racial Studies* 27, no. 6 (November 2004): 931–50.
19 Ian Haney-Lopez, *White by Law: The Legal Construction of Race* (New York: New York University Press 2006); Michael Omi and Howard Winant, *Racial Formation in the United States*, 3rd ed. (Milton Park, UK: Routledge, 2014).
20 Linda Villarosa, *Under the Skin: Racism, Inequality and the Health of a Nation* (New York: Penguin Random House, 2022).
21 A hookup is a "casual, unplanned sexual encounter that occurs outside of an established relationship." Elizabeth McClintock, "When Does Race Matter? Race, Sex, and Dating at an Elite University," *Journal of Marriage and Family* 72, no. 1 (January 2010): 45–72.
22 Jeffrey Jones, "Most Americans Approve of Interracial Dating," Gallup, October 7, 2005, https://gallup.com.
23 Kara Joyner and Grace Kao, "Interracial Relationships and the Transition to Adulthood," *American Sociological Review* 70, no. 4 (August 2005): 563–81. Sixty percent of 18–29-year-olds who participated in the Gallup poll reported that they had dated interracially as did 53 percent of individuals ages 30–49, 46 percent of individuals ages 50–64, and 28 percent of individuals 65 and older. Sixty-nine percent of Latinos, 52 percent of African Americans, and 45 percent of Whites reported the same. Jones, Most Americans Approve.

24 McClintock, "When Does Race Matter?"; Shana Levin, Pamela L. Taylor, and Elena Caudle, "Interethnic and Interracial Dating in College: A Longitudinal Study," *Journal of Social and Personal Relationships* 24, no. 3 (June 2007): 323–41.
25 Melissa R. Herman and Mary E. Campbell, "I Wouldn't, but You Can"; Attitudes toward Interracial Relationships," *Social Science Research* 41, no. 2 (March 2012): 343–58; Martin S. Fiebert, Dusty Nugent, Scott L Hershberger, and Margo Kasdan, "Dating and Commitment Choices as a Function of Ethnicity among American College Students in California," *Psychological Reports* 94, no. 33 (June 2004): 1293–1300, https://doi.org/10.2466/pro.94.3c.1293-1300; George Yancey, "Who Interracially Dates: An Examination of the Characteristics of Those Who Have Interracially Dated," *Journal of Comparative Family Studies* 33, no. 2 (Spring 2002): 179–90; Debra L. Blackwell and Daniel T. Lichter, "Homogamy among Dating, Cohabiting and Married Couples," *Sociological Quarterly* 45, no. 4 (2004): 719–37.
26 Zhenchao Qian and Daniel T. Lichter, "Changing Patterns of Interracial Marriage in a Multiracial Society," *Journal of Marriage and Family* 73, no. 5 (September 2011): 1065–84, https://doi.org/10.1111/j.1741-3737.2011.00866.x. In 2010, 18.3 percent of cohabiting different-sex couples were interracial as compared to 9.5 percent of married different-sex couples. Daphne Lofquist, Terry Lugaila, Martin O'Connell, and Sarah Feliz, "Households and Families: 2010," U.S. Census Bureau (April 2012): 18–19 and table 7. Interracial cohabiting couples are 60 percent as likely as same-race cohabiting couples to marry. Joyner and Kao, "Interracial Relationships."
27 Patricia S. Pittman Calderon, Jed D. Wong, and Barbara T. Hodgdon, "A Scoping Review of the Physical Health and Psychological Well-Being in Individuals in Interracial Romantic Relationships," *Family Relations* 71, no. 5 (September 2022): 2011–29, https://doi.org/10.1111/fare.1276; "Interracial Marriages Now More Common, but Not Without Challenges," *CBS News*, June 13, 2021, https://cbsnews.com/news.
28 Hongyu Wang, Grace Kao, and Kara Joyner "Stability of Interracial and Intraracial Romantic Relationships among Adolescents," *Social Science Research* 35, no. 2 (June 2006): 435–53, https://doi.org/10.1016/j.ssresearch.2004.10.001; Qian and Lichter, "Changing Patterns"; Elizabeth Vaquera and Grace Kao, "Private and Public Displays of Affection among Interracial and Intraracial Adolescent Couples," *Social Science Quarterly* 86, no. 2 (April 2005): 484–508, https://doi.org/10.1111/j.0038-4941.2005.00314.x.
29 Wendy Wang, "Interracial Marriage, 'Who Is Marrying Out?,'" Pew Research Center, June 12, 2015, https://pewresearch.org.
30 Immigrants from South and East Asia are less likely than immigrants from Southeast Asia to have a U.S.-born White spouse. Pratikshya Bohra-Mishra and Douglas Massey, "Intermarriage among New Immigrants in the USA," *Ethnic and Racial Studies* 38, no. 5 (2015): 734–58, https://doi.org/10.1080/01419870.2014.937726; "The Rise of Asian Americans," Pew Research Center, June 19, 2012, https://pewresearch.org.

31 Gretchen Livingston and Anna Brown, "Intermarriage in the U.S. 50 Years after Loving v. Virginia," Pew Research Center, May 18, 2017, https://pewresearch.org/.
32 Qian and Lichter, "Changing Patterns."
33 Qian and Lichter, "Changing Patterns"; Kim Parker, Juliana Menasce Horowitz, Rich Morin and Mark Hugo Lopez, "Multiracial in America: Proud, Diverse and Growing in Numbers," Pew Research Center, June 11, 2015, https://pewresearch.org.
34 Livingston and Brown, "Intermarriage in the U.S."
35 The gender disparity is even greater between foreign-born Asian men and women. Foreign-born Asian American women are three times as likely as their male counterparts to marry out (34 percent versus 11 percent); Wendy Wang, "The Rise of Intermarriage: Race, Characteristics Vary by Race and Gender," Pew Research Center, February 16, 2012, https://pewresearch.org.
36 Wang, "Interracial Marriage" (reporting that in 2013, "61 percent of American Indian female newlyweds married outside their race, compared with 54 percent of American Indian male newlyweds.").
37 Xuanning Fu, "Marital Assimilation and Family Financial Resources of US-Born Hispanics," *Open Society Journal* 2 (June 2009): 10–22, doi: 0.2174/1874946100902 010010.
38 Wang, "The Rise of Intermarriage." U.S.-born Asians are one and a half times as likely as their foreign-born counterparts to marry out. Latinos' and Asians' rate of intermarriage with Whites has decreased since the 1990s, but that decrease is largely attributable to the decrease in the intermarriage rate of immigrants. The rate of intermarriage of U.S.-born Asian Americans and Latinos has remained virtually unchanged since the 1980s. In fact, the difference between the intermarriage rate of U.S.-born Asian Americans and Latinos and that of their immigrant counterparts was even higher for Latinos and Asian Americans who married out in 2008—39 percent versus 12 percent and 46 percent versus 26 percent, respectively. See Jeffrey S. Passel, Wendy Wang, and Paul Taylor, "One-in-Seven New U.S. Marriages is Interracial or Interethnic," Pew Research Center, June 4, 2010, https://pewresearch.org. There is no significant difference between the intermarriage rate of U.S.-born and foreign-born Blacks. See Qian and Lichter, "Changing Patterns."
39 Wang, "The Rise of Intermarriage," 6.
40 Livingston and Brown, "Intermarriage in the U.S." (reporting that 16 percent of Latinos with a high school diploma or less are intermarried as compared to 46 percent of Latinos with at least a bachelor's degree); Paul Taylor, D'Vera Cohn, Wendy Wang, Gretchen M. Livingston, Cary Funk, and Rich Morin, "Second Generation Americans: A Portrait of the Adult Children of Immigrants," Pew Research Center, 68, February 7, 2013, https://pewresearch.org (reporting that 60 percent of Asian Americans who intermarried with Whites in 2010 had a college degree as compared to 49 percent of all Asian American adults in the United States); Wang, "The Rise of Intermarriage"; Paul Taylor, D'Vera Cohn, Wendy

Wang, Jeffrey S. Passel, Rakesh Kochhar, Richard Fry, Kim Parker, Cary Funk, and Gretchen M. Livingston, "The Rise of Asian Americans," Pew Research Center, April 4, 2013, https://pewresearch.org. Another study found that "educational attainment among Blacks in 2008 was significantly associated with marriages to Whites. When both partners had at least a college education, the odds of marrying out were more than two times higher than when both partners had only a high school diploma or less." Qian and Lichter, "Changing Patterns," 1077.

41 Zhenchao Qian, "Breaking the Last Taboo: Interracial Marriage in America," *Contexts* 4, no. 4 (November 2005): 33–37, https://doi.org/10.1525/ctx.2005.4.4.33.

42 Aaron Gullickson and Vincent Kang Fu, "Comment: An Endorsement of Exchange Theory in Mate Selection," *American Journal of Sociology* 115, no. 4 (January 2010): 1243–51, https://doi.org/10.1086/649049; Vincent Kang Fu, "Racial Intermarriage Pairings," *Demography* 38, no. 2 (May 2001): 147–59, https://doi.org/10.2307/3088297.

43 Wang, "The Rise of Intermarriage," 14. One study of the three largest Latino groups—Mexican Americans, Cuban Americans, and Puerto Ricans—found that for all three groups, members who intermarried with Whites enjoyed higher financial resources than counterparts who married other Latinos. Fu, "Marital Assimilation and Family."

44 Wang, "The Rise of Intermarriage," 14. White/Asian newlyweds of 2008 through 2010 had median combined annual earnings of $70,952 as compared to $60,000 for White/White couples and $62,000 for Asian/Asian couples.

45 Qian, "Breaking the Last Taboo."

46 Qian, "Race and Social Distance: Intermarriage with Non-Latino Whites," *Race & Society* 5 (December 2002): 33. Latinos who identified as White were twice as likely as Latinos who identified as Black to be married to non-Latino Whites. Haeyoun Park, "Who Is Marrying Whom?," *New York Times*, January 29, 2011, https://nytimes.com.

47 Qian, "Race and Social Distance," 45.

48 Qian, "Breaking the Last Taboo."

49 Angeliki Kastanis and Bianca Wilson, "Race/Ethnicity, Gender, and Socioeconomic Wellbeing of Individuals in Same-Sex Couples," Williams Institute, UCLA School of Law, February 2014), https://williamsinstitute.law.ucla.edu.

50 Amanda Barroso and Richard Fry, "On Some Demographic Measures, People in Same-Sex Marriages Differ from Those in Opposite-Sex Marriages," Pew Research Center, July 7, 2021, https://pewresearch.org.

51 Kastanis and Wilson, "Race/Ethnicity, Gender."

52 Cynthia Feliciano, Rennie Lee, and Belinda Robnett, "Racial Boundaries among Latinos: Evidence from Internet Daters' Racial Preferences," *Social Problems* 58, no. 2 (May 2011): 195, https://doi.org/10.1525/sp.2011.58.2.189.

53 Voon Chin Phua and Gayle Kaufman, "The Crossroads of Race and Sexuality: Date Selection among Men in Internet 'Personal' Ads," *Journal of Family Issues* 24, no. 8 (November 2003): 981–94, https://doi.org/10.1177/0192513X03256607

("Preferences for minorities often are tinted with stereotypical images: Asians as exotic, docile, loyal partners; Hispanics as passionate, fiery lovers; and Blacks as 'well-endowed,' forbidden partners.").

54 Gerald A. Mendelsohn, Lindsay Shaw Taylor, Andrew T. Fiore, and Coye Cheshire, "Black/White Online Dating: Interracial Courtship in the 21st Century," *Psychology of Popular Media Culture* 3, no. 1 (2014): 2–18; Belinda Robnett and Cynthia Feliciano, "Patterns of Racial-Ethnic Exclusion by Internet Daters," *Social Forces* 89, no. 3 (2011): 807–28; Gunther Hitsch, Ali Hortaçsu, and Dan Ariely, "What Makes You Click—Mate Preferences in Online Dating," *Quantitative Marketing and Economics* 8, no. 4 (December 2010): 393–427, doi:10.1007/s11129-010-9088-6.

55 Paul W. Eastwick and Eli J. Finkel, "Sex Differences in Mate Preferences Revisited: Do People Know What They Initially Desire in a Romantic Partner?," *Journal of Personality and Social Psychology* 94, no. 2 (February 2008): 245–64; Dylan F. Selterman, Elizabeth Chagnon, and Sean P. Mackinnon, "Do Men and Women Exhibit Different Preferences for Mates? A Replication of Eastwick and Finkel," *SAGE Open* 5, no. 3 (2008), https://doi.org/10.1177/2158244015605160.

56 Ken-Hou Lin and Jennifer Lundquist, "Mate Selection in Cyberspace: The Intersection of Race, Gender, and Education," *American Journal of Sociology* 119, no. 1 (July 2013): 183, 203; Christian Rudder, *Dataclysm: Love, Sex, Race, and Identity—What Our Online Lives Tell Us about Our Offline Selves* (New York: Crown Publishing, 2014), 10.

57 Lin and Lundquist, "Mate Selection"; Mary Madden and Amanda Lenhart, "Online Dating: Americans Who Are Seeking Romance Use the Internet to Help Them in Their Search, but There Is Still Widespread Public Concern about the Safety of Online Dating," Pew Internet and American Life Project, Pew Research Center, March 5, 2006, https://pewresearch.org; Dan Slater, *Love in the Time of Algorithms: What Technology Does to Meeting and Mating* (New York: Penguin, 2013), 2; Michael J. Rosenfeld and Reuben J. Thomas, "Searching for a Mate: The Rise of the Internet as a Social Intermediary," *American Sociological Review* 77, no. 4 (2012): 523–47, https://doi.org/10.1177/0003122412448050.

58 Gary Becker, "A Theory of Marriage, Part I," *Journal of Political Economy* 81, no. 4 (1973): 813–46; Martin Browning, Pierre-André Chiappori, and Yoram Weiss, *The Economics of the Family* (Cambridge: Cambridge University Press, 2014); Matthijs Kalmijn, "Intermarriage and Homogamy: Causes, Patterns, Trends," *Annual Review of Sociology* 24 (August 1998): 395–421.

59 Kalmijn, "Intermarriage and Homogamy."

60 Emma Pierson, "In the End, People May Really Just Want to Date Themselves," *Five Thirty Eight*, April 9, 2014, https://fivethirtyeight.com.

61 Hitsch, Hortaçsu, and Ariely, "What Makes You Click," 415–17. Other studies have similarly found that date-seekers prefer attractive partners. See Eastwick and Finkel, "Sex Differences in Mate Preferences Revisited," 245; Raymond Fisman, Sheena S. Iyengar, Emir Kamenica, and Itamar Simonson, "Gender Differences

in Mate Selection: Evidence from a Speed Dating Experiment," *Quarterly Journal of Economics* 121, no. 2 (2006): 673–97 https://doi.org/10.1162/qjec.2006.121.2.673; Pamela C. Regan, Lauren Levin, Susan Sprecher, F. Scott Christopher, and Rodney Gate, "Partner Preferences: What Characteristics Do Men and Women Desire in Their Short Term Sexual and Long Run Romantic Partners," *Journal of Psychology and Human Sexuality* 12, no. 3 (2000): 1–21; Gunther Hitsch, Ali Hortaçsu, and Dan Ariely, "Matching and Sorting in Online Dating," *American Economic Review* 100, no. 1 (2010); Fisman et al., "Gender Differences."

62 David M. Buss, "The Strategies of Human Mating," *American Scientist* 82, no. 3 (May–June 1994): 238–49; Pamela Regan, "Minimum Mate Selection Standards as a Function of Perceived Mate Value, Relationship Context, and Gender," *Journal of Psychology & Human Sexuality* 10, no. 1 (1998): 53–73.

63 Eduardo Bonilla-Silva and Gianpaolo Baiocchi, "Anything but Racism: How Sociologists Limit the Significance of Racism," *Race & Society* 4, no. 2 (2001): 117–31, https://doi.org/10.1016/S1090-9524(03)00004-4; Charles Gallagher, "The End of Racism as the New Doxa: New Strategies for Researching Race," in *White Logic, White Methods: Racism and Methodology*, ed. Tukufu Zuberi and Eduardo Bonilla-Silva (Lanham, MD: Rowman & Littlefield, 2008), 163.

64 Rudder, *Dataclysm*, 104, 112–13.

65 Hitsch, Hortaçsu, and Ariely, "What Makes You Click," 424. Another study found similar results. Raymond Fisman, Sheena S. Iyengar, Emir Kamenica, and Itamar Simonson, "Racial Preferences in Dating," *Review of Economic Studies* 75 (May 2008): 117–32.

66 Cynthia Feliciano, Belinda Robnett, and Golnaz Komaie, "Gendered Racial Exclusion among White Internet Daters," *Social Science Research* 38, no. 1 (March 2009): 9–54, https://doi.org/10.1016/j.ssresearch.2008.09.004.

67 George Yancey, "Crossracial Differences in the Racial Preferences of Potential Dating Partners: A Test of the Alienation of African Americans and Social Dominance Orientation," *Sociological Quarterly* 50, no. 1 (Winter 2009): 121–43, https://doi.org/10.1111/j.1533-8525.2008.01135.x; Glenn T. Tsunokai, Augustine J. Kposowa, and Michele A. Adams, "Racial Preferences in Internet Dating: A Comparison of Four Birth Cohorts," *Western Journal of Black Studies* 33, no. 1 (2009): 1–15; Rudder, *Dataclysm*, 102.

68 Celeste Vaughan Curington, Ken-Hou Lin, and Jennifer Hickes Lundquist, "Positioning Multiraciality in Cyberspace: Treatment of Multiracial Daters in an Online Dating Website," *American Sociological Review* 80, no. 4 (August 2015): 10; Rudder, *Dataclysm*, 116–17.

69 Feliciano, Robnett, and Komaie, "Gendered Racial Exclusion."

70 Rudder, *Dataclysm*, 103–7; Celeste Vaughan Curington, Jennifer H. Lundquist, and Ken-Hou Lin, *The Dating Divide: Race and Desire in the Era of Online Romance* (Oakland: University of California Press, 2021), 116.

71 Curington, Lin, and Lundquist, "Positioning Multiraciality," 773; Lin and Lundquist, "Mate Selection," 205.

72 Curington, Lin, and Lundquist, "Positioning Multiraciality."
73 Feliciano, Robnett, and Komaie, "Gendered Racial Exclusion," 49–50.
74 Christian Rudder, "Race and Attraction, 2009–2014," *Ok Trends* (September 10, 2014), https://web.archive.org; Rudder, *Dataclysm*, 109.
75 Hitsch, Hortaçsu, and Ariely, "What Makes You Click," 19.
76 Feliciano, Robnett, and Komaie, "Gendered Racial Exclusion"; Tsunokai, Kposowa, and Adams, "Racial Preferences."
77 Lin and Lundquist, "Mate Selection."
78 Robnett and Feliciano, "Patterns of Racial-Ethnic Exclusion" (finding that while a majority of straight White women stated that they preferred to date only White men, only 6 percent of Asian American women and 16 percent of Latina women preferred to date only men of their same race); Gerald Mendelsohn et al., "Black/White Online Dating."
79 Robnett and Feliciano, "Patterns of Racial-Ethnic Exclusion."
80 Robnett and Feliciano, "Patterns of Racial-Ethnic Exclusion."
81 Curington, Lin, and Lundquist, "Positioning Multiraciality"; Lin and Lundquist, "Mate Selection," 203; Rudder, "Race and Attraction."
82 James H. Liu, Susan Miller Campbell, and Heather Condie, "Ethnocentrism in Dating Preferences for an American Sample: The Ingroup Bias in Social Context," *European Journal of Social Psychology* 25, no. 1 (1995): 95–115, https://doi.org/10.1002/ejsp.2420250108.
83 Robnett and Feliciano, "Patterns of Racial-Ethnic Exclusion," 818.
84 Yancey, "Crossracial Differences"; Robnett and Feliciano, "Patterns of Racial-Ethnic Exclusion."
85 Robnett and Feliciano, "Patterns of Racial-Ethnic Exclusion," 816.
86 Robnett and Feliciano, "Patterns of Racial-Ethnic Exclusion."
87 Mendelsohn et al., "Black/White Online Dating."
88 Mendelsohn et al., "Black/White Online Dating"; Curington, Lin, and Lundquist, "Positioning Multiraciality"; Lin and Lundquist, "Mate Selection."
89 Curington, Lin, and Lundquist, "Positioning Multiraciality," 765; Lin and Lundquist, "Mate Selection," 196; Rudder, *Dataclysm*.
90 Curington, Lin, and Lundquist, "Positioning Multiraciality"; Lin and Lundquist, "Mate Selection," 202–9; Christian Rudder, "How Your Race Affects the Messages You Get," *OkTrends*, October 5, 2009, blog.okcupid.com; Rudder, "Race and Attraction."
91 Brandon Andrew Robinson, "'Personal Preference' as the New Racism: Gay Desire and Racial Cleansing in Cyberspace," *Sociology of Race and Ethnicity*, 1, no. 2 (2015): 317–30.
92 Phua and Kaufman, "The Crossroads of Race and Sexuality," 981, 988, 989.
93 Lundquist and Lin, "Is Love (Color) Blind?," 1441.
94 Lundquist and Lin, "Is Love (Color) Blind?," 1438; Rudder, "How Race Affects."
95 Lundquist and Lin, "Is Love (Color) Blind?," 1424.

96 Tsunokai, Kposowa, and Adams, "Racial Preferences"; Glenn T. Tsunokai, Allison R. McGrath, and Jillian K. Kavanagh, "Online Dating Preferences of Asian Americans," *Journal of Social and Personal Relationships* 31, no. 6 (September 2014): 798, https://doi.org/10.1177/0265407513505925; Lundquist and Lin, "Is Love (Color) Blind?"; Russell K. Robinson, "Structural Dimensions of Romantic Preferences," *Fordham Law Review* 76, no. 6 (2008): 2787; Rudder, "How Race Affects"; Phua and Kaufman, "The Crossroads of Race and Sexuality"; Patrick A. Wilson, Pamela Valera, Ana Ventuneac, Ivan Balan, Matt Rowe, and Alex Carballo-Dieguez, "Race-Based Sexual Stereotyping and Sexual Partnering among Men Who Use the Internet to Identify Other Men for Bareback Sex," *Journal of Sex Research* 46, no. 5 (2009): 399–413; Robinson, "'Personal Preference' as the New Racism."
97 Phua and Kaufman, "The Crossroads of Race and Sexuality," 989.
98 Tsunokai, McGrath, and Kavanagh, "Online Dating," 808.
99 Wilson et al., "Race-Based Sexual Stereotyping."
100 Phua and Kaufman, "The Crossroads of Race and Sexuality," 988; Wilson et al., "Race-Based Sexual Stereotyping."
101 Lundquist and Lin, "Is Love (Color) Blind?"; Voon Chin Phua, "Contesting and Maintaining Hegemonic Masculinities: Gay Asian American Men in Mate Selection," *Sex Roles: A Journal of Research*, 57, nos. 11–12 (2007): 909–18; Maurice Kwong-Lai Poon and Peter Trung-Thu Ho, "Negotiating Social Stigma among Gay Asian Men," *Sexualities* 11, nos. 1–2 (2008): 245–68; Robinson, "Personal Preference."
102 Patricia Hill Collins, *Black Sexual Politics: African Americans, Gender, and the New Racism* (Milton Park: Routledge, 2005), 44, 102–3.
103 Robinson, "Structural Dimensions," 2817.
104 Wilson et al., "Race-Based Sexual Stereotyping."
105 "Internet/Broadband Fact Sheet," Pew Research Center, April 7, 2021, http://pewinternet.org.
106 Rudder, *Dataclysm*, 27.
107 "Social Media Use in 2021," Pew Research Center, April 7, 2021, https://pewresearch.org
108 Madden and Lenhart, "Online Dating."
109 Fisman et al., "Racial Preferences"; Fisman et al., "Gender Differences."
110 Christian Rudder, "Race and Attraction, 2009–2014," *Oktrends*, September 10, 2014, https://gwern.net.
111 Rudder, *Dataclysm*, 108.
112 Michael Omi and Howard Winant, *Racial Formation in the United States*, 2nd ed. (Milton Park: Routledge, 1994), 68.
113 Rudder, *Dataclysm*, 97, 102, 106–7. The researchers controlled for physical attractiveness so the ratings are not attributable to objective differences in attractiveness of the photos. In fact, online daters rated the profiles and photos of Asian American, Latina, and White women as *more* attractive than the average woman.

114 Approximately 80 percent of Asian American, African American, and Latino students as compared to 49 percent of White students reported racial preferences. Eighty percent of Asian American, 66 percent of Latino, and 49 percent of White students excluded African Americans as potential dates. James A. Bany, Belinda Robnett, and Cynthia Feliciano, "Gendered Black Exclusion: The Persistence of Racial Stereotypes among Daters," *Race & Social Problems* 6, no. 3 (September 2014): 201–13.

115 Bany, Robnett, and Feliciano, "Gendered Black Exclusion," 206–8.

116 Bany, Robnett, and Feliciano, "Gendered Black Exclusion," 208.

117 Kimberly Jade Norwood, *Color Matters: Skin Tone Bias and the Myth of a Post-Racial America* (Milton Park: Routledge, 2013); Collins, *Black Sexual Politics*, 194; Verna Keith, "A Colorstruck World: Skin Tone, Achievement, and Self-Esteem among African American Women," in *Shades of Difference: Why Skin Color Matters*, ed. Evelyn Nakano Glenn (Stanford, CA: Stanford University Press, 2009), 25–38; Christie D. Batson, Zhenchao Qian, and Daniel Lichter, "Interracial and Intraracial Patterns of Mate Selection among America's Diverse Black Populations," *Journal of Marriage and Family* 68, no. 3 (2006): 658–72; M. Belinda Tucker and Claudia Mitchell-Kernan, "Social Structural and Psychological Correlates of Interethnic Dating," *Journal of Social & Personal Relationships* 12, no. 3 (1995): 341–61 https://doi.org/10.1177/0265407595123002.

118 Joanne L. Rondilla and Paul Spickard, *Is Lighter Better? Skin-Tone Discrimination among Asian Americans* (Lanham, MD: Rowman & Littlefield, 2007), 21, 90, 128; Keith, "A Colorstruck World"; Andres Villarreal, "Stratification by Skin Color in Contemporary Mexico," *American Sociological Review* 75, no. 5 (2010): 652–78.

119 Mark Hill, "Skin Color and the Perception of Attractiveness among African American: Does Gender Make a Difference?," *Social Psychology Quarterly*, 65, no. 1 (2002): 77, 83.

120 Selena Bond and Thomas F. Cash, "Black Beauty: Skin Color and Body Images among African American College Women," *Journal of Applied Social Psychology*, 22, no. 11 (1992): 874–88; Ronald E. Hall, "Bias among African Americans Regarding Skin Color: Implications for Social Work Practice," *Research on Social Work Practice* 2, no. 4 (1992): 479–86, https://doi.org/10.1177/104973159200200404; Ronald E. Hall, "Skin Color Bias: A New Perspective on an Old Problem," *Journal of Psychology* 132, no. 2 (1998): 238–40.

121 Evelyn Nakano Glenn, "Consuming Lightness: Segmented Markets and Global Capital in the Skin-Whitening Trade," in *Shades of Difference: Why Skin Color Matters*, ed. Evelyn Nakano Glenn (Stanford, CA: Stanford University Press, 2009), 168; Charles Blow, "A Bias More than Skin Deep," *New York Times*, July 13, 2015, https://nytimes.com.; Monisha Rajesh, "India's Unfair Obsession with Lighter Skin," *The Guardian*, August 14, 2013, https://www.theguardian.com; G. P. Abuja, "Beauty in Nigeria: Lighter Shades of Skin," *The Economist*, September 28, 2012, https://www.economist.com; Priya Arora and Sapna Maheshwari, "Criticism

of Skin Lighteners Brings Retreat by Unilever and Johnson & Johnson," *New York Times*, June 25, 2020, https://nytimes.com.
122 Keith, "A Colorstruck World."
123 Yesha Callahan, "Viola Davis Responds to Being Called 'Less Classically Beautiful': 'You Define You,'" *The Root*, September 26, 2014, https://www.theroot.com.
124 Siobhan Brooks, *Unequal Desires: Race and Erotic Capital in the Stripping Industry* (Albany, NY: State University of New York Press, 2010), 90–91.
125 David Buss, *The Dangerous Passion* (New York: Free Press, 2000); Adam D. Galinsky, Erika V. Hall, and Amy J. C. Cuddy, "Gendered Races: Implications for Interracial Marriage, Leadership Selection, and Athletic Participation," *Psychological Science* 24, no. 4 (2013): 498–506.
126 Collins, *Black Sexual Politics*, 44; Wilson et al., "Race-Based Sexual Stereotyping."
127 For example, Kerry Washington, who plays the lead character in the television drama *Scandal*, is African American. Shonda Rhimes, the creator of *Scandal*, is African American.
128 Collins, *Black Sexual Politics*.
129 Elahe Izadi, "Shonda Rhimes Has Thoughts About That 'Angry Black Woman' Column," *Washington Post*, September 19, 2014, https://washingtonpost.com.
130 Collins, *Black Sexual Politics*.
131 Feliciano, Robnett, and Komaie, "Gendered Racial Exclusion."
132 Galinsky, Hall, and Cuddy, "Gendered Races."
133 Kerri L. Johnson, Johnathan B. Freeman, and Kristin Pauker, "Race Is Gendered: How Covarying Phenotypes and Stereotypes Bias Sex Categorization," *Journal of Personality and Social Psychology*, 102, no. 1 (2011): 116–31; Galinsky, Hall, and Cuddy, "Gendered Races," 498–506.
134 Hill, "Skin Color," 79.
135 Phillip Atiba Goff, Margaret A. Thomas, and Matthew Christian Jackson, "Ain't I a Woman: Towards an Intersectional Approach to Person Perceptions and Group-Based Harms," *Sex Roles* 59 (August 2008): 392–403; Margaret Thomas and Phillip Atiba Goff, "Pain at the Crossroads: How Intersectionality Works and Hurts," cited in Elizabeth F. Emens, "Intimate Discrimination: The State's Role in the Accidents of Sex and Love," *Harvard Law Review* 122, no. 5 (March 2009): 1307, 1321; Johnson, Freeman, and Pauker, "Race Is Gendered."
136 Feliciano, Robnett, and Komaie, "Gendered Racial Exclusion."
137 Gail Dines, "The White Man's Burden: Gonzo Pornography and the Construction of Black Masculinity," *Yale Journal of Law and Feminism* 18, no.1 (2006): 283, 291–92; Randall Kennedy, *Interracial Intimacies: Sex, Marriage, Identity, and Adoption* (New York: Vintage Books, 2004).
138 Salvador Vidal-Ortiz, Brandon Andrew Robinson, and Cristina Khan, *Race and Sexuality* (Cambridge: Polity Press, 2018); Jared Sexton, *Amalgamation Schemes: Antiblackness and the Critique of Multiracialism* (Minneapolis: University of Minnesota Press, 2008).
139 Bany, Robnett, and Feliciano, "Gendered Black Exclusion," 208.

140 Bany, Robnett, and Feliciano, "Gendered Black Exclusion," 208–9.
141 Rose Weitz and Leonard Gordon, "Images of Black Women among Anglo College Students," *Sex Roles* 28 (January 1993): 19–34, https://doi.org/10.1007/BF00289745.
142 Bany, Robnett, and Feliciano, "Gendered Black Exclusion," 208.
143 Wilson et al., "Race-Based Sexual Stereotyping."
144 Bany, Robnett, and Feliciano, "Gendered Black Exclusion," 206–8.
145 Sixty-one percent of Asian American women as compared to 48 percent of Asian American men and 48 percent of Latinas as compared to 20 percent of Latino men cited social disapproval as a concern. Bany, Robnett, and Feliciano, "Gendered Black Exclusion," 205, 207.
146 Eduardo Bonilla-Silva and Tyrone A. Forman, "'I Am Not a Racist but . . .': Mapping White College Students' Racial Ideology in the USA," *Discourse & Society*, 11, no. 1 (2000): 60–62.
147 "Interracial Marriage Now More Common."
148 Erica Morales, "Parental Messages Concerning Latino/Black Interracial Dating: An Exploratory Study among Latina/o Young Adults," *Latino Studies* 10, no. 3 (September 2012): 314–33; Jennifer Lee and Frank D. Bean, "America's Changing Color Lines: Immigration, Race/Ethnicity, and Multiracial Identification," *Annual Review of Sociology* 30 (March 2004): 221–42.
149 Morales, "Parental Messages," 316.
150 George Yancey, *Who Is White? Latinos, Asians, and the New Black/Non-Black Divide* (Boulder, CO: Lynne Rienner Publishers, 2003); Wang, "The Rise of Intermarriage"; Morales, "Parental Messages"; Eileen O'Brien, *The Racial Middle: Latinos and Asian Americans Living beyond the Racial Divide* (New York: New York University Press, 2008), 109–16, 120; Cynthia Feliciano, Rennie Lee, and Belinda Robnett, "Racial Boundaries."
151 Morales, "Parental Messages," 316.
152 R. A. Lenhardt, "Understanding the Mark: Race, Stigma, and Equality in Context," *New York University Law Review* 79, no. 3 (June 2004): 803, 809–10.
153 Morales, "Parental Messages," 316; Suzanne Oboler, *Ethnic Labels, Latino Lives: Identity and the Politics of (Re)Presentation in the United States* (Minneapolis: University of Minnesota Press, 1995); Tatcho Mindiola Jr., Yolanda Flores Niemann, and Néstor Rodriguez, *Black-Brown Relations and Stereotypes* (Austin: University of Texas Press, 2002). Numerous scholars have noted that all racial groups agree that "Whites have the highest social status followed by Asians, Latinos, and Blacks." Arnold Ko, Jim Sidanius, Daniel T Levin, and Mahzarin R Banaji, "Evidence for Hypodescent and Racial Hierarchy in the Categorization and Perception of Biracial Individuals," *Journal of Personality and Social Psychology* 100 (March 2011): 492. See also Kimberly Kanh, Arnold K. Ho, Jim Sidanius, and Felicia Pratto, "The Space between Us and Them: Perceptions of Status Differences," *Group Processes and Intergroup Relations* 12 (August 2009): 591.
154 Maria Root, *Love's Revolution: Interracial Marriage* (Philadelphia, PA: Temple University Press, 2001), 60.

155 Tucker and Mitchell-Kernan, "Social Structural and Psychological Correlates"; Morales, "Parental Messages," 317; Eria Chito Childs, "Families on the Color-Line: Patrolling Borders and Crossing Boundaries," *Race and Society* 5, no. 2 (2002): 139–61; Heather Dalmage, *Tripping on the Color Line: Black-White Multiracial Families in a Racially Divided World* (New Brunswick, NJ: Rutgers University Press, 2000), 153; Erica Chito Childs, *Navigating Interracial Borders: Black/White Couples and Their Social Worlds* (New Brunswick, NJ: Rutgers University Press, 2005).

156 Root, *Love's Revolution*, 60; Suzanne C. Miller, Michael A. Olson, and Russell H. Fazio, "Perceived Reactions to Interracial Romantic Relationships: When Race Is Used as a Cue to Status," *Group Processes Intergroup Relations* 7, no. 4 (2004): 354–69, https://doi.org/10.1177/1368430204046143.

157 Morales, "Parental Messages," 315.

158 Jones, "Most Americans Approve."

159 Kumiko Nemoto, *Racing Romance: Love, Power, and Desire among Asian American/White Couples* (New Brunswick, NJ: Rutgers University Press, 2009).

160 Lawrence Bobo and Ryan A. Smith, "From Jim Crow Racism to Laissez-Faire Racism: The Transformation of Racial Attitudes," in *Beyond Pluralism: The Conception of Group and Group Identities in America*, ed. W. Katkin, N. Landsman and A. Tyree (Champaign: University of Illinois Press, 1998); Eduardo Bonilla-Silva, *Racism without Racists*, 6th ed. (Lanham, MD: Rowman & Littlefield, 2022).

161 Rachel L. Swarns, "For Asian American Couples, a Tie That Binds," *New York Times*, March 30, 2012, https://nytimes.com; Russell K. Robinson, "Perceptual Segregation," *Columbia Law Review* 108, no. 5 (June 2008): 1093.

162 Derald Wing Sue, "Whiteness and Ethnocentric Monoculturalism: Making the 'Invisible' Visible," *American Psychologist* 59, no. 8 (November 2004):761–69, doi: 10.1037/0003-066X.59.8.761.

163 Project Implicit, accessed September 10, 2023, https://implicit.harvard.edu.

164 John T. Jost, Mahzarin R. Banaji, and Brian A. Nosek, "A Decade of System Justification Theory: Accumulated Evidence of Conscious and Unconscious Bolstering of the Status Quo," *Political Psychology* 25, no. 6 (2004): 881–919.

165 Mahzarin R. Banaji and Anthony G. Greenwald, *Blindspot: Hidden Biases of Good People* (New York: Delacorte Press, 2013); Jerry Kang, "Trojan Horses of Race," *Harvard Law Review* 118 (March 2005): 1489, 1512; Project Implicit, The Implicit Association Test.

166 Banaji and Greenwald, *Blindspot*; Brian A. Nosek, Frederick L. Smyth, Jeffrey J. Hansen, Thierry Devos, Nicole M. Lindner, Kate A. Ranganath, Colin Tucker Smith, Kristina R. Olson, Dolly Chugh, Anthony G. Greenwald, and Mahzarin R. Banaji, "Pervasiveness and Correlates of Implicit Attitudes and Stereotypes," *European Review of Social Psychology* 18, no. 1 (2008): 36–88; Joshua Correll, Geoffrey R. Urland, and Tiffany A. Ito, "Event-Related Potentials and the Decision to Shoot: The Role of Threat Perception and Cognitive Control," *Journal of Experimental Social Psychology* 42, no. 1 (2006): 120–28, https://doi.org/10.1016/j

.jesp.2005.02.006; Joshua Correll, Bernadette Park, Charles M. Judd, and Bernd Wittenbrink, "The Police Officer's Dilemma: Using Ethnicity to Disambiguate Potentially Threatening Individuals," *Journal of Personality & Social Psychology* 83, no. 6 (2002): 1314–29, https://doi.org/10.1037/0022-3514.83.6.1314; Alexander R. Greene, Dana R. Carney, Daniel J. Pallin, Long H. Ngo, Kristal L. Raymond, Lisa I. Iezzoni, and Mahzarin R. Banaji, "Implicit Bias among Physicians and Its Prediction of Thrombolysis Decisions for Black and White Patients," *Journal of General Internal Medicine* 22, no. 9 (2007): 31–1238.

167 Jerry Kang, "Trojan Horses," 1534; Feliciano, Lee, and Robnett, "Racial Boundaries."

CHAPTER 2. HOW LAW REGULATED INTERRACIAL INTIMACY AND ITS EFFECTS TODAY

1 Loving v. Virginia, 388 U.S. 1 (1967).
2 South Carolina and Alabama did not repeal their anti-miscegenation laws until 1998 and 2000, respectively. Hrishi Karthikeyan and Gabriel J. Chin, "Preserving Racial Identity: Population Patterns and the Application of Anti-Miscegenation Statutes to Asian Americans, 1910–1950," *Asian Law Journal* 9 (January 2002): 35. Forty percent of Alabama voters opposed repealing the anti-miscegenation law. Elizabeth Becker, Abby Goodnough, Laura Mansnerus, Todd S. Purdum, Diana Jean Schemo, Jacques Steinberg, and Matthew L. Wald, "The 2000 Elections: State by State," *New York Times*, November 9, 2000, https://nytimes.com.
3 Peggy Pascoe, *What Comes Naturally: Miscegenation Law and the Making of Race in America* (New York: Oxford University Press, 2010), 9.
4 Ian Haney Lopez, *White by Law: The Legal Construction of Race*, 10th ed. (New York: New York University Press, 2006), 3.
5 Buchanan v. Warley, 245 U.S. 60 (1917); Harmon v. Tyler, 273 U.S. 668 (1927); Rice v. Gong, 104 So. 105 (1925).
6 "Irish Nell Butler," Maryland State Archives: Biographical Series, *MSA SC 5496-000534*, accessed September 1, 2023, https://msa.maryland.gov.
7 "Irish Nell Butler."
8 One of Nell and Charles' enslaved children escaped and later purchased his freedom. In the late 1700s, enslaved descendants of Nell Butler successfully sued to obtain their freedom on the ground that their ancestor was a white woman. "Irish Nell Butler."
9 Rachel F. Moran, *Interracial Intimacy: The Regulation of Race and Romance*, (Chicago: University of Chicago Press, 2003), 20.
10 A. Leon Higginbotham Jr. and Barbara K. Kopytoff, "Racial Purity and Interracial Sex in the Law of Colonial and Antebellum Virginia," *Georgetown Law Journal* 77, no. 6 (August 1989): 1967–2030.
11 Moran, *Interracial Intimacy*, 4
12 Pascoe, *What Comes Naturally*, 20.
13 Higginbotham and Kopytoff, "Racial Purity and Interracial Sex," 1995 (citing Act XVI, 3 Laws of Va. 86, 86–87 (Hening 1823) (enacted 1691)).

14 Higginbotham and Kopytoff, "Racial Purity and Interracial Sex," 2006 (citing Act XVI, 3 Laws of Va. 86, 87 (Hening 1823) (enacted 1671)).
15 Pascoe, *What Comes Naturally*, 20; Moran, *Interracial Intimacy*, 19–20.
16 Pascoe, *What Comes Naturally*, 21.
17 Republic of Texas Laws (1837) (providing that marriages between "any person of European blood or their descendants" and "Africans, or the descendants of Africans . . . shall be null and void") (cited in Pascoe, *What Comes Naturally*, 17); Oregon Laws (1866) (prohibiting marriages between whites and various groups and providing that such marriages were null and void) (cited in Pascoe, *What Comes Naturally*, 77).
18 Succession of Minvielle, 15 La. Ann. 342, 342–43 (1860) (holding that "The law is of that rigorous nature that it will not permit a marriage to exist between persons of the two different races for a moment. No suit is needed to declare the nullity of such an union. Either party may disregard it, and neither can pretend to derive from it any of the consequences of a lawful marriage").
19 Pace v. Alabama, 106 U.S. 583 (1883).
20 Deniz Gevrek, "Interracial Marriage, Migration and *Loving*," *National Economic Association* 41, no. 1 (January 2014), table 1. However, interracial couples in all states faced significant social opposition even in the states without antimiscegenation laws. Angela Onwuachi-Willig, *According to Our Hearts: Rhinelander v. Rhinelander and the Law of the Multiracial Family* (New Haven, CT: Yale University Press, June 2013).
21 Pascoe, *What Comes Naturally*, 92, 99, 118–119. See also Kirby v. Kirby, 206 P. 405, 406 (Ariz. 1922); Perez v. Sharp, 32 Cal. 2d 711 (Cal. 1948); *In re* Paquet's Estate, 200 P. 911 (Or. 1921).
22 James Davis, *Who Is Black: One Nation's Definition* (Philadelphia: Penn State University Press, 2001).
23 Act of Sept. 6, 1927, No. 626, s 5, 1927 Ala. Acts 716, 717 (defining as Black any person "descended on the part of the father or mother from negro ancestors, without reference to or limit of time or number of generations removed") (cited in Peter Wallenstein, "Race, Marriage, and the Law of Freedom: Alabama and Virginia, 1860s–1960s," *Chicago Kent Law Review* 70, no. 2 (December 1994): 371, 437]; Ark. Stat. Ann. Chap. 109, section 4, 9 (1858) (defining as Black "any person who has in his or her veins any Negro blood whatever").
24 Lopez, *White by Law*, 83; Christine Hickman, "The Devil and the One Drop Rule: Racial Categories, African Americans, and the U.S. Census," *Michigan Law Review* 95 (March 1997): 1161, 1190; Pascoe, *What Comes Naturally*, 116.
25 Miss. Code Ann. Chap. 90, § 2859 (1892).
26 Pascoe, *What Comes Naturally*, 144.
27 Lopez, *White by Law*, 83; Cheryl Harris, "Whiteness as Property," *Harvard Law Review* 106, no. 8 (June 1993): 1738.
28 Pascoe, *What Comes Naturally*, 141.
29 Loving, 388 U.S. at 5 n.4 (citing Va. Code Ann. 20-54 (1960 Repl.Vol.)).

30 Loving, 388 U.S. at 5 n.4 (citing Va. Code Ann. 20-54 (1960 Repl.Vol.)); Kevin Maillard, "The Pocahontas Exception: The Exemption of American Indian Ancestry from Racial Purity Law," *Michigan Journal of Race and Law* 12 (Spring 2007): 351.
31 Lopez, *White by Law*, 12.
32 George Martinez, "The Legal Construction of Race: Mexican Americans and Whiteness," *Harvard Latino Law Review* 322 (Fall 1997): 325.
33 Loving v. Virginia, 388 U.S. 1, 5, n.4 (1967).
34 Pascoe, *What Comes Naturally*, 94, 95; Barbara C. Cruz, and Michael J. Berson, "The American Melting Pot? Miscegenation Laws in the United States," *OAH Magazine of History* 15, no. 4 (Summer 2001): 80–84, https://doi.org/10.1093/magh/15.4.80 (discussing Thomas Jefferson and Patrick Henry's support of marriages between Whites and American Indians).
35 Maillard, "The Pocahontas Exception," 360–62.
36 Richard Chused, "Married Women's Property Law: 1800–1850," *Georgetown Law Journal* 71 (Summer 1992): 1361.
37 Pascoe, *What Comes Naturally*, 103–4.
38 Pascoe, *What Comes Naturally*, 103–4. The U.S. Supreme Court recognized these marriages as valid in Meister v. Moore, 96 U.S. 76 (1877) (recognizing the relationship between a White man and an American Indian woman as a common law marriage).
39 Gevrek, "Interracial Marriage, Migration and *Loving*," table 1; Pascoe, *What Comes Naturally*, 99.
40 Pascoe, *What Comes Naturally*, 77 (emphasis added).
41 Pascoe, *What Comes Naturally*, 99.
42 Deenesh Sohoni, "Unsuitable Suitors: Anti-Miscegenation Laws, Naturalization Laws, and the Construction of Asian Identities," *Law & Society Review* 41 (September 2007): 597. Nevada passed the first statute prohibiting marriages between Whites and Chinese persons in 1861. Nev. Terr. Laws Ch. 32, § 1, 3 (1861). Pascoe, *What Comes Naturally*, 81–84. Fifteen states forbade marriage between Asians and Whites. Leti Volpp, "American Mestizo: Filipinos and Antimiscegenation Laws in California," *University of California, Davis Law Review* 33, no. 4 (2000): 798n12 (listing "Arizona, California, Georgia, Idaho, Maryland, Mississippi, Missouri, Montana, Nebraska, Nevada, Oregon, South Dakota, Utah, Virginia, and Wyoming").
43 Cal. Civ. Code § 69 (1880).
44 Pascoe, *What Comes Naturally*, 89.
45 Pascoe, *What Comes Naturally*, 118.
46 Sohoni, "Unsuitable Suitors," 598 (noting that the majority of states that "passed anti-miscegenation laws against ethnic groups from Asia would use the racial identifier *Mongolian*"); Susan Koshy, *Sexual Naturalization: Asian American and Miscegenation* (Stanford, CA: Stanford University Press, 2005), 7 (noting that anti-miscegenation laws used the term "Mongolians" to include Chinese, Japanese, and Koreans).

47 Pascoe, *What Comes Naturally*, 154–59; Roldan v. Los Angeles County, 126 Cal. App. 267 (1933); Cal. Compiled Laws of California Chapter 104 Section 60 (Cal. Stat. 1933). By the time California amended its law to prohibit marriages between Whites and "Malays," several other states had done the same. Nev. Rev. Laws Sec. 6514 (1912) ("It shall be unlawful for any person of the Caucasian or white race to intermarry with any person of the Ethiopian or black race, Malay or brown race, Mongolian or yellow race, or the American Indian or red race, within the State of Nevada."); S.D. Laws Ch. 266 (1913) (prohibiting Whites from marrying or cohabitating with "persons belonging to the African, Corean [sic], Malayan, or Mongolian race"); Wyo. Laws. Ch. 57, Sec. 1 & 2 (1913) (prohibiting "all marriages of white persons with Negroes, Mulattoes, Mongolians or Malays").
48 Theda Perdue, *"Mixed Blood" Indians: Racial Construction in the Early South* (Athens and London: University of Georgia Press, 2005), 52–53. For a discussion of "custom marriages" between white traders and American Indian women and their importance to trade, see Catherine J. Denial, *Making Marriage: Husbands, Wives and the American State in Dakota and Ojibwe Country* (Minneapolis: Minnesota Historical Society Press, 2013), 35.
49 Due to restrictive immigrations laws, until 1906 women comprised 5 percent or less of the Chinese population in the United States and only 20 percent of the Korean population in the United States By 1914, less than 1 percent (.24 percent) of the Asian Indian population in the United States were women. In 1930 Filipino women comprised less than 4 percent of the adult Filipino population in the United States. Koshy, *Sexual Naturalization*, 8.
50 Rachel F. Moran, "Love with a Proper Stranger: What Anti-Miscegenation Laws Can Tell Us about the Meaning of Race, Sex, and Marriage," *Hofstra Law Review* 32 (January 2004), 1663, 1666–67; Volpp, "American Mestizo," 819; Pascoe, *What Comes Naturally*, 90 (discussing scandals surrounding relationships between Japanese men and White woman). Koshy, *Sexual Naturalization*, 5–9.
51 Pascoe, *What Comes Naturally*, 78; Karthikeyan, "Preserving Racial Identity," 26–27; Ronald Takaki, *Strangers from a Different Shore: A History of Asian Americans* (Boston, MA: Little, Brown and Company, 1989), 330.
52 Takaki, *Strangers from a Different Shore*, 417.
53 Inland Steel Co. v. Barcena, 39 N.E.2d 800 (Ind. 1942) (stating that about 20 percent of people in Mexico are White, 40 percent are Indian and the rest are of mixed-blood). But see Laura Gómez, "Off-White in an Age of White Supremacy: Mexican Elites and the Rights of Indians and Blacks in Nineteenth-Century New Mexico," *UCLA Chicano-Latino Law Review* 25, no. 9 (2005): 59n21 ("by 1810, eighty percent of Mexico's population was either mestizo or Indian," citing Martha Menchaca, *Recovering History, Constructing Race: The Indian, Black, and White Roots of Mexican Americans* (Austin, TX: University of Texas Press, 2001), 158.
54 Martinez, "The Legal Construction of Race," 321.
55 Treaty of Peace, Friendship, Limits and Settlement, February 2, 1848, U.S.-Mex., 9 Stat. 922 (commonly known as the Treaty of Guadalupe-Hidalgo).

56 The Naturalization Act of February 18, 1875, limited citizenship to "aliens being free white persons, and to aliens of African nativity, and to persons of African descent." Naturalization Act, Ch. 80, 18 Stat. 318 (1875).
57 In re Rodriguez, 81 F. 337 (W.D. Tex. 1897).
58 Martinez, "The Legal Construction of Race," 327.
59 Kirby v. Kirby, 206 P. 405, 406 (Ariz. 1922).
60 Kirby, 206 P. at 406.
61 Perez v. Sharp, 32 Cal.2d. 711, 721 (1948).
62 Robert v. Dodge, *Andrea and Sylvester: Challenging Marriage Taboos and Paving the Road to Same-Sex Marriage* (New York: Algora, 2015), 53.
63 Dara Orenstein, "Void for Vagueness: Mexicans and the Collapse of Miscegenation Law in California," *Pacific Historical Review* 74 (August 2005): 379; Robin Lenhardt, "Forgotten Lessons on Race, Law, and Marriage: The Story of Perez v. Sharp," in *Race Law Stories*, ed. Rachel F. Moran and Devon W. Carbado (New York: Thomson Reuters/Foundation Press, 2008), 343–79; R. A. Lenhardt, "Beyond Analogy: Perez v. Sharp," *California Law Review* 96 (August 2008): 839.
64 Westminster v. Mendez, 161 F.2d 774 (9th Cir. 1947). School districts in other states also segregated Mexican American children; Ruben Donato, "Porque tenían sangre de 'NEGROS': The Exclusion of Mexican Children from a Louisiana School, 1915–1916," *Association of Mexican American Educators Journal* 2, no. 1 (2017): 137, https://doi.10.24974/amae.11.335. Ruben Donato, "*Francisco Maestas et al. v. George H. Shone et al.*: Mexican American Resistance to School Segregation in the Hispano Homeland, 1912–1914," *Journal of Latinos & Education* 16, no. 1 (2017): 13, https://doi.10.1080.15348431/2016/1179190.
65 Westminster, 161 F.2d at 776, 781. Although California law did not authorize educational segregation of children of Mexican and Latino descent, such segregation was "practiced under regulations, customs and usages adopted more or less as a common plan and enforced by [trustees and superintendents of several school districts and members of the board of education]." Westminster, 161 F.2d at 779. California statutes did authorize segregation of American Indian children and "children of Chinese, Japanese or Mongolian parentage." Westminster, 161 F.2d at 780.
66 Karla M. McKanders, "Sustaining Tiered Personhood: Jim Crow and Anti-Immigrant Laws," *Harvard Journal on Racial & Ethnic Justice* 26 (July 2010): 199 (citing James Loewen, *Sundown Towns: A Hidden Dimension of American Racism* [New York: The New Press, 2005], 4).
67 Laura Gómez, *Inventing Latinos: A New Story of American Racism* (New York: The New Press, 2020), 105. Jeanne Powers, "Forgotten History: Mexican American School Segregation in Arizona from 1900–1951," *Equity & Excellence in Education* 41, no. 4 (2008): 471.
68 Hernandez v. Texas, 347 U.S. 475, 479–80 (1954) (concluding that residents of the Jackson County, Texas, "community distinguished between 'white' and 'Mexican'" based on evidence that until recently, "children of Mexican descent were required

to attend a segregated school for the first four grades," that "[a]t least one restaurant in town prominently displayed a sign announcing 'No Mexicans Served,'" and that the courthouse had a separate bathroom marked "Colored Men" and "Hombres Aqui" [Men Here]); Lopez v. Seccombe, 71 F. Supp. 769, 770 (S.D. Cal. 1944); George Martinez, "African Americans, Latinos and the Construction of Race: Toward an Epistemic Coalition," *Chicano-Latino Law Review* 19 (Fall 1998): 219; Richard Valencia, *Chicano Students and the Courts: The Mexican American Legal Struggle for Education Equality* (New York: New York University Press, 2008), 7.

69 Fernanda Echavarri and Marlon Bishop, "'No Mexicans Allowed': School Segregation in the Southwest," *LatinoUSA*, March 17, 2017, https://latinousa.org; Suzanne Gamboa, "History of Racism against Mexican Americans Clouds Texas Immigration Law," *NBC News*, June 3, 2017, https://nbcnews.com.

70 Dodge, *Andrea and Sylvester*, 53.

71 Social scientists at the time believed that mestizos (persons with Spanish ancestry) were inferior to both Whites and American Indians. One commentator noted that "American visitors to the Mexican frontier were nearly unanimous in commenting on the dark skin of Mexican mestizos who, it was generally agreed, had inherited the worst qualities of Spaniards and Indians to produce a 'race' still more despicable than that of either parent." Juan F. Perea, "Los Olvidados: On the Making of Invisible People," *New York University Law Review* 70 (October 1995): 976 (quoting David J. Weber, Editor's Introduction, "Yankee Infiltration and the Hardening of Stereotypes," in *Foreigners in Their Native Land: Historical Roots of the Mexican Americans*, ed. David J. Weber (Albuquerque: University of New Mexico Press, 1973), 59–60).

72 Moran, "Love with a Proper Stranger," 1670; Moran, *Interracial Intimacy*, 57; Koshy, *Sexual Naturalization*, 6.

73 *Perez*, 32 Cal.2d at 729–32.

74 *Perez*, 32 Cal.2d at 722.

75 *Perez*, 32 Cal.2d at 712.

76 *Perez*, 32 Cal.2d at 721 (citing United States v. Bhagat Singh Thind, 261 U.S. 204, 215 (1923) (holding that Hindus were not White).

77 *Perez*, 32 Cal.2d at 721.

78 *Perez*, 32 Cal.2d at 721.

79 *Perez*, 32 Cal.2d at 729.

80 *Perez*, 32 Cal.2d at 730–31.

81 *Perez*, 32 Cal.2d at 731.

82 *Perez*, 32 Cal.2d at 728.

83 *Perez*, 32 Cal.2d at 722.

84 Chinese Exclusion Act, ch. 126, 22 Stat. 58 (1882) (repealed 1943).

85 Paul Finkelman, "Coping with a New 'Yellow Peril': Japanese Immigration, the Gentlemen's Agreement, and the Coming of World War II," *West Virginia Law Review* 117 (April 2015): 1409; Bill Ong Hing, "Institutional Racism, ICE Raids,

and Immigration Reform," *University of San Francisco Law Review* 44 (December 2009): 335–36 (discussing the Gentlemen's Agreement of 1908).
86 Immigration Act of 1917, Ch. 29, § 3, 39 Stat. 874.
87 Immigration Act of 1924, Ch. 190, § 9, 43 Stat. 153.
88 Laura E. Gómez, *Inventing Latinos: A New Story of American Racism* (New York: The New Press, 2020), 28.
89 Undesirable Aliens Act, 45 Stat. 1551 (1929).
90 United States v. Machic-Xiap, No. 3:19-CR-407-SI, 2021 WL 3362738, at *11 (D. Or. August 3, 2021).
91 *Machic-Xiap*, 2021 WL 3362738, at *11 (quoting 70 Cong. Rec. 2462 (1928) (statement of Hon. Robert Alexis Green read into the record)).
92 *Machic-Xiap*, 2021 WL 3362738, at *7.
93 *Machic-Xiap*, 2021 WL 3362738, at *7.
94 Ozawa v. United States, 260 U.S. 178, 198 (1922); *Thind*, 261 U.S. 204 (1923).
95 *Ozawa*, 260 U.S. at 178.
96 *Ozawa*, 260 U.S. at 178.
97 *Ozawa*, 260 U.S. at 197.
98 *Ozawa*, 260 U.S. at 198.
99 *Thind*, 261 U.S. at 215.
100 In re Balsara, 171 F. 294, 295 (C.C.S.D.N.Y. 1909); see also United States v. Balsara, 180 F. 694, 696 (2d Cir. 1910). In re Akhay Kumar Mozumdar, 207 F. 115, 118 (E.D. Wash. 1913).
101 *Thind*, 261 U.S. at 215.
102 *Ozawa*, 260 U.S. at 198.
103 *Ozawa*, 260 U.S. at 196–97.
104 *Ozawa*, 260 U.S. at 198 (emphasis added).
105 *Thind*, 261 U.S. at 213.
106 *Thind*, 261 U.S. at 210.
107 *Thind*, 261 U.S. at 215.
108 *Thind*, 261 U.S. at 215
109 *Thind*, 261 U.S. at 210.
110 *Thind*, 261 U.S. at 215.
111 Karthikeyan and Chin, "Preserving Racial Identity," 14–16.
112 Hart-Celler Act, Pub. L. No. 89-236, 79 Stat. 911 (1965).
113 Robert Chang, "The Invention of Asian Americans," *University of California Irvine Law Review* 3, no. 4 (December 2013): 947; Frank Wu, "Where Are You Really From? Asian Americans and the Perpetual Foreigner Syndrome," *Civil Rights Journal* 6 (Winter 2002): 14; Vinay Harpalani, "Racial Triangulation, Interest-Convergence, and the Double-Consciousness of Asian Americans," *Georgia State University Law Review* 6 (November 2021): 1.
114 Erika Lee, *The Making of Asian America: A History* (New York: Simon & Schuster, 2016), 8–9, 402.

115 From 1924 to 1933, after controlling for different population numbers, only 16 out of 1,000 recorded marriages in Los Angeles county for Chinese or Japanese persons had a White spouse and fewer than 1 out of 1,000 recorded marriages for Black persons had a White spouse. In contrast 393 out of 1,000 recorded marriages for Mexicans had a White spouse and 333 out of 1,000 recorded marriages for American Indians had a White spouse. Pascoe, *What Comes Naturally*, 152.
116 *Perez*, 32 Cal.2d at 722.
117 Rose Villazor, "The Other *Loving*: Uncovering the Federal Government's Racial Regulation of Marriage," *New York University Law Review* 86 (November 2011): 1361.
118 Immigration Act of 1924, Ch. 190, § 9, 43 Stat. 153.
119 Naturalization Act, Ch. 80, 18 Stat. 318 (1875).
120 *Ozawa*, 260 U.S. at 198; *Thind*, 261 U.S. at 215.
121 The only exception were Filipinos/as the Philippines was a U.S. territory and Filipinos could therefore enter the United States without restrictions until 1934, when the Tydings-McDuffie Act providing for Philippine Independence was signed. Philippine Independence Act (Tydings-McDuffie Act), Pub. L. No. 73–127, 48 Stat. 456 (March 24, 1934).
122 Under the 1907 Expatriation Act, a U.S. citizen woman lost her citizenship if she married a man who was not a U.S. citizen. Act of Mar. 2, 1907, ch. 2534, §§ 3–4, Pub. L. No. 59–193, 34 Stat. 1228, 1228–29 (1907); Mackenzie v. Hare, 239 U.S. 299, 312 (1915) (upholding the 1907 Expatriation Act). Kristin Collins, "Illegitimate Borders: Jus Sanguinis Citizenship and the Legal Construction of Family, Race, and Nation," *Yale Law Journal* 123 (May 2014): 2134. Although the Cable Act of 1922 allowed her to regain U.S. citizenship if and when her husband became a U.S. citizen, a woman who married a man who was *ineligible* to become naturalized citizens permanently lost her own citizenship. Married Women's Independent Nationality Act (Cable Act), ch. 411, § 3, Pub. L. No. 346, 42 Stat. 1021, 1022 (1922). Leti Volpp, "Divesting Citizenship: On Asian American History and the Loss of Citizenship through Marriage," *UCLA Law Review* 53 (December 2005): 443–47. These laws were repealed in 1931. See Act of March 3, 1931, ch. 442, Pub. L. No. 71–829, 46 Stat. 1511; 8 U.S.C. 397 (1931).
123 American Indian men born on tribal land were also ineligible for U.S. citizenship until 1924. Indian Citizenship Act of 1924, Pub. L. No. 68–175, 43 Stat. 253 (1924). Indigenous men from other countries were also ineligible for naturalization. See In re Camille, 6 F. 256, 256 (C.C.D. Or. 1880) (holding that a Canadian national who is half White and half Indian is not White and thus is not eligible to become a naturalized U.S. citizen).
124 Villazor, "The Other *Loving*," 1362n1.
125 Villazor, "The Other *Loving*," 1381.
126 Villazor, "The Other *Loving*," 1365.

127 Villazor, "The Other *Loving*," 1382n121. Although the War Brides Act also applied to husbands and children of U.S. citizen military personnel, the majority of its beneficiaries were women.
128 Bonham v. Bouiss, 161 F.2d 678, 679 (9th Cir. 1947) (denying admission to a war bride because she was "not eligible to [sic] citizenship by reason of her Japanese blood").
129 Villazor, "The Other *Loving*," 1361, 1411.
130 Villazor, "The Other *Loving*," 1367n34.
131 Villazor, "The Other *Loving*," 1400n270; Rachel Moran, "Loving and the Legacy of Unintended Consequences," *Wisconsin Law Review* 239 (January 2007): 250–52; Jesse H. Choper, "Consequences of Supreme Court Decisions Upholding Individual Rights," *Michigan Law Review* 83 (October 1984): 29.
132 Villazor, "The Other *Loving*," 1415. Pascoe, *What Comes Naturally*, 198–99.
133 In 1947, Congress amended the War Brides Act to provide that the "alien spouse of an American citizen . . . shall not be considered as inadmissible because of race, if otherwise admissible." Act of July 22, 1947, 61 Stat. 401 (1947). Immigration and Nationality Act of 1952 (McCarran-Walter Act), ch. 477, 66 Stat. 163 (1952).
134 Arlisha Norwood, "Rosa Parks," National Women's History Museum, 2017, https://womenshistory.org.
135 Brown v. Bd. of Educ., 347 U.S. 483, 495 (1954).
136 Reginald Oh, "Interracial Marriage in the Shadows of Jim Crow: Racial Segregation as a System of Racial and Gender Subordination," *University of California, Davis Law Review* 39 (March 2006): 1324 (arguing that "a central purpose of racial segregation was to prevent the development of intimate social relationships between blacks and whites"); Sohoni, "Unsuitable Suitors," 589 (arguing that "many of the motivations for other forms of racial discrimination have their roots in the fear that social contact between groups eventually leads to racial mixing"); Gunnar Myrdal, *An American Dilemma: The Negro Problem and Modern Democracy* (New York: Harper & Row, 1962), 606 (stating that "no excuse for other forms of social segregation is so potent as the one that sociable relations on an equal basis between members of the two races may possibly lead to intermarriage").
137 Theodore Bilbo, *Take Your Choice: Separation or Mongrelization* (Poplarville, MS: Dream House Publishers, 1947), 223.
138 Buchanan v. Warley, 245 U.S. 60, 71 (1917).
139 *Buchanan*, 245 U.S. at 81.
140 *Buchanan*, 245 U.S. at 81.
141 City of Richmond v. Deans, 37 F.2d 712, 713 (4th Cir. 1930); S. S. Field, "The Constitutionality of Segregation Ordinances," *Virginia Law Review* 5, no. 2 (1917): 89. (asserting that segregation ordinances sought to "prevent cross-breeding between the races"); Richard Rothstein, *The Color of Law: A Forgotten History of How Our Government Segregated America* (New York: W. W. Norton, 2018).
142 An Act to Preserve Racial Integrity, ch. 371, § 5099a, 1924 Va. Acts 534 (repealed 1975).

143 R. A. Lenhardt, "*According to Our Hearts* and Location: Toward a Structuralist Approach to the Study of Interracial Families," *Gender Race & Justice* 16 (Summer 2013): 764.
144 Plessy v. Ferguson, 163 U.S. 537 (1896).
145 Plessy v. Ferguson, 163 U.S. at 545.
146 Plessy, 163 U.S. at 545 (1896) (citing State v. Gibson, 36 Ind. 389 [1871]). Daniel Lyons, "The Negro in America," *Studies: An Irish Quarterly Review* 40, no. 157 (1951): 70 (arguing that segregation laws, such as those segregating buses and restaurants, were created to safeguard laws against interracial marriage); Bilbo, *Take Your Choice*, 222–29 (arguing that racial segregation and physical separation are necessary to prevent racial mixing and preserve a "white America for all time to come").
147 Oh, "Interracial Marriage in the Shadows of Jim Crow," 1340 (citing Heart of Atlanta Motel, Inc. v. U.S., 379 U.S. 241 (1964) (racially segregated hotels); Plessy v. Ferguson, 163 U.S. 537 (1896) (racially segregated transportation); Turner v. City of Memphis, 369 U.S. 350 (1962) (racially segregated public restaurants); Dawson v. Baltimore, 220 F.2d 386 (4th Cir. 1955) (racially segregated public beaches); Palmer v. Thompson, 403 U.S. 217 (1971) (racially segregated public swimming pools).
148 Fritz Harsdorff, "Desegregation of Public Schools Is Carried Out without Violence," *Times-Picayune*, November 15, 1960, https://teepee12.files.wordpress.com/2018/06/ruby-bridges-times-picayune.jpg. "Angry Women Set upon White Mother of Pupil," *Times-Picayune*, November 15, 1960, https://bloximages.newyork1.vip.townnews.com/nola.com/content/tncms/assets/v3/editorial/6/c9/6c94f00e-b941-55f9-ac1e-7c41e8661070/5d13d8a927250.image.jpg.
149 Oh, "Interracial Marriage in the Shadows of Jim Crow," 1338n108 (citing Josephine Ross, "The Sexualization of Difference: A Comparison of Mixed-Race and Same-Gender Marriage," *Harvard Civil Rights-Civil Liberties Law Review* 37 [Summer 2002]: 268; Charles Herbert Stember, *Sexual Racism: The Emotional Barrier to an Integrated Society* [New York: Elsevier, 1976]).
150 People ex rel. King v. Gallagher, 93 N.Y. 438, 442 (1883) (holding that the school board had "full legislative authority, in the exercise of its discretionary powers, to maintain separate schools for the education of white and colored children"); Westminster Sch. Dist. of Orange Cty. v. Mendez, 161 F.2d 774, 780 (9th Cir. 1947) (citing California law that permitted segregation of American Indian children and "children of Chinese, Japanese or Mongolian parentage"). Act amendatory of, and supplementary to, An Act to establish, support, and regulate, common schools, and to repeal former Acts concerning the same (California School of Law of 1860), CA State Assembly, ch. 329, § 8 (April 28, 1860) (providing that "Negroes, Mongolians and Indians shall not be admitted into the public schools"); Ho by Ho v. S.F. Unified Sch. Dist., 147 F.3d 854, 863 (9th Cir. 1998) (describing state mandated segregation of Chinese children in California public schools until 1947); Joyce Kuo, "Excluded, Segregated and Forgotten: A Historical View of the

Discrimination of Chinese Americans in Public Schools," *Asian Law Journal* 5, (January 1998): 206; David Brudnoy, "Race and the San Francisco School Board Incident: Contemporary Evaluations," *California Historical Quarterly* 50, no. 3 (1971): 97. The San Francisco Board of Education did not officially rescind the 1906 resolution segregating children of Asian ancestry and requiring them to attend an "Oriental school" until 2017. See San Francisco Unified School District, "SF Board of Education Rescinds 1906 Resolution That Excluded Asians from 'Normal Schools,'" January 25, 2017, https://sfusd.edu. Although California law did not authorize educational segregation of children of Mexican and Latino descent, such segregation was "practiced under regulations, customs and usages adopted more or less as a common plan and enforced by [trustees and superintendents of several school districts and members of the board of education]." Westminster Sch. Dist. of Orange Cty. v. Mendez, 161 F.2d 774, 779 (9th Cir. 1947).

151 Gong v. Rice, 275 U.S. 78, 87 (1927).
152 Oh, "Interracial Marriage in the Shadows of Jim Crow," 1333. See also Lyons, "The Negro in America," 70 (arguing that segregation laws, such as those that segregated schools, were created to safeguard laws against interracial marriage).
153 Rice v. Gong, 104 So. 105 (Miss. 1925), aff'd sub nom. Gong Lum v. Rice, 275 U.S. 78 (1927).
154 Rice, 104 So. at 108.
155 Rice, 104 So. at 110.
156 Oh, "Interracial Marriage in the Shadows of Jim Crow," 1336.
157 Oh, "Interracial Marriage in the Shadows of Jim Crow," 1336.
158 Gong Lum, 275 U.S. at 79–80.
159 Laura Meckler and Hannah Natanson, "New Critical Race Theory Laws Have Teachers Scared, Confused and Self-Censoring," *Washington Post*, February 14, 2022, https://washingtonpost.com; Eesha Pendharkar, "Efforts to Ban Critical Race Theory Could Restrict Teaching for a Third of America's Kids," *Education-Week*, January 27, 2022, https://edweek.org; Madeleine Carlisle, "LGBTQ Teachers Struggle to Navigate Florida's So-Called 'Don't Say Gay' Law," *Time*, August 25, 2022, https://time.com; Katie Reilly, "For Black Parents Resisting White-Washed History, Homeschooling Is an Increasingly Popular Option," *Time*, February 28, 2022, https://time.com; Emma Colton, "CRT and COVID Policies in Virginia Spark Huge Jump in Homeschooling," *Fox News*, January 12, 2022, https://foxnews.com.
160 *Brown*, 347 U.S. at 493.
161 Oh, "Interracial Marriage in the Shadows of Jim Crow," 1328.
162 Loving v. Virginia, 388 U.S. 1, 7 (1967) (concluding that there was no explanation for a law that sought "to preserve the racial integrity of its citizens" and to prevent "the corruption of blood" and "a mongrel breed of citizens," other than as "an endorsement of the doctrine of White Supremacy"). The law is replete with examples of its promotion of White supremacy. See People v. Hall, 4 Cal. 399, 404 (1854) (declaring that the Chinese were a "race of people whom nature has

marked as inferior"); Scott v. State, 39 Ga. 321, 323 (1869) (proclaiming that "amalgamation of the races . . . never elevate[s] the inferior race to the position of the superior, but they bring down the superior to that of the inferior"); Rice v. Gong, 104 So. 105, 108 (Miss. 1925) (noting that preservation of the "integrity and purity of the white race" was "the dominant purpose" of its state constitution), aff'd sub nom. Gong Lum v. Rice, 275 U.S. 78 (1927); Perez v. Sharp, 32 Cal.2d. 711 (Cal. 1948) (lamenting that "[m]any courts in this country have assumed that human beings can be judged by race and that other races are inferior to the Caucasian"); Clark v. Crosland, 17 Ark. 43, 45 (1856) (stating that American Indians are "an inferior race, many of them ignorant"); U.S.A. v. Lucero, 1 N.M. 422 (1869) (noting that "[w]hen the term Indian is used in our acts of congress, it means that savage and roaming race of red men given to war and the chase for a living, and wholly ignorant of the pursuits of civilized man").

163 Pascoe, *What Comes Naturally*, 103; Inland Steel v. Barcena, 110 Ind. App. 551 (1942) (concluding that a Mexican husband was not White).
164 *Machic-Xiap*, 2021 WL 3362738, at * 5 and 11.
165 Pascoe, *What Comes Naturally*, 122–23.
166 Pascoe, *What Comes Naturally*, 99.
167 Higginbotham and Kopytoff, "Racial Purity and Interracial Sex," 1977.
168 Pascoe, *What Comes Naturally*, 77 (citing An Act to Regulate Marriages, sec. 3, 1862 Or. Gen. Laws 85; H. B. no. 1, "House Bills no. 1–111," Box 13, 1866 Legislature, 4th Session, Record Group 61–117, Secretary of State, Oregon State Archives, Salem) (emphasis added).
169 Pascoe, *What Comes Naturally*, 99.
170 In re Camille, 6 F. 256 (D. Or. 1880).
171 All forty-one states with anti-miscegenation laws prohibited Whites from marrying African Americans, fifteen states prohibited Whites from marrying persons of Asian ancestry, and seven states prohibited Whites from marrying American Indians. Gevrek, "Interracial Marriage, Migration and *Loving*," table 1; Pascoe, *What Comes Naturally*, 92, 99, 118.
172 Moran, "Love with a Proper Stranger," 1679.
173 Stevens v. United States, 146 F.2d 120, 123 (10th Cir. 1944).
174 Pascoe, *What Comes Naturally*, 100–104.
175 Immigration and Nationality Act of 1952 (McCarran-Walter Act), ch. 477, 66 Stat. 163 (1952).
176 Hart-Celler Act, Pub. L. No. 89–236, 79 Stat. 911 (1965).
177 Lee, *The Making of Asian America*, 285. Ninety-three percent of immigrants from India admitted to the United States in 1975 were either professional/technical workers or the spouses of such workers, and 81 percent of recent Indian immigrants have a college degree. Lee, *The Making of Asian America*, 296. Jennifer Lee, "Asian Americans, Affirmative Action & the Rise in Anti-Asian Hate," *Daedalus* 150, no. 2 (Spring 2021), https://amacad.org (noting that as a result of U.S. immigration policy, "contemporary Asian immigrants in the United States are,

on average, more likely to have graduated from college than their nonmigrant counterparts in their countries of origin, and also more likely to hold a college degree than the U.S. mean"). Fifty-five percent of Chinese immigrants in the United States have graduated from college compared with only 3.6 percent of adults in China. Indian immigrants in the United States are ten times more likely to have a bachelor's degree than their nonmigrant counterparts in India, and Vietnamese, Korean, and Filipino immigrants in the United States are three to four times more likely to have a college degree than their respective nonmigrant counterparts.

178 Lee, *The Making of Asian America*, 285. Although Congress later passed the Immigration Act of 1990, which made it more difficult for immigrants to obtain permanent resident status and granted them temporary work visas instead, the majority of skilled guest workers today come from Asia. Asian immigrants receive about 75 percent of H-1B visas. Since the 1980s, one-third of engineers and medical professionals in the United States come from India, the Philippines, China, and Taiwan. Lee, *The Making of Asian America*, 286.

179 Harpalani, "Racial Triangulation," 1374–75 (noting that post-1965 Asian American immigrants and their "children had the additional advantage of growing up in educated home environments and the social, cultural, and economic capital that comes with education").

180 Harpalani, "Racial Triangulation," 1375.

181 Koshy, *Sexual Naturalization*, 11 (citing Yen Le Espiritu, *Asian American Women and Men: Labor, Laws and Love* [Thousand Oaks, CA: SAGE, 1996], 45–46).

182 Jennifer Lee, "From Undesirable to Marriageable: Hyper-Selectivity and the Racial Mobility of Asian Americans," *Annals of the American Academy of Political and Social Science* 662, no. 1 (2015): 79–93 (stating that "the passage of the 1965 Immigration and Nationality Act altered the socioeconomic profiles of Asian immigrants . . . thereby making them more desirable partners in the marriage market"); Jennifer Lee and Min Zhou, "From Unassimilable to Exceptional: The Rise of Asian Americans and 'Stereotype Promise,'" *New Diversities* 16 , no. 1 (2014): 7–22, https://newdiversities.mmg.mpg.de.

183 In addition, Americans grew more accustomed to seeing White men with Asian women as a result of the law's facilitation of immigration of mail order brides. The majority of American men who seek foreign brides are White, and foreign brides are disproportionately from Asia. Marianne Blair, Merle Weiner, Barbara Stark and Solangel Maldonado, *Family Law in the World Community: Cases, Materials, and Problems in Comparative and International Family Law*, 3rd ed. (Durham, NC: Carolina Academic Press, 2015), 147–48; Frank McAndrew, "'Mail Order Brides' Still Exist," *Psychology Today*, November 24, 2015, https://psychologytoday .com; "Asian Mail Order Bride Full Guide: Why, Where, and How to Find Asian Brides," *San Francisco Weekly*, August 4, 2021, https://sfweekly.com.

184 Pascoe, *What Comes Naturally*, 21–22.

185 This was known as the "other white strategy." Michael Olivas, "Review Essay—The Arc of Triumph and the Agony of Defeat: Mexican Americans and the Law,"

Journal of Legal Education 60 (November 2010): 354–67; Gomez, *Inventing Latinos*, 105–6; Martinez, "The Legal Construction of Race," 2–3.
186 Gong Lum, 275 U.S. at 83.
187 Suzanne Oboler, *Ethnic Labels, Latino Lives: Identity and the Politics of (Re)Presentation in the United States* (Minneapolis: University of Minnesota Press, 1995); Tatcho Mindiola, Yolanda Flores Niemann, and Néstor Rodríguez, *Black-Brown Relations and Stereotypes* (Austin: University of Texas Press, 2002); Arnold K. Ho, Jim Sidanius, Daniel T. Levin, Mahzarin R. Banaji, "Evidence for Hypodescent and Racial Hierarchy in the Categorization and Perception of Biracial Individuals," *Journal of Personality and Social Psychology* 100 (March 2011): 492, doi: 10.1037/a0021562; Kimberly Kahn, Jim Sidanius, Arnold K. Ho, and Felicia Pratto, "The Space between Us and Them: Perceptions of Status Differences," *Group Processes and Intergroup Relations* 12 (August 2009): 591, https://doi.org/10.1177/1368430209338716.
188 Tanya K. Hernandez, *Racial Innocence: Unmasking Latino Anti-Black Bias and the Struggle for Equality* (Boston: Beacon Press, 2022); Gomez, *Inventing Latinos*, 66–67, 82.
189 Derald Wing Sue, "Whiteness and Ethnocentric Monoculturalism: Making the 'Invisible' Visible," *American Psychologist* 59, no. 8 (November 2004):761–69. doi: 10.1037/0003-066X.59.8.761.
190 Lopez, *White by Law*, 10.
191 Ediberto Román, "Who Exactly Is Living la Vida Loca? The Legal and Political Consequences of Latino-Latina Ethnic and Racial Stereotypes in Film and Other Media," *Journal of Gender Race & Justice* 4 (January 2000): 62.
192 See Calif. Anti-Vagrancy Act of 1855, known as the Greaser Act because it targeted and referred to persons "commonly known as 'Greasers' or the issue of Spanish and Indian blood." Steven W. Bender, *Greasers and Gringos: Latinos, Law, and the American Imagination* (New York: New York University Press, 2003), xiii. "Greasers" was a derogatory and racial slur that Whites adopted based on "the practice of Mexican laborers in the Southwest greasing their backs to facilitate the unloading of hides and cargo" during the Mexican-American War. The term was also used to refer to Mexicans' and Mexican Americans' darker skin tone and assumptions about their hygiene. For discussion of stereotypes about Latinos, see Cynthia Willis-Esqueda, "Bad Characters and Desperados: Latinxs and Causal Explanations for Legal System Bias," *UCLA Law Review* 67 (November 2020): 1214–15.
193 Machic-Xiap, 2021 WL 3362738, at *5 and *11.
194 Michelle Alexander, *The New Jim Crow: Mass Incarceration in the Age of Colorblindness* (New York: The New Press, 2012), 106.
195 Paul Finkelman, "The Crime of Color," *Tulane Law Review* 67 (June 1993): 2063–64.
196 N. Jeremi Duru, "The Central Park Five, the Scottsboro Boys, and the Myth of the Bestial Black Man," *Cardozo Law Review* 25 (Fall 2004): 1322. For discussion of

cases involving innocent Black and Latino men charged and convicted of crimes against White victims, see Carl Suddler, *Presumed Criminal: Black Youth and the Justice System in Postwar New York* (New York: New York University Press, 2019).

197 Finkelman, "The Crime of Color," 2093.

198 Calhoun v. United States, 133 S. Ct. 1136, 1136–37 (2013) (concluding that by asking the jury "You've got African–Americans, you've got Hispanics, you've got a bag full of money. Does that tell you—a light bulb doesn't go off in your head and say, This is a drug deal?," the prosecutor inappropriately sought to appeal to the jury's prejudices and "tapped a deep and sorry vein of racial prejudice that has run through the history of criminal justice in our Nation" and "a time when appeals to race were not uncommon in the courtroom). *Calhoun*, 133 S Ct at 1138 (citing cases in which prosecutors appealed to racial prejudice).

199 Finkelman, "The Crime of Color," 2063.

200 Ian Haney Lopez, *Dog Whistle Politics: How Coded Racial Appeals Have Reinvented Racism and Wrecked the Middle Class* (New York: Oxford University Press, 2014), 58–59.

201 Marguerite Ward, "How Decades of US Welfare Policies Lifted Up the White Middle Class and Largely Excluded Black Americans," *Insider*, August 11, 2020, https://businessinsider.com.

202 Meghan Keneally, "Hillary Clinton's Long History with Black Voters," *ABC News*, September 9, 2016, https://abcnews.go.com; Julia Jacobo, "Donald Trump Says He Will Get 'Bad Hombres' out of US," *ABCNews*, October 19, 2016, https://abcnews.go.com.

203 Kevin Johnson, "Race, the Immigration Laws, and Domestic Race Relations: A 'Magic Mirror' into the Heart of Darkness," *Indiana Law Journal* 73, no. 4 (Fall 1998): 1111.

204 Peter Baker, "Bush Made Willie Horton an Issue in 1988, and the Racial Scars Are Still Fresh," *New York Times*, December 3, 2018, https://nytimes.com.

205 Lee, "Asian Americans, Affirmative Action," 185.

206 Frank Wu, *Yellow: Race in America beyond Black and White* (New York: Basic Books 2003), 79; Kevin R. Johnson, "Racial Hierarchy, Asian Americans and Latinos as 'Foreigners,' and Social Change: Is Law the Way to Go?" *Oregon Law Review* 76 (January 1997): 347; Natsu Taylor Saito, "Aliens and Non-Aliens Alike: Citizenship, 'Foreignness,' and Racial Hierarchy in American Law," *Oregon Law Review* 76 (January1997): 262. President Trump certainly signaled to his followers that Asian Americans, Latinos, anyone with ancestors in the Middle-East, and even African Americans are not true Americans when he tweeted that four congresswomen should "go back" to where they came from. The congresswomen are, of course, all U.S. citizens, and three were born in the United States. Devon Cole, "Trump tweets racist attacks at progressive Democratic congresswomen," CNN Politics, July 14, 2019, https://cnn.com.

207 Hyunyi Cho, Wenbo Li, Julie Cannon, Rachel Lopez, Chi Chuck Song, "Testing Three Explanations for Stigmatization of People of Asian Descent during

COVID-19: Maladaptive Coping, Biased Media Use, or Racial Prejudice?," *Ethnicity & Health* 26, no. 1 (January 2021): 94–109, https://doi.org/10.1080/13557858.2020.1830035; Anna Purna Kambhampaty, "'I Will Not Stand Silent.' 10 Asian Americans Reflect on Racism during the Pandemic and the Need for Equality," *Time*, June 25, 2020. https://time.com; "More than 9,000 Anti-Asian Incidents Have Been Reported Since the Pandemic Began," *NPR*, August 12, 2021, https://npr.org.
208 People v. Hall, 4 Cal. 399, 404 (1854).
209 Ozawa, 260 U.S. 178; Thind, 261 U.S. 204.
210 John Eligon, "Quadroon? Moor? Virginia Sued for Making Those Who Wed Say What They Are," *New York Times*, September 8, 2019, https://nytimes.com.
211 Rogers v. Virginia State Registrar, No. 119CV01149RDAIDD, 2020 WL 3246327, at *1 (E.D. Va. Jan. 23, 2020).

CHAPTER 3. FREEDOM OF ASSOCIATION VERSUS DISCRIMINATION IN INTIMATE SPHERES

1 42 U.S.C. § 2000e (employment); 42 U.S.C. § 3604 (housing); 42 U.S.C. § 2000a (public accommodations).
2 42 U.S.C. § 2000e.
3 42 U.S.C. § 3603(b)(2) (providing exemption from law prohibiting discrimination in the sale or rental of housing for "rooms or units in dwellings containing living quarters occupied or intended to be occupied by no more than four families living independently of each other, if the owner actually maintains and occupies one of such living quarters as his residence"); 42 U.S.C. §2000a(b)(1) (providing exemption from law prohibiting discrimination in public accommodations for "any inn, hotel, motel, or other establishment which provides lodging to transient guests, other than an establishment located within a building which contains not more than five rooms for rent or hire and which is actually occupied by the proprietor of such establishment as his residence").
4 42 U.S.C. § 2000a(e).
5 Sonu Bedi, *Private Racism: Intimacy as a Matter of Justice* (New York: Cambridge University Press, 2019); Russell K. Robinson and David M. Frost, "LGBT Equality and Sexual Racism," *Fordham Law Review* 86, no. 6 (July 2018): 2739.
6 Amy Thomson, Olivia Carville, and Nate Lanxon, "Match Opts to Keep Race Filter for Dating as Other Sites Drop It," Bloomberg, June 8, 2020, https://bloomberg.com.
7 Jevan Hutson, Jessie G. Taft, Solon Barocas, and Karen Levy, "Debiasing Desire: Addressing Bias and Discrimination on Intimate Platforms," *Proceedings of the ACM on Human-Compute Interaction* 73 (November 2018): 7n4, https://doi.10.1145/3274342.
8 Raj Kaur Bilkhu, "Shaadi.com: Dating Site Removes Skin Tone Filter after Backlash," *BBC News*, June 23, 2020, https://bbc.com.
9 "Match Is Owned by Match Group, a Tech Company That Houses . . . Tinder, Hinge, OkCupid, Match, Plenty of Fish, OurTime, Meetic and Pairs," *Forbes*, November 17, 2022, https://forbes.com.

10 Christian Rudder, *Dataclysm: Love, Sex, Race, and Identity—What Our Online Lives Tell Us about Our Offline Selves* (New York: Crown, 2014).
11 Elizabeth F. Emens, "Intimate Discrimination: The State's Role in the Accidents of Sex and Love," *Harvard Law Review* 122, no. 5 (March 2009): 1307, 1323.
12 eHarmony, accessed June 13, 2018, https://eharmony.com.
13 42 U.S.C. §3604.
14 Fair Housing Council of San Fernando Valley v. Roommate.com, LLC, 666 F.3d 1216 (9th Cir. 2012).
15 42 U.S.C. § 3603(b)(2). Some states, however, allow discrimination only where the owner-occupied dwelling has two or fewer units. Mass. Gen. Laws. ann. ch. 151B, § 4(7) (West 2022); N.Y. Hum. Rts L. § 296(5)(a) (West 2022). Robert G. Schwemm, "Discriminatory Housing Statements and Section 3604(c): A New Look at the Fair Housing Act's Most Intriguing Provision," *Fordham Urban Law Journal* 29 (January 2001): 187, 221, nn402–4, app.
16 S. Michael Gaddis, Nicholas DiRago, and Raj Ghoshal, "Moving to the City: An Audit Study Examining the Consequences of Racial/Ethnic Discrimination on Residential Segregation," *Social Science Research Network*, December 9, 2020, http://dx.doi.org/10.2139/ssrn.2605853.
17 Benjamin Edelman, Michael Luca, and Dan Svirsky, "Racial Discrimination in the Sharing Economy: Evidence from a Field Experiment," *American Economic Journal* 9, no. 22 (2017): 1–22, https://pubs.aeaweb.org.
18 Selden v. Airbnb, Inc., 2016 U.S. Dist. LEXIS 150863; Alison Griswold, "The Dirty Secret of Airbnb Is That It's Really, Really White," *Quartz*, June 23, 2016, https://qz.com; Elaine Glusac, "As Airbnb Grows, So Do Claims of Discrimination," *New York Times*, June 21, 2016, https://nytimes.com; Maggie Penman, Shankar Vendatam, and Max Nesterak, "#AirbnbWhileBlack: How Hidden Bias Shapes the Sharing Economy," NPR, April 26, 2016, https://npr.org.
19 42 U.S.C. §2000a(b)(1).
20 Allison K. Bethel, "The Contemporary Face of Housing Discrimination and the Fair Housing Act: A New Home for Haters—Online Home Sharing Platforms: A Look at the Applicability of the Fair Housing Act to Home Shares," *University of Richmond Law Review* 53, no. 3 (March 2019): 903; Brenna R. McLaughlin, "#airbnbwhileblack: Repealing the Fair Housing Act's Mrs. Murphy Exemption to Combat Racism on Airbnb," *Wisconsin Law Review* 2018, no. 1 (May 2018): 149, 151; James D. Walsh, "Reaching Mrs. Murphy: A Call for Repeal of the Mrs. Murphy Exemption to the Fair Housing Act," *Harvard Civil Rights-Civil Liberties Law Review* 34 (Winter 1999): 605, 607.
21 Hernandez, *Racial Innocence*, 87–88; Kenneth L. Karst, "The Freedom of Intimate Association," *Yale Law Journal* 89 (March 1980): 624, 638.
22 42 U.S.C. § 2000e-2(a).
23 42 U.S.C. § 2000e(b).
24 See, e.g., Alaska Stat. Ann. § 18.80.300 (West 2023) (any person with one or more employees); Ariz. Rev. Stat. Ann. § 41–1461 (West 2023) (same); Colo. Rev. Stat.

Ann. § 24-34-401 (West 2023) (same); D.C. Code Ann. § 2–1402 (West 2023) (same); Haw. Rev. Stat. Ann. § 378–1 (West 2023) (same); Me. Stat. Ann. Tit. 5, § 4553 (West 2023) (same); Mich. Comp. Laws §37–2202 (West 2023) (same); Minn. Stat. Ann. § 363A.03 (West 2023) (same); N.J. Stat. Ann. § 10:5–12 (West 2023) (same); N.D. Laws § 14–02.4–02 (West 2023) (same); 25 Okla. Stat. Ann. § 1301 (West 2023) (same); S.D. Codified Laws § 20-13-1 (West 2023) (same); Vt. Stat. Ann. Tit. 21, § 495d (West 2023) (same); Wis. Stat. Ann. §111.32 (West 2023) (same). But see Va. Code Ann. 2.1–714 (West 2023) (any person employing more than five but less than fifteen employees); Wash. Rev. Code Ann. §49.60.040 (West 2023) (any person employing eight or more employees).

25 N.J. Stat. Ann. § 10:5–5 (West 2023).

26 D.C. Stat. Ann. § 2–1401.02(10) (West 2022); Haw. Rev. Stat. Ann. § 378–1 (West 2022); Rebecca Tan, "D.C. Protects Most Workers from Discrimination. But Not Nannies or Housekeepers," *Washington Post*, August 22, 2019, https://washingtonpost.com.

27 Jennifer Steinhauer, "Domestic Workers Face Blatant Discrimination, Investigation Reveals," *New York Times*, June 1, 2005, https://nytimes.com. For discussion of the harms caused by discrimination against domestic workers, see Naomi Schoenbaum, "The Law of Intimate Work," *Washington Law Review* 90 (June 2015): 1167.

28 42 U.S.C. § 2000a(a) ("All persons shall be entitled to the full and equal enjoyment of the goods, services, facilities, privileges, advantages, and accommodations of any place of public accommodation, as defined in this section, without discrimination or segregation on the ground of race, color, religion, or national origin").

29 For a list of these laws, see National Council of State Legislatures, "State Public Accommodation Laws," June 25, 2021, http://ncsl.org. Some states define a place of public accommodation broadly. For example, New Jersey law provides that

> "a place of public accommodation" shall include, but not be limited to: any tavern, roadhouse, hotel, motel, trailer camp, summer camp, day camp, or resort camp, whether for entertainment of transient guests or accommodation of those seeking health, recreation, or rest; any producer, manufacturer, wholesaler, distributor, retail shop, store, establishment, or concession dealing with goods or services of any kind; any restaurant, eating house, or place where food is sold for consumption on the premises; any place maintained for the sale of ice cream, ice and fruit preparations or their derivatives, soda water or confections, or where any beverages of any kind are retailed for consumption on the premises; any garage, any public conveyance operated on land or water or in the air or any stations and terminals thereof; any bathhouse, boardwalk, or seashore accommodation; any auditorium, meeting place, or hall; any theatre, motion-picture house, music hall, roof garden, skating rink, swimming pool, amusement and recreation park, fair, bowling alley, gymnasium, shooting gallery,

billiard and pool parlor, or other place of amusement; any comfort station; any dispensary, clinic, or hospital; any public library; and any kindergarten, primary and secondary school, trade or business school, high school, academy, college and university, or any educational institution under the supervision of the State Board of Education or the Commissioner of Education of the State of New Jersey. (N.J. Stat. Ann. § 10:5–5[l] [West 2022])

30 42 U.S.C. § 2000a(e). See also N.J. Stat. Ann. § 10:5–5 (West 2022); Commonwealth of Ky. v. Pendennis Club, Inc., 153 S.W.3d 784, 789 (Ky. 2004) (holding that "truly private clubs have a constitutional right to discriminate because of race").

31 Jennifer Jolly Ryan, "Chipping Away at the Discrimination at the Country Club," *Pepperdine Law Review* 25 (January 1998): 495, 496; "Discrimination Remains a Policy and a Practice at Many Clubs," *New York Times*, September 13, 1976, https://nytimes.com.

32 Richard Fausset, "Latent Prejudice Stirs When a Black Man Tries to Join a Charleston Club," *New York Times*, December 18, 2018, https://nytimes.com.

33 Roberts v. United States Jaycees, 468 U.S. 609, 617–18 (1984); Karst, "The Freedom of Intimate Association," 626–47.

34 Boy Scouts of America v. Dale, 530 U.S. 640, 648 (2000) (emphasis added) (quoting Roberts, 468 U.S. at 623).

35 Shayak Sarkar, "Intimate Employment," *Harvard Journal of Law & Gender* 39 (Winter 2016): 429, 450–51 (discussing concerns about intimate association surrounding Title VII and the Fair Housing Act); Nancy Leong, "The First Amendment and Fair Housing in the Platform Economy," *Ohio State Law Journal* 78 (October 2017): 1001, 1011–14.

36 Runyon v. McCrary, 427 U.S. 160, 187–88 (1976) (Powell, J., concurring).

37 Thomas v. Dosberg, 249 A.D.2d 999, 1000 (N.Y. App. Div. 1998).

38 *Fair Housing Council*, 666 F.3d at 1221–22.

39 United States v. Hunter, 459 F.2d 205, 213 (4th Cir. 1972) (holding that "while the owner or landlord of an exempted dwelling is free to indulge his discriminatory preferences in selling or renting that dwelling, neither the [Fair Housing] Act nor the Constitution gives him a right to publicize his intent to so discriminate").

40 42 U.S.C. § 3604(c).

41 The ban on publication of discriminatory preferences applies to both written advertisements and verbal statements. 42 U.S.C. § 3604(c); Ragin v. N.Y. Times Co., 923 F.2d 995, 1000 (2d Cir. 1991); Corey v. Sec'y, United States HUD, 719 F.3d 322, 326 (4th Cir. 2013).

42 *Hunter*, 459 F.2d at 213 (holding that newspaper violated law by publishing a discriminatory ad posted by a Mrs. Murphy owner listing an apartment in a "white home"); U.S. Department of Housing and Urban Development, Guidance Regarding Advertisements Under Sec 804(c) of the Fair Housing Act (1995).

43 *Fair Housing Council*, 666 F.3d at 1221.

44 "Fair Housing Is Everyone's Right," Craigslist, accessed September 6, 2023, https://craigslist.org (stating that "under federal Fair Housing law, the prohibition on discriminatory advertisements applies to all situations except [that] . . . if you are advertising a shared housing unit, in which tenants will be sharing a bathroom, kitchen, or other common area, you may express a preference based upon sex only"); "Advertising for Roommates or Housemates," Housing Opportunities Made Equal of Virginia, Inc., accessed September 6, 2023, https://homeofva.org (stating that "in most circumstances a person seeking a roommate/housemate could refuse to rent to someone just because of a protected class . . . but they could not post an ad identifying that intention or preference to discriminate"); "Advertising for Roommates or Housemates," Fair Housing Center of Central Indiana, accessed September 6, 2023, https://fhcci.org (same). For discussion of racial discrimination in advertisements for roommates, see Gaddis, DiRago, and Ghoshal, "Moving to the City."
45 Schwemm, "Discriminatory Housing Statements," 212.
46 Stewart v. Furton, 774 F.2d 706, 710 (6th Cir. 1985); United States v. Space Hunters, Inc., 429 F.3d 416, 424–26 (2d Cir. 2005). For additional cases, see Schwemm, "Discriminatory Housing Statements," 232–34, 241, 249, nn298–300.
47 Rigel C. Oliveri, "Discriminatory Housing Advertisements On-Line: Lessons from Craigslist," *Indiana Law Review* 43 (January 2010): 1125, 1131.
48 *Ragin*, 923 F.2d at 1005; Ragin v. Harry Macklowe Real Estate Co., 6 F.3d 898, 907–09 (2d Cir. 1993); Saunders v. Gen. Servs. Corp., 659 F. Supp. 1042, 1053 (E.D. Va. 1987).
49 Schwemm, "Discriminatory Housing Statements," 223–24.
50 *Hunter*, 459 F.2d at 214.
51 Mayers v. Ridley, 465 F.2d 630 (D.C. Cir. 1972); Schwemm, "Discriminatory Housing Statements," 275–76.
52 Schwemm, "Discriminatory Housing Statements," 249–50; Spann v. Colonial Village, Inc., 899 F.2d 24, 27 (D.C. Cir. 1990).
53 "Advertising for Roommates or Housemates."
54 42 U.S.C. § 3603(b)(1).
55 If the owner does not reside in the house at the time it is sold, the exemption from the anti-discrimination law only applies to only "one such sale within any twenty-four month period." 42 U.S.C. § 3603(b)(1).
56 42 U.S.C. § 3603(b)(1) provides that

> the sale or rental of any such single-family house shall be excepted from the application of this subchapter only if such house is sold or rented (A) without the use in any manner of the sales or rental facilities or the sales or rental services of any real estate broker, agent, or salesman, or of such facilities or services of any person in the business of selling or renting dwellings, or of any employee or agent of any such broker, agent, salesman, or person and (B) without the publication, posting or mailing, after notice, of any advertisement or written notice in violation of section 3604(c) of this title.

57 National Association of Realtors, "Code of Ethics and Standards of Practice of the National Association of Realtors Standard of Practice 10-1," January 2023, https://www.nar.realtor (prohibiting realtors from volunteering "information regarding the racial, religious or ethnic composition of any neighborhood").

58 Kenneth R. Harney, "Some Realty Sites Describe Neighborhoods' Racial and Ethnic Makeup: Is That Legal?," *Washington Post*, June 20, 2014, https://washingtonpost.com.

59 42 U.S.C. § 3601 et seq.; "5 Things You Should Know About the Prohibition of Racial Steering in New Jersey," NJ Office of the Attorney General, Division on Civil Rights, https://www.nj.gov.

60 "Coverage of Employment Agencies," U.S. Equal Employment Opportunity Commission, accessed August 31, 2023, https://eeoc.gov (emphasis added).

61 "Coverage of Employment Agencies."

62 New York State Office of the Attorney General, "Press Release, Eight Employment Agencies to End Discriminatory Practicesg [sic]," May 31, 2005, https://ag.ny.gov.; Steinhauer, "Domestic Workers Face Blatant Discrimination."

63 New York State, "Press Release, Eight Employment Agencies."

64 Complaint, People ex rel. Spitzer v. Best Domestic Placement Service, Inc., 2005 WL 1502529 (S.D.N.Y. May 31, 2005) (No. 05CV5130); Pavillion Agency, Inc. v. Spitzer, 9 Misc. 3d 626 (N.Y. Sup. Ct. 2005).

65 New York amended its law in 2021 and now includes domestic workers within the protections of its Human Rights Law. See NY Legis 830 (2021), 2021 Sess. Law News of N.Y. Ch. 830 (S. 5064) (McKinney's).

66 Pavillion, 9 Misc. 3d at 631.

67 Pavillion, 9 Misc. 3d at 631.

68 Solangel Maldonado, "Discouraging Racial Preferences in Adoptions," *University of California, Davis Law Review* 39, no. 4 (April 2006): 1415, 1426; Barbara Fedders, "Race and Market Values in Domestic Infant Adoption," *North Carolina Law Review* 88 (June 2010): 1687, 1708–9.

69 Maldonado, "Discouraging Racial Preferences in Adoptions," 1426.

70 R. Richard Banks, "The Color of Desire: Fulfilling Adoptive Parents' Racial Preferences through Discriminatory State Action," *Yale Law Journal* 107 (January 1998): 875; Maldonado, "Discouraging Racial Preferences."

71 For example, the private adoption agency Adoptions from the Heart only accepts applications from "families open to all racial backgrounds and ethnic heritage." Adoptions from the Heart, accessed September 6, 2023, https://afth.org.

72 Title VI provides that "no person in the United States shall, on the ground of race, color, or national origin, be excluded from participating in, be denied the benefits of, or be subjected to discrimination under any program or activity receiving Federal financial assistance." 42 U.S.C. § 2000d.

73 42 U.S.C.A. § 1996b.

74 42 U.S.C.A. § 1996b.

75 Ralph Richard Banks, "The Multiethnic Placement Act and the Troubling Persistence of Race Matching," *Capital University Law Review* 38 (Winter 2009): 271.
76 Letter from Roosevelt Freeman, Regional Manager, Office for Civil Rights, Dep't of Health & Human Servs. to Kim S. Aydlette, State Dir., S.C. Dep't of Social Services, October 31, 2005, 9, https://hhs.gov.
77 Randall Kennedy, *Interracial Intimacies: Sex, Marriage, Identity, and Adoption* (New York: Pantheon, 2003), 27–28.
78 Sonu Bedi, "Sexual Racism: Intimacy as a Matter of Justice," *Journal of Politics* 77 (October 2015): 998, 1005; Matt Zwolinski, "Why Not Regulate Private Discrimination?," *San Diego Law Review* 43 (Fall 2006): 1043, 1052.
79 Zach Stafford, "That Dating Site for White People? It's Racist, No Matter How It's Justified," *The Guardian*, January 8, 2016, https://theguardian.com (emphasis in original).
80 Ashley Brown, "'Least Desirable'? How Racial Discrimination Plays Out in Online Dating," NPR, January 9, 2018, https://npr.org.
81 Chris Stokel-Walker, "Why Is It OK for Online Daters to Block Whole Ethnic Groups?," *The Guardian*, September 29, 2018, https://theguardian.com.
82 Hutson et al., "Debiasing Desire," 7.
83 Lore Yessuff, "Trying to Feel Love-Worthy (While Working for a Dating App)," *New York Times*, July 17, 2020. https://nytimes.com.
84 Yessuff, "Trying to Feel Love-Worthy."
85 Germine H. Awad, Carolette Norwood, Desire S. Taylor, Mercedes Martinez, Shannon McClain, Bianca Jones, Andrea Holman, and Collette Chapman-Hilliard, "Beauty and Body Image Concerns among African American College Women," *Journal of Black Psychology* 41, no. 6 (December 2015): 540, 550.
86 Kindr, "Grindr Users Talk about Sexual Racism | Kindr ep. 1," video, September 18, 2018, https://kindr.grindr.com.
87 Hutson et al., "Debiasing Desire," 7.
88 Denton Callander, Christy E. Newman, and Martin Holt, "Is Sexual Racism Really Racism? Distinguishing Attitudes toward Sexual Racism and Generic Racism among Gay and Bisexual Men," *Archives of Sexual Behavior*, 44, no. 7 (2015): 1991, 1995; Emens, "Intimate Discrimination," 1310; Note, "Racial Steering in the Romantic Marketplace," *Harvard Law Review* 107 (February 1994): 877, 883–84, 889; Hutson et al., "Debiasing Desire," 5, note 17.
89 Bedi, *Private Racism*, 83.
90 Bedi, *Private Racism*, 133; Russell K. Robinson, "Structural Dimensions of Romantic Preferences," *Fordham Law Review* 76, no. 6 (2008): 2787; Hutson et al., "Debiasing Desire."
91 42 U.S.C. § 1981.
92 Nancy Leong and Aaron Belzer, "The New Public Accommodations: Race Discrimination in the Platform Economy," *Georgetown Law Journal* 105 (January 2017): 1271, 1302.

93 Hutson et al., "Debiasing Desire," 7.
94 Leong and Belzer, "The New Public Accommodations," 1298–1301; Bedi, *Private Racism*, 113, 133–35; Colin Crawford, "Cyberplace: Defining a Right to Internet Access through Public Accommodation Law," *Temple Law Review* 76 (Summer 2003): 225, 249; Shani Else, "Court Must Welcome the Reality of the Modern World: Cyberspace Is a Place under Title III of the Americans with Disabilities Act," *Washington & Lee Law Review* 65 (Summer 2008): 1121, 1157; Tara Thompson, "Locating Discrimination: Interactive Web Sites as Public Accommodations under Title II of the Civil Rights Act," *University of Chicago Legal Forum* 2002, no. 15 (2002): 409, 411. For cases interpreting public accommodations broadly, see Carparts Distrib. Ctr., Inc. v. Auto. Wholesaler's Ass'n of New England Inc., 37 F.3d 12, 19 (1st Cir. 1994); Doe v. Mut. of Omaha Ins. Co., 179 F.3d 557, 559 (7th Cir. 1999).
95 Leong and Belzer, "The New Public Accommodations," 1301.
96 Hutson et al., "Debiasing Desire," 6; Karen Levy and Solon Barocas, "Designing against Discrimination in Online Markets," *Berkeley Tech Law Journal* 32 (December 2017): 1183–1237.
97 Michael J. Rosenfeld, Reuben J. Thomas, and Sonia Hausen, "Disintermediating Your Friends: How Online Dating in the United States Displaces Other Ways of Meeting," *Proceedings of the National Academy of Sciences* 116, no. 36 (2019): 17753–58, https://doi.org/10.1073/pnas.1908630116.
98 Hutson et al. "Debiasing Desire," 8.
99 Communications Decency Act, 47 U.S.C. § 230(c)(1) (1996) (providing that "no provider or user of an interactive computer service shall be treated as the publisher or speaker of any information provided by another information content provider").
100 David Bernstein, "Does the Right to Choose a Roommate Include a Right to Advertise Discriminatory Preferences?," Volokh Conspiracy, February 8, 2012, https://volokh.com (emphasis in original).
101 Anne Elizabeth Brown, "Ridehail Revolution: Ridehail Travel and Equity in Los Angeles," thesis, University of California, Los Angeles, 2018, https://escholarship.org; Jorge Meija and Chris Parker, "When Transparency Fails: Bias and Financial Incentives in Ridesharing Platforms," *Management Science* 67, no. 1 (2020), https://doi.org/10.1287/mnsc.2019.3525; Benjamin Edelman, Michael Luca, and Dan Svirsky, "Racial Discrimination in the Sharing Economy: Evidence from a Field Experiment," *American Economic Journal* 9, no. 2 (2017): 1, https://aeaweb.org.
102 Communications Decency Act, 47 U.S.C. § 230(c)(1) (1996).
103 Although the law does not require websites to remove discriminatory content posted by their users, it provides immunity for websites that do remove such content. See Communications Decency Act, 47 U.S.C. § 230(c)(2) (1996) (providing that "no provider or user of an interactive computer service shall be held liable on account of . . . any action voluntarily taken in good faith to restrict access to or availability of material that the provider or user considers to be obscene,

lewd, lascivious, filthy, excessively violent, harassing, or otherwise objectionable, whether or not such material is constitutionally protected").

104 Airbnb, Nondiscrimination Policy, February 2022, https://airbnb.com.
105 Uber, Uber Non-Discrimination Policy, January 2020, https://uber.com.
106 "Fair Housing Is Everyone's Right."
107 Ollie Locke and Jack Rogers, "How One Gay App Is Fighting Racist Body-Shamers," *The Advocate*, January 4, 2018, https://advocate.com.
108 Hutson et al., "Debiasing Desire," 11; Hornet, Guidelines, accessed September 9, 2023, https://hornet.com ("We don't tolerate mocking or rejecting other users just because they don't fit your search range. Any content of such nature will be removed. This applies to any kind of discrimination, namely: Race, ethnicity, nationality, religion; Orientation, gender identity; Age, height, or weight; Disability, genetic information"). Hornet Live Guidelines, accessed September 9, 2023, https://hornet.com (prohibiting "racial slurs or discriminatory language").
109 Abram Brown, "Race Protests Are Forcing Dating Apps to Reconsider the Value of Their 'Ethnicity Filters,'" *Forbes*, June 2, 2020, https://forbes.com; Hugo Greenhalgh, "LGBT+ Dating Apps Ditch Ethnicity Filters to Fight Racism amid U.S. Protests," Reuters, June 2020, https://reuters.com.
110 Kevin Truong, "Asian American Man Plans Lawsuit to Stop 'Sexual Racism' on Grindr," *NBC News*, July 13, 2018, https://www.nbcnews.com.
111 Kindr About Grindr, accessed September 6, 2023, https://kindr.grindr.com; Kindr, "Grindr Users Talk about Sexual Racism."
112 Sonia Elks, "Gay Dating App Announces 'Zero Tolerance' of Racism, Transphobia," Reuters, September 18, 2018, https://reuters.com. Grindr also prohibited hate speech defined to include content that "promotes or condones racism." Grindr, Community Guidelines, accessed September 9, 2023, https://grindr.com.
113 Greenhalgh, "LGBT+ Dating Apps Ditch Ethnicity Filters."
114 Julia Angwin and Terry Parris Jr., "Facebook Lets Advertisers Exclude by Race," Pro Publica, October 28, 2016, https://propublica.org. For example, Facebook did not take action until it was sued. Ariana Tobin and Ava Kofman, "Facebook Finally Agrees to Eliminate Tool That Enabled Discriminatory Advertising," Pro Publica, June 22, 2022, https://propublica.org; Settlement Agreement, United States. v. Meta Platforms, Inc., 22 Civ. 5187 (S.D.N.Y., June 21, 2022), https://justice.gov.
115 Zwolinski, "Why Not Regulate Private Discrimination?" 1048.

CHAPTER 4. HOW LAW SHAPES OPPORTUNITY FOR INTERRACIAL INTIMACY

1 William H. Frey, "Even as Metropolitan Areas Diversify, White Americans Still Live in Mostly White Neighborhoods," The Brookings Institution, March 23, 2020, https://brookings.edu/; U.S. Census Bureau, "Quick Facts," July 1, 2021, https://census.gov (reporting that 13.6 percent of the U.S. population is African American and 18.9 percent is Latino).

2 "K–12 Education: Student Population Has Significantly Diversified, but Many Schools Remain Divided Along Racial, Ethnic, and Economic Lines," U.S. Government Accountability Office, June 16, 2022, https://gao.gov; Erica Frankenberg, Jongyeon Ee, Jennifer B. Ayscue, Gary Orfield, "Harming Our Common Future: America's Segregated Schools 65 Years After *Brown*," 25–31 (May 10, 2019), The Civil Rights Project, University of California, Los Angeles, https://civilrightsproject.ucla.edu.

3 Jon Marcus, "Facts about Race and College Admission," *Hechinger Report*, July 6, 2018, https://hechingerreport.org ("Enrollment in the 468 best-funded and most selective four-year institutions is 75 percent white").

4 As many commentators have noted, the term is a misnomer, as "every job, no matter what it is, requires a unique set of skills and knowledge. There is no such thing as a low-skill or unskilled worker." "There's No Such Thing as a 'Low-Skill Worker,'" National Fund for Workplace Solutions, January 6, 2022, https://nationalfund.org; Jerusalem Demsas, "Stop Calling Workers 'Low-Skill.' Essential Workers Aren't 'Low-Skill,' They're Low-Wage," Vox, January 11, 2022, https://www.vox.com.

5 John-Paul Ferguson and Rembrand Koning, "Firm Turnover and the Return of Racial Establishment Segregation," *American Sociological Review* 83, no. 3 (June 2018): 445–74.

6 Beverly Daniel Tatum, *Why Are All the Black Kids Sitting Together in the Cafeteria? And Other Conversations About Race*, rev. ed. (New York: Basic Books, 2003), 55.

7 Robert P. Jones, "Self-Segregation: Why It's So Hard for Whites to Understand Ferguson," *The Atlantic*, August 21, 2014, https://theatlantic.com; Tanya K. Hernandez, *Racial Innocence: Unmasking Latino Anti-Black Bias and the Struggle for Equality* (Boston: Beacon Press, 2022), 20, 91, 101.

8 For example, the rate of interracial marriage is 17 percent, but it would be 44 percent if race did not play a role in our intimate choices. See Chapter 1.

9 See Elizabeth Emens, "Intimate Discrimination: The State's Role in the Accidents of Sex and Love," *Harvard Law Review* 122 (March 2009): 1307; Dorothy E. Roberts, "Crossing Two Color Lines: Interracial Marriage and Residential Segregation in Chicago," *Capital University Law Review* 45 (Winter 2017): 1; Russell K. Robinson, "Structural Dimensions of Romantic Preferences," *Fordham Law Review* 76 (May 2008): 2787; Rose Cuison Villazor, "Residential Segregation and Interracial Marriages," *Fordham Law Review* 86 (May 2018): 2717.

10 Fair Housing Act, 42 U.S.C. § 3601 et seq.; Mass. Gen. Laws Ann. ch. 151B, § 4(7) (West 2022); N.J. Stat. Ann. § 10:5–12 (West 2021); N.Y. Exec. Law § 296(5)(a) (McKinney 2022).

11 Brown v. Bd. of Educ., 347 U.S. 483 (1954).

12 Title VII of the Civil Rights Act of 1964, 42 U.S.C. § 2000e et seq.

13 Gary Orfield and Danielle Jarvie, "Black Segregation Matters: School Resegregation and Black Educational Opportunity," The Civil Rights Project, University of California, Los Angeles, December 2020, https://civilrightsproject.ucla.edu.

14 Hilary White, "According to New Stats, Weddings Are the Place to Meet Someone Special," POPSUGAR Love & Sex, June 19, 2018, https://popsugar.com.
15 "New Jersey 2020 Census: New Jersey Population Topped 9 Million in Last Decade," August 25, 2021, https://census.gov.
16 Alana Semuels, "The U.S. Is Increasingly Diverse, So Why Is Segregation Getting Worse?," *Time*, June 21, 2021, https://time.com.
17 Richard Rothstein, *The Color of Law: A Forgotten History of How Our Government Segregated America* (New York: W. W. Norton, 2018).
18 U.S. Department of Housing and Urban Development, "Affirmatively Furthering Fair Housing (AFFH)," accessed December 28, 2022, https://hud.gov.
19 Buchanan v. Warley, 245 U.S. 60, 70 (1917).
20 *Buchanan*, 245 U.S. at 81; City of Richmond v. Deans, 37 F.2d 712, 713 (4th Cir. 1930). S. S. Field, "The Constitutionality of Segregation Ordinances," *Virginia Law Review* 5 (November 1917): 81–91, 89.
21 *Buchanan*, 245 U.S. 60.
22 Rothstein, *The Color of Law*, 70.
23 Village of Euclid v. Ambler Realty Co., 272 U.S. 365, 394 (1926).
24 E. Badger and Q. Bui, "Cities Start to Question an American Ideal: A House with a Yard on Every Lot," *New York Times*, June 28, 2019, https://nytimes.com; Alex Baca, Patrick McAnaney, and Jenny Schuetz, "'Gentle' Density Can Save Our Neighborhoods," The Brookings Institution, December 4, 2019, https://brookings.edu.
25 Rothstein, *The Color of Law*, 86.
26 Ta Nehisi Coates, "The Case for Reparations," *The Atlantic*, June 2014, https://theatlantic.com.
27 Rothstein, *The Color of Law*, 96.
28 Dorothy A. Brown, "Your Home's Value Is Based on Racism," *New York Times*, March 20, 2021, https://nytimes.com.
29 Rothstein, *The Color of Law*, 30.
30 Rothstein, *The Color of Law*, 90–91.
31 Campbell Gibson and Kay Jung, "Historical Census Statistics on Population Totals by Race, 1970 to 1990, and by Hispanic Origin, 1970 to 1990, for Large Cities and Other Urban Places in the United States," U.S. Census Bureau (September 2002), https://census.gov.
32 U.S. Census Bureau, "Population Estimates," 2021, https://census.gov.
33 Rothstein, *The Color of Law*, 101. See also Paul Dictos, "Racially Restrictive Covenants," Office of the Assessor-Reporter, September 17, 2021, https://co.fresno.ca.us (identifying thousands of racially restrictive covenants in deeds in California including one deed of a home built in 1952 that provided "[t]his property is sold on condition it is not resold to or occupied by the following races: Armenian, Mexican, Japanese, Korean, Syrian, Negros, Filipinos or Chinese").
34 Rothstein, *The Color of Law*, 113.

35 See Corrigan v. Buckley, 271 U.S. 323, 331 (1926); Mays v. Burgess, 147 F.2d 869 (D.C. Cir. 1945); Steward v. Cronan, 98 P.2d 999 (Colo. 1940); 3 A.L.R.2d 466 (originally published in 1949) (listing cases).
36 Shelley v. Kramer, 334 U.S. 1 (1948), overruled *Corrigan*. For extensive discussion of racially restrictive covenants, even after *Shelley*, see Richard R. W. Brooks and Carol M. Rose, *Saving the Neighborhood: Racially Restrictive Covenants, Law, and Social Norms* (Cambridge, MA: Harvard University Press, 2013).
37 Rothstein, *The Color of Law*, 105–7.
38 Rothstein, *The Color of Law*, 93.
39 Richard Rothstein, "The Neighborhoods We Will Not Share," *New York Times*, January 20, 2020, https://nytimes.com; Rothstein, *The Color of Law*, 84.
40 In 2019, Parkchester was 4 percent White. "Parkchester Neighborhood in Bronx, New York (NY), 10462 Detailed Profile," City-Data.com, 2019, http://city-data.com.
41 In 2020, Stuyvesant Town was 89 percent White and less than 1 percent African American. Census Reporter, "Stuyvesant Town, Columbia County, NY," 2020, https://censusreporter.org.
42 Dictos, "Racially Restrictive Covenants" (identifying thousands of racially restrictive covenants in deeds in California and finding that such deeds were filed as late as the 1950s, several years after the Supreme Court's decision in *Shelley*); Cheryl W. Thompson, Cristina Kim, and Natalie Moore, "Racial Covenants, a Relic of the Past, Are Still on the Books across the Country," NPR, November 17, 2021, https://npr.org.
43 Rothstein, *The Color of Law*, 166.
44 Richard Kahlenberg, "An Economic Fair Housing Act," The Century Foundation, August 3, 2017, https://tcf.org; Rothstein, *The Color of Law*, 85, 166.
45 Monica Bell, "Anti-Segregation Policing," *New York University Law Review* 95 (June 2020): 650, 717; Matthew D. Lassiter and Susan Cianci Salvatore, "Civil Rights in America: Racial Discrimination in Housing," 51, National Park Service, March 2021, https://nps.gov; Matthew Fleischer, "Opinion: How White People Used Police to Make L.A. One of the Most Segregated Cities in America," *Los Angeles Times*, August 11, 2020, https://latimes.com.
46 Richard Rothstein, "The Black Lives Next Door," *New York Times*, August 14, 2020, https://nytimes.com.
47 Rothstein, *The Color of Law*, 11.
48 Villazor, "Residential Segregation," 2718–22.
49 42 U.S.C. § 3601, et. seq.
50 42 U.S.C. § 3604.
51 See, e.g., Mass. Gen. Laws Ann. ch. 151B, § 4(7) (West 2022); N.J. Stat. Ann. § 10:5–12 (West 2021); N.Y. Exec. Law § 296(5)(a) (McKinney 2022).
52 Rothstein, *The Color of Law*, 8.
53 Rothstein, *The Color of Law*, 182; Ingrid Gould Ellen, Keren Horn, Yiwen Kuai, Roman Pazuniak, and Michael David Williams, "Effect of QAP Incentives on

the Location of LIHTC Properties," 4, U.S. Department of Housing and Urban Development Office of Policy Development and Research, April 7, 2015, https://furmancenter.org; Jacqueline Rabe Thomas, "Separated by Design: Why Affordable Housing Is Built in Areas with High Crime, Few Jobs and Struggling Schools," ProPublica, November 25, 2019, https://propublica.org. See Ingrid Gould Ellen and Keren Mertens Horn, "Do Federally Assisted Households Have Access to High Performing Public Schools?" Poverty & Race Research Action Council, 2012, http://prrac.org.

54 Meghan M. O'Neil, "Housing Policy, Race, Inequality, and Disparate Impact," *Phylon* 55, no. 1 & 2 (2018): 60, 63, 72.

55 Rothstein, "The Black Lives Next Door."

56 Neil Bhutta, Andrew C. Chang, Lisa J. Dettling, and Joanne W. Hsu, with assistance from Julia Hewitt, "Disparities in Wealth by Race and Ethnicity in the 2019 Survey of Consumer Finances," Federal Reserve, September 28, 2020, https://federalreserve.gov.

57 "Quarterly Residential Vacancies and Homeownership, Third Quarter 2022," table 7, November 2, 2022, U.S. Census, https://census.gov.

58 Anna Bahney, "The Black Homeownership Rate Is Now Lower than It Was a Decade Ago," CNN Business, February 25, 2022, https://cnn.com.

59 Richard Rothstein, "The Neighborhoods We Will Not Share," *New York Times*, January 20, 2020, https://nytimes.com.

60 African Americans, regardless of income, are more likely than any other group to reside in African American neighborhoods. Michela Zonta, "Racial Disparities in Home Appreciation," The Center for American Progress, July 15, 2019, https://americanprogress.org; Jenny Schuetz, "Metro Areas Are Still Racially Segregated," The Brookings Institution, December 8, 2017, https://brookings.edu; John R. Logan, "The Persistence of Segregation in the Metropolis," *City & Community* 12, no. 2 (June 2013), https://doi.org/10.1111%2Fcico.12021; Sean F. Reardon, Lindsay Fox, and Joseph Townsend, "Neighborhood Income Composition by Household Race and Income, 1990–2009," *Annals of the American Academy of Political and Social Science* 660, no. 1 (2015): 78, 85–90, https://doi.org/10.1177/0002716215576104; Patrick Sharkey, "Spatial Segmentation and the Black Middle Class," *American Journal of Sociology* 119, no. 4 (2014): 903–54, https://doi.org/10.1086/674561.

61 Emily Badger, "How Redlining's Racist Effects Lasted for Decades," *New York Times*, August 24, 2017, https://nytimes.com; Jonathan Rothwell and Andre M. Perry, "Biased Appraisals and the Devaluation of Housing in Black Neighborhoods," The Brookings Institution, November 17, 2021, https://brookings.edu. One study found that "in the average U.S. metropolitan area, homes in neighborhoods where the share of the population is 50 percent Black are valued at roughly half the price as homes in neighborhoods with no Black residents." Andre M. Perry, Jonathan Rothwell, and David Harshbarger, "The Devaluation of Assets in Black Neighborhoods," The Brookings Institution, November 27, 2018, https://brookings

.edu; Zonta, "Racial Disparities"; Sarah Mikhitarian, "Home Values Remain Low in Vast Majority of Formerly Redlined Neighborhoods," Zillow, April 25, 2018, https://zillow.com.

62 Daniel Aaronson, Daniel Hartley, and Bhash Mazumder, "The Effects of the 1930s HOLC 'Redlining' Maps," *American Economic Journal: Economic Policy* 13, no. 4 (November 2021): 355–92, https://doi.org/10.1257/pol.20190414; U.S. Department of Justice, "Press Release, Justice Department Announces New Initiative to Combat Redlining," October 22, 2021, https://www.justice.gov.

63 Emily Badger, "How Redlining's Racist Effects Lasted for Decades," *New York Times*, August 24, 2017, https://nytimes.com.

64 Ryan Best and Elena Mejia, "The Lasting Legacy of Redlining," FiveThirtyEight, February 9, 2022, https://fivethirtyeight.com; Stephen Menendian, Samir Gambhir, and Arthur Gailes, "The Roots of Structural Racism Project," Othering & Belonging Institute, June 30, 2021, https://belonging.berkeley.edu.

65 U.S. Department of Justice, "Press Release, Justice Department Announces New Initiative."

66 "NAR President Charlie Oppler Apologizes for Past Policies That Contributed to Racial Inequality," National Association of Realtors, November 19, 2020, https://nar.realtor.

67 "Steer Clear of 'Steering,'" National Association of Realtors, July 10, 2020, https://nar.realtor.

68 Ann Choi, Keith Herbert, and Olivia Winslow, "Long Island Divided," *Newsday*, November 17, 2019, https://newsday.com.

69 Rothstein, "The Neighborhoods We Will Not Share."

70 Andrew Hacker, *Two Nations: Black and White, Separate, Hostile, Unequal* (New York: Scribner, 2010).

71 Bhutta et al., "Disparities in Wealth by Race and Ethnicity"; Richard D. Kahlenberg, "Tearing Down the Walls: How the Biden Administration and Congress Can Reduce Exclusionary Zoning," The Century Foundation, April 18, 2021, https://tcf.org; Richard Fry, Jesse Bennett, and Amanda Barroso, "Racial and Ethnic Gaps in the U.S. Persist on Key Demographic Indicators," Pew Research Center, January 12, 2021, https://pewresearch.org.

72 See Matthew Resseger, "The Impact of Land Use Regulation on Racial Segregation: Evidence from Massachusetts Zoning Borders," Mercatus Research Paper, October 2022, http://dx.doi.org/10.2139/ssrn.4244120; Jonathan T. Rothwell, "Racial Enclaves and Density Zoning: The Institutionalized Segregation of Racial Minorities in the United States," *American Law and Economics Review* 13, no. 1 (2011): 290–358, https://doi.org/10.1093/aler/ahq015; Thomas, "Separated by Design"; Ellen et al., "Effect of QAP Incentives."

Although some states, such as New Jersey, require every municipality to allocate a certain percentage of new homes for low- and moderate-income families, in practice these units are usually located in poorer and predominantly minority areas. Even when they are located in White suburbs, they are placed in the least desirable part of town, away from the single-family homes in which the majority of Whites reside.

73 Junia Howell and Elizabeth Korver-Glenn, "The Increasing Effect of Neighborhood Racial Composition on Housing Values, 1980–2015," *Social Problems* 68, no. 4 (November 2021): 1051–71, https://doi.10.1093/socpro/spaa033.
74 Richard D. Kahlenberg, "The Walls We Won't Tear Down," *New York Times*, August 3, 2017, https://nytimes.com.
75 Richard D. Kahlenberg, "The 'New Redlining' Is Deciding Who Lives in Your Neighborhood," *New York Times*, April 19, 2021, https://nytimes.com.
76 Kahlenberg, "An Economic Fair Housing Act."
77 42 U.S.C. § 3603(b)(2).
78 Hernandez, *Racial Innocence*, 87–88; Kenneth L. Karst, "The Freedom of Intimate Association," *Yale Law Journal* 89 (March 1980): 624, 638.
79 Hernandez, *Racial Innocence*, 88.
80 347 U.S. 483 (1954).
81 Brown v. Board of Education (*Brown II*), 349 U.S. 294, 301 (1955).
82 Orfield and Jarvie, "Black Segregation Matters"; Frankenberg et al., "Harming Our Common Future"; Gary Orfield, John Kucsera, and Genevieve Siegel-Hawley, "E Pluribus . . . Separation: Deepening Double Segregation for More Students," The Civil Rights Project, University of California, Los Angeles, September 19, 2012, https://civilrightsproject.ucla.edu.
83 Frankenberg et al., "Harming Our Common Future," 31–33; "K–12 Education: Student Population Has Significantly Diversified, but Many Schools Remain Divided along Racial, Ethnic, and Economic Lines," U.S. Government Accountability Office, June 16, 2022, https://gao.gov.
84 Matthew F. Delmont, *Why Busing Failed: Race, Media, and the National Resistance to School Desegregation* (Oakland: University of California Press, 2016), 3–6.
85 Swann v. Charlotte-Mecklenburg Board of Education, 402 U.S. 1 (1971).
86 Milliken v. Bradley, 418 U.S. 717 (1974).
87 *Milliken*, 418 U.S. at 745.
88 Bradley v. Milliken, 338 F. Supp. 582, 587 (E.D. Mich. 1971), aff'd, 484 F.2d 215 (6th Cir. 1973), rev'd, 418 U.S. 717 (1974).
89 Matthew D. Lassiter, "How White Americans' Refusal to Accept Busing Has Kept Schools Segregated," *Washington Post*, April 20, 2021, https://washingtonpost.com.
90 U.S. Congress Joint Economic Committee, "Zoned Out: How School and Residential Zoning Limit Educational Opportunity," November 2019, https://jec.senate.gov; Kahlenberg, "An Economic Fair Housing Act."
91 See, e.g., N.J. Stat. Ann. § 18A:38–1 (West 2022).
92 LaToya Baldwin Clark, "Stealing Education," *UCLA Law Review*, 68 (October 2021): 566, 573–74.
93 Amended Complaint for Declaratory Judgment and Other Relief, Latino Action Network v. New Jersey, No. MER-L-001076-18 (N.J. Super. Ct. Law Div. Aug. 2, 2019), 18.

94 Cranford Township School District, NJ; Mountainside Borough School District, NJ; Westfield Town School District, NJ, Census Reporter, accessed September 24, 2022, https://censusreporter.org. The median household income of parents with children in public schools in Plainfield, which is predominantly African American and Latino, is $59,241 as compared to Westfield's $250,001. Plainfield City School District, NJ, Westfield Town School District, NJ, National Center for Education Statistics, accessed September 24, 2022, https://nces.ed.gov.

95 "New York State Education at a Glance," N.Y. State Education Department, accessed September 24, 2022, https://data.nysed.gov; Bronxville Union Free School District, NY, Mount Vernon School District, NY, National Center for Education Statistics, accessed September 24, 2022, https://nces.ed.gov.

96 Kimiko de Freytas-Tamura, "A Suburb Believed in Liberal Ideals. Then Came a New Busing Plan," *New York Times*, August 30, 2019, https://nytimes.com.

97 See Chapter 2. Reginald Oh, "Interracial Marriage in the Shadows of Jim Crow: Racial Segregation as a System of Racial and Gender Subordination," *University of California, Davis Law Review* 39 (March 2006): 1321, 1339–30.

98 Nikole Hannah-Jones, "It Was Never about Busing," *New York Times*, July 12, 2019, https://nytimes.com.

99 Students for Fair Admissions, Inc. v. President & Fellows of Harvard College, 143 S. Ct. 2141, 2226 (2023) (Sotomayor, J., dissenting).

100 See Jeannine Bell, "The Hidden Fences Shaping Resegregation," *Harvard Civil Rights–Civil Liberties Law Review* 54, no. 2 (2019): 814; Kimberly Jenkins Robinson, "The High Cost of Education Federalism," *Wake Forest Law Review* 48 (Spring 2013): 287, 319–20; Derek W. Black, "Middle-Income Peers as Educational Resources and the Constitutional Right to Equal Access," *Boston College Law Review* 53 (March 2012): 373, 404–5.

101 *Brown I*, 347 U.S. at 493; Sheff v. O'Neill, 678 A.2d 1267, 1289–90 (Conn. 1996); Booker v. Bd. of Ed. of City of Plainfield, Union Cnty., 212 A.2d 1 (N.J. 1965); In re North Haledon, 854 A.2d 327 (N.J. 2004).

102 NAEP Report Card: Reading, accessed September 30, 2022, https://nationsreportcard.gov.

103 NAEP Report Card: Mathematics, accessed September 30, 2022, https://nationsreportcard.gov. The COVID-19 pandemic will likely exacerbate the achievement gap for years to come. See generally Department of Education Office for Civil Rights, "Education in a Pandemic: The Disparate Impact of COVID-19 on America's Students," 2021; Emma Dorn, Bryan Hancock, Jimmy Sarakatsannis, and Ellen Viruleg, COVID-19 and Education: The Lingering Effects of Unfinished Learning," McKinsey & Co., July 27, 2021, https://mckinsey.com; Sarah Mervosh, "The Pandemic Erased Two Decades of Progress in Math and Reading," *New York Times*, September 1, 2022, https://nytimes.com.

104 See Hanna Dumont and Douglas D. Ready, "Do Schools Reduce or Exacerbate Inequality?: How the Associations between Student Achievement and Achievement Growth Influence Our Understanding of the Role of Schooling," *American*

Educational Research Journal 57, no. 2 (2019): 728, 733–34, https://doi.org/10.3102/0002831219868182; Roslyn Arlin Mickelson, "School Integration and K–12 Outcomes: An Updated Quick Synthesis of Social Science Evidence," Institute of Education Sciences, 2016, 5–6, nn23–29, https://eric.ed.gov; Roslyn Arlin Mickelson, "Subverting Swann: First- and Second-Generation Segregation in the Charlotte-Mecklenburg Schools," *American Educational Research Journal* 38, no. 2 (2001): 215, 243.

105 Black, "Middle-Income Peers as Educational Resources," 407.

106 David Dante Troutt, *The Price of Paradise: The Costs of Inequality and a Vision for a More Equitable America* (New York: New York University Press, 2013), 217.

107 *Students for Fair Admissions*, 143 S. Ct. at 2236 (Sotomayor, J., dissenting) (citing Department of Education, National Center for Education, Institute of Educational Science, The Condition of Education 2022, 24 (2020) (fig. 16)).

108 Erianna Jiles, "Student Voice: Having 'the Hardest Year of My Life' at 'a School That's Mostly White, Conservative and Isolated—Everything I Wasn't,'" *Hechinger Report*, March 19, 2020, https://hechingerreport.org; Katherine Long, "What It's Like to Be Black on Campus: Isolated, Exhausted, Calling for Change," *Seattle Times*, April 9, 2016, https://seattletimes.com; Report and Recommendations of the Brigham Young University Committee on Race, Equity, and Belonging, February 2021, https://race.byu.edu; Tomas Monarrez and Kelia Washington, "Racial and Ethnic Segregation within Colleges," Urban Institute, December 2020, https://urban.org..

109 Rachel D. Godsil and L. Song Richardson, "Racial Anxiety," *Iowa Law Review* 102, no. 5 (July 2017): 2235, 2239.

110 Emlice Santana, "Friendship Is Skin (Color) Deep: The Role of Skin Color in Cross-Ethnoracial Friendships," *Du Bois Review: Social Science Research on Race* 19, no. 1, 147–73. https://doi.org/10.1017/S1742058X21000291; Daniel Cox, Juhem Navarro-Rivera, and Robert P. Jones, "Race, Religion, and Political Affiliation of Americans' Core Social Networks," Public Religion Research Institute, August 3, 2016, https://prri.org.

111 James A. Bany, Belinda Robnett, and Cynthia Feliciano, "Gendered Black Exclusion: The Persistence of Racial Stereotypes among Daters," *Race & Social Problems* 6 (July 2014): 201–13.

112 Sarah Hanlon, "These Are the Best Dating Apps for Marriage, According to Data," The Knot, December 16, 2022, https://theknot.com; Esther Lee, "Dating Apps Are Officially the Most Popular Way to Meet a Spouse," The Knot, October 30, 2019, https://theknot.com; Cara Newlon, "College Students Still Often Find Spouses on Campus," *USA Today College*, October 17, 2013, https://usatoday.com.

113 Sally H. Jacobs, "Ketanji Brown Jackson's Ancestors Were Enslaved. Her Husband's Were Enslavers," *Washington Post*, June 19, 2023, https://washingtonpost.com; Emily Burack, "Everything to Know about Dr. Patrick Jackson, Husband of Judge Ketanji Brown Jackson," *Town & Country*, April 7, 2022, https://townandcountrymag.com.

114 "MRS Degree," Urban Dictionary, April 7, 2007, https://urbandictionary.com.
115 Hilary Droke, "Top 10 Schools to Find a Husband," *College Magazine*, April 18, 2017, https://collegemagazine.com; Charles Fain Lehman, "The Mr. & Mrs. Degree: Which Colleges Have the Highest Marriage Rates?," Institute for Family Studies, April 25, 2022, https://ifstudies.org.
116 The Marriage Pact, 2023, accessed June 20, 2023, https://marriagepact.com.
117 The Marriage Pact.
118 Students for Fair Admissions, Inc. v. President & Fellows of Harvard College, 143 S. Ct. 2141 (2023).
119 *Students for Fair Admissions*, 143 S. Ct. at 2260 (Sotomayor, J., dissenting) (warning that the majority's ban on affirmative action "will cause a sharp decline in the rates at which underrepresented minority students enroll in our Nation's colleges and universities").
120 Kevin Carey, "A Detailed Look at the Downside of California's Ban on Affirmative Action," *New York Times*, October 18, 2021, https://nytimes.com (citing Zachary Bleemer, "Affirmative Action, Mismatch, and Economic Mobility after California's Proposition 209," August 2020, https://cshe.berkeley.edu).
121 Lee, "Dating Apps."
122 Elise C. Boddie, "Racial Territoriality," *UCLA Law Review* 58 (December 2010): 401.
123 Elijah Anderson, "The White Space," *Sociology of Race & Ethnicity* 1, no. 1 (2015): 10; Elijah Anderson, *Black in White Space: The Enduring Impact of Color in Everyday Life* (Chicago: University of Chicago Press, 2022).
124 Zenitha Prince, "Eleven O'clock on Sundays Is Still the Most Segregated Hour in America," *Louisiana Weekly*, June 15, 2016, http://louisianaweekly.com. Racial and ethnic minorities have expressed a variety of reasons for flocking to churches where the majority of congregants are of their same race and ethnicity, "including the comfort associated with familiar styles of worship and music, sermons that are relevant to the distinctive struggles of Black Americans, and avoidance of the discrimination and discomfort that some of them have felt in non-Black religious spaces." Besheer Mohamed, Kiana Cox, Jeff Diamant, and Claire Gecewicz, "Faith among Black Americans," Pew Research Center, February 16, 2021, https://pewresearch.org, 26–32. See also "Changing Faiths: Latinos and the transformation of American Religion," Pew Research Center, April 25, 2007, https://pewresearch.org; Nikki Tundel, "Monocultural Churches Still the Norm in Diverse US Society" *MPR News*, June 7, 2012, https://mprnews.org.
125 Hurubie Meko and Dan Higgins, "Buffalo Gunman Pleads Guilty in Racist Attack That Left 10 Dead," *New York Times*, November 28, 2022, https://nytimes.com; Simon Romero, Manny Fernandez, and Mariel Padilla, "Massacre at a Crowded Walmart in Texas Leaves 20 Dead," *New York Times*, August 3, 2019, https://nytimes.com; Jason Horowitz, Nick Corasaniti, and Ashley Southall, "Nine Killed in Shooting at Black Church in Charleston," *New York Times*, June 17, 2015,

https://nytimes.com; Nicholas Bogel-Burroughs, "Atlanta Spa Shootings Were Hate Crimes, Prosecutor Says," *New York Times*, May 11, 2021, https://nytimes.com.

126 Boddie, "Racial Territoriality," 401.
127 See Chapter 2.
128 Sharon Lafraniere and Andrew W. Lehren, "The Disproportionate Risks of Driving While Black," *New York Times*, October 25, 2015, https://nytimes.com; *Driving While Black: Race, Space and Mobility in America*, video, PBS, October 13, 2020, https://pbs.org.
129 Colleen O'Dea, "State Police Arrest, Charge More Black, Hispanic Drivers than White," *NJ Spotlight News*, July 9, 2021, https://njspotlightnews.org; Remy Samuels, "Westfield Police Accused of Racial Profiling, Discrimination: Lawsuit," Patch, April 14, 2022, https://patch.com.
130 Mark P. Denbeaux, Kelley Kearns, and Michael J. Ricciardelli, "Racial Profiling Report: Bloomfield Police and Bloomfield Municipal Court," Seton Hall University School of Law Center for Policy and Research, April 9, 2016, http://dx.doi.org/10.2139/ssrn.2760382.
131 Bell, "The Hidden Fences," 817; Jessica Mazzola, "Toll So Far for Town's 1 Awful Night: 2 Ousted Cops, $280K and a Lawsuit," NJ.com, October 3, 2017, https://nj.com; Disha Raychaudhuri and Stephen Stirling, "Black People in N.J. Say They're More Likely to Be Punched, Kicked by Cops. Now, Data Backs That Up," NJ.com, January 19, 2019, https://nj.com.
132 Abby Goodnough, "Harvard Professor Jailed; Officer Is Accused of Bias," *New York Times*, July 20, 2009, https://nytimes.com.
133 Angela Onwuachi-Willig, "Policing the Boundaries of Whiteness: The Tragedy of Being 'Out of Place' from Emmett Till to Trayvon Martin," *Iowa Law Review* 102 (March 2017): 1113; Serge F. Kovaleski and Campbell Robertson "New Details Are Released in Shooting of Trayvon Martin," *New York Times*, May 17, 2012, https://nytimes.com
134 Richard Fausset, "What We Know about the Shooting Death of Ahmaud Arbery," *New York Times*, August 8, 2022, https://nytimes.com.
135 The Marshall Project, "Driving While Black, December 15, 2022, https://themarshallproject.org; Frank Baumgartner, Derek Epp, and Kelsey Shoub, *Suspect Citizens: What 20 Million Traffic Stops Tells Us about Policing and Race* (New York: Cambridge University Press, 2018); Victoria M. Massie, "What Philando Castile's Death Says about the Dangers of 'Driving While Black,'" *Vox*, July 10, 2016, https://vox.com; Christopher Wright Durocher, "How the Supreme Court Helped Create 'Driving While Black,'" *Politico Magazine*, April 17, 2021, https://politico.com.
136 Topher Sanders, Kate Rabinowitz, and Benjamin Conarck, "Walking While Black: Jacksonville's Enforcement of Pedestrian Violations Raises Concerns That It's Another Example of Racial Profiling," ProPublica, November 16, 2017, https://propublica.org/; Amy Goodman with Denis Moynihan, "Trayvon Martin:

Walking While Black: The Killing of Trayvon Martin," *Democracy Now!*, March 22, 2012, https://democracynow.org; Ness White, "The Dangers of Walking While Black," Yahoo News, May 16, 2016, https://news.yahoo.com.

137 Matthew Futterman and Talya Minsberg, "After a Killing, 'Running While Black' Stirs Even More Anxiety," *New York Times*, May 8, 2020, https://nytimes.com

138 Deborah N. Archer, "Transportation Policy and the Underdevelopment of Black Communities," *Iowa Law Review* 106, no. 5 (July 2021): 2125, 2143–47; Regina Austin, "'Not Just for the Fun of It!': Governmental Restraints on Black Leisure, Social Inequality, and the Privatization of Public Space," *Southern California Law Review* 71 (May 1998): 667, 669; Sarah Schindler, "Architectural Exclusion: Discrimination and Segregation through Physical Design of the Built Environment," *Yale Law Journal* 124, no. 6 (April 2015): 1934, 1961–65.

139 Schindler, "Architectural Exclusion," 1961–65.

140 Cheektowaga was 95 percent White and 3 percent African American. U.S. Census Bureau, 2000 Census of Population and Housing, Summary Population and Housing Characteristics, PHC-1-34, New York, Table 3 (July 2002), https://census.gov

141 David W. Chen, "Suit Accusing Shopping Mall of Racism over Bus Policy Settled," *New York Times*, November 18, 1999, https://nytimes.com; Lynn Duke, "Buffalo Family Seeking Millions for Fatal Lack of a Bus Stop," *Washington Post*, November 18, 1999, washingtonpost.com.

142 Chen, "Suit Accusing Shopping Mall."

143 Malcolm Gladwell, "Symbol of Suburban Separatism," *Washington Post*, February 6, 1996, https://washingtonpost.com.

144 Schindler, "Architectural Exclusion," 1963.

145 Anderson, *Black in White Space*.

146 Godsil and Richardson, "Racial Anxiety," 2242–43.

CHAPTER 5. PERPETUATING INEQUALITY

Epigraph: Orly Lobel, *The Equality Machine: Harnessing Digital Technology for a Brighter, More Inclusive Future* (New York: Public Affairs, 2022), 258.

1 Suzann Pileggi Pawelski, "The Happy Couple," *Scientific American* 25 (March 2016): 87.

2 Sonu Bedi, "Sexual Racism: Intimacy as a Matter of Justice," *Journal of Politics* 77, no. 4 (October 2015): 998–1011.

3 Cheryl Harris, "Whiteness as Property," *Harvard Law Review* 106, no. 8 (June 1993): 1709; Stephanie M. Wildman and Adrienne D. Davis, "Language and Silence: Making System of Privilege Visible," *Santa Clara Law Review* 35, no. 3 (1995): 894 (defining White privilege as "an invisible package of unearned assets"); Khiara Bridges, "Race, Pregnancy, and the Opioid Epidemic: White Privilege and Criminalization of Opioid Use During Pregnancy," *Harvard Law Review* 133 (January 2020): 770 (discussing the "[coexistence] of white privilege with white disadvantage").

4   Eduardo Bonilla-Silva, "From Bi-Racial to Tri-Racial: Towards a New System of Racial Stratification in the USA," *Ethnic & Racial Studies* 27, no. 6 (November 2004): 931–50, doi:10.1080/0141987042000268530; Eduardo Bonilla-Silva and David R. Dietrich, "The Latin Americanization of U.S. Race Relations: A New Pigmentocracy," in *Shades of Difference: Why Skin Color Matters*, ed. Evelyn Nakano Glenn (Stanford, CA: Stanford University Press, 2009), 40–60.
5   "Wedding Services in the US—Market Size 2005–2029 IBISWorld, August 30, 2022, https://ibisworld.com
6   Sam Roberts, "Want Your Union to Last? Marry in New Jersey," *New York Times*, October 12, 2012, https://nytimes.com.
7   Seth Motel and Meredith Dost, "Half of Unmarried LGBT Americans Say They Would Like to Wed," Pew Research Center, June 26, 2015, https://pewresearch.org; "The Decline of Marriage and Rise of New Families, Part Three: Marriage," Pew Research Center, November 18, 2010, https://pewresearch.org.
8   Zachary Evans, "U.S. Marriage Rate Dropped to 50-Year Low in 2020 *National Review*, May 17, 2022, https://nationalreview.com; Richard Fry, "New Census Data Show More Americans Are Tying the Knot, but Mostly It's the College-Educated," Pew Research Center, February 6, 2014, https://pewresearch.org; A. W. Geiger and Gretchen Livingston, "8 Facts about Love and Marriage in America," Pew Research Center, February 13, 2019, https://pewresearch.org.
9   Juliana Horowitz, Nikki Graf, and Gretchen Livingston, "Marriage and Cohabitation in the U.S.," Pew Research Center, November 6, 2019, https://pewresearch.org.
10 See Andrew Cherlin, "Marriage Has Become a Trophy," *The Atlantic*, March 20, 2018, https://theatlantic.com; Kathryn Edin and Maria Kefalas, *Promises I Can Keep: Why Poor Women Put Motherhood before Marriage* (Oakland: University of California Press, 2005); June Carbone and Naomi Cahn, *Marriage Markets: How Inequality Is Remaking the American Family* (New York: Oxford University Press, 2005). A study conducted by the Pew Research Center found that two-thirds of cohabiting adults who report that they would like to get married someday cite either their own or their partner's finances as a reason why they are not engaged or married. Another 45 percent cite not being far enough along in their job or career. About 60 percent of participants reported that it is very important for a person to have a steady job before getting married. Study participants without a bachelor's degree were more likely than college graduates to report that it is very important for a person to have a steady job (68 percent vs. 50 percent) or to be financially stable (47 percent vs. 38 percent) before getting married. Horowitz, Graf, and Livingston, "Marriage and Cohabitation in the U.S."
11 Ariel J. Binder and John Bound, "The Declining Labor Market Prospects of Less Educated Men," *Journal of Economic Perspectives* 33, no. 2 (Spring 2019): 163; Elena Holodny, "Americans Who Haven't Gone to College Are Worse Off Today than 40 Years Ago," *Business Insider*, November 11, 2017, https://businessinsider.com; Julian Mark, "'Unluckiest Generation' Falters in Boomer-Dominated Market for

Homes," *Washington Post*, August 12, 2023, https://www.washingtonpost.com; Alice Kantor, "Half of Millennials Own Homes. The Rest Fear They Never Will," *Bloomberg*, April 19, 2023, https://www.bloomberg.com. The Millennial generation includes persons born between 1981 and 1996; the Gen. Z. generation includes persons born in 1997 or later. See Michael Dimock, "Defining Generations: Where Millennials End and Generation Z Begins," Pew Research Center, January 17, 2019, https://pewresearch.org

12 Geiger and Livingston, "8 Facts about Love and Marriage"; Kim Parker and Renee Stepler, "Americans See Men as the Financial Providers Even as Women's Contributions Grow," Pew Research Center, September 20, 2017, https://pewresearch.org. Only one-third of Americans believe that for a woman to be a good wife or partner, it is very important that she be able to support a family financially.

13 Geiger and Livingston, "8 Facts about Love and Marriage."
14 Obergefell v. Hodges, 576 U.S. 644 (2015).
15 *Obergefell*, 576 U.S. at 657.
16 *Obergefell*, 576 U.S. at 681.
17 *Obergefell*, 576 U.S. at 657.
18 *Obergefell*, 576 U.S. at 666.
19 *Obergefell*, 576 U.S. at 646.
20 *Obergefell*, 576 U.S. at 667.
21 For discussion of the many scholarly critiques of *Obergefell*, see Gregg Strauss, "What's Wrong with *Obergefell*?," *Cardozo Law Review* 40, no. 2 (2018): 631.
22 *Obergefell*, 576 U.S. at 669 (quoting Maynard v. Hill, 125 U.S. 190, 211 (1888)).
23 *Obergefell*, 576 U.S. at 669.
24 Goodridge v. Dep't of Pub. Health, 798 N.E.2d 941, 955 (Mass. 2003).
25 United States v. Windsor, 570 U.S. 744, 773 (2013); *Goodridge*, 798 N.E.2d at 955–57.
26 *Goodridge*, 798 N.E.2d at 955–57
27 *Obergefell*, 576 U.S. at 669 (emphasis added).
28 *Windsor*, 570 U.S. at 773.
29 *Windsor*, 570 U.S. at 773 (citing 20 C.F.R. § 404.335).
30 "A Survey of LGBT Americans, Chapter 4: Marriage and Parenting," Pew Research Center, June 13, 2013, https://pewresearch.org.
31 *Obergefell*, 576 U.S. at 668.
32 *Obergefell*, 576 U.S. at 668.
33 *Obergefell*, 576 U.S. at 668; *Windsor*, 570 U.S. at 772.
34 Goodridge v. Dep't of Pub. Health, 798 N.E.2d 941, 956 (Mass. 2003).
35 *Goodridge*, 798 N.E.2d at 956–7.
36 *Goodridge*, 798 N.E.2d at 957. See also Solangel Maldonado, "Illegitimate Harm: Law, Stigma, and Discrimination against Nonmarital Children," *Florida Law Review* 63, no. 2 (2011): 345; Cynthia Grant Bowman, "The New Illegitimacy: Children of Cohabiting Couples and Step Children," *American University Journal of Gender Social Policy & the Law* 20, no. 3 (2012): 437; Todd D. Kendall and

Robert Tamura, "Unmarried Fertility, Crime, & Social Stigma," *Journal of Law & Economics* 53 (February 2010): 185–221.

37 Horowitz, Graf, and Livingston, "Marriage and Cohabitation in the U.S."
38 Gretchen Livingston, "The Changing Profile of Unmarried Parents," Pew Research Center, April 25, 2018, https://pewresearch.org.
39 *Obergefell*, 576 U.S. at 681, 667. For critiques of *Obergefell*, see Michael Cobb, "The Supreme Court's Lonely Hearts Club," *New York Times*, June 30, 2015, https://nytimes.com; Strauss, "What's Wrong with *Obergefell*?"
40 Kristen Schultz Lee and Hiroshi Ono, "Marriage, Cohabitation, and Happiness: A Cross-National Analysis of 27 Countries," *Journal of Marriage and Family* 74, no. 5 (September 2012), https://doi.org/10.1111/j.1741-3737.2012.01001.x; Alois Stutzer and Bruno S. Frey, "Does Marriage People Make Happy, or Do Happy People Get Married?," *Journal of Socio-Economics* 35, no. 2 (April 2006): 326–347, https://doi.org/10.1016/j.socec.2005.11.043; Malgorzata Mikucka, "The Life Satisfaction Advantage of Being Married and Gender Specialization," *Journal of Marriage and Family* 78, no. 3 (June 2016): 759–79, https://doi.org/10.1111/jomf.12290.
41 "Marriage and Committed Relationships Reduce Production of Stress Hormones," *Uchicago News*, August 18, 2010, https://news.uchicago.edu; Dario Maestripieri, Nicole M. Baran, Paola Sapienza, and Luigi Zingales, "Between- and within-Sex Variation in Hormonal Responses to Psychological Stress in a Large Sample of College Students," *Stress* 13, no. 5 (September 2010): 413–24, https://doi.org/10.3109/10253891003681137.
42 Tara Parker-Pope, "Is Marriage Good for Your Health?" *New York Times*, April 14, 2010, https://nytimes.com; William M. Schultz et al., "Marital Status and Outcomes in Patients with Cardiovascular Disease," *Journal of the American Heart Association* 6 (December 2017): e005890, https://doi.org/10.1161/JAHA.117.005890; "Marriage Helps Cancer Survival," *Telegraph*, April 11, 2016, https://telegraph.co.uk.
43 The positive health effects of marriage may be greater for men. Rebekah Wanic and James Kulik, "Toward an Understanding of Gender Differences in the Impact of Marital Conflict on Health," *Sex Roles* 65 (May 2011): 297–312, https://doi.org/10.1007/s11199-011-9968-6 (reporting that "while the married fair [sic] better than the unmarried overall in terms of morbidity and mortality . . . the health protective effect of marriage is stronger for males than females" and that "men consistently report higher marital satisfaction than women do"); Alexandra Sifferlin, "Do Married People Really Live Longer?," *Time*, February 12, 2015, https://time.com.
44 Richard Fry and D'Vera Cohn, "Women, Men and the New Economics of Marriage," Pew Research Center, January 19, 2010, https://pewresearch.org; Jay L. Zagorsky, "Marriage and Divorce's Impact on Wealth," *Journal of Sociology* 41, no. 4 (2005), 406–24, https://doi.org/10.1177/1440783305057847.
45 Erez Aloni, "The Marital Wealth Gap," *Washington Law Review* 93, no. 1 (2018): 46; Zagorsky, "Marriage and Divorce's Impact on Wealth" (reporting that married couples are more likely to receive money from their families than single or

cohabitating couples—money for the wedding or as a wedding present, as well as help with a down payment for a home).

46 Guillaume Vandenbroucke, "Married Men Sit atop the Wage Ladder," Economic Research: Federal Reserve Bank of St. Louis, 2018, https://research.stlouisfed.org; Jay L. Zagorsky, "Marriage and Divorce's Impact on Wealth," *Journal of Sociology* 71, no. 4 (December 2005): 406–10, doi: 10.1177/1440783305058478.

47 Lori Ann Campbell and Robert L Kaufman, "Racial Differences in Household Wealth: Beyond Black and White," *Research in Social Stratification and Mobility* 24 (February 2006): 131, 136, https://doi.org/10.1016/j.rssm.2005.06.001.

48 Elyakim Kislev, "Are Married People Happier? Think Again," *Psychology Today*, January 20, 2019, https://psychologytoday.com; Matthijs Kalmijn, "The Ambiguous Link between Marriage and Health: A Dynamic Reanalysis of Loss and Gain Effects," *Social Forces* 95 (June 2017): 1607, https://doi.org/10.1093/sf/sox015; Theodore F. Robles, "Marital Quality and Health: Implications for Marriage in the 21st Century," *Current Directions in Psychological Science* 23, no. 6 (December 2014): 6, https://doi.org/10.1177/0963721414549043; John E. Murray, "Marital Protection and Marital Selection: Evidence from a Historical-Prospective Sample of American Men," *Demography* 37, no. 4 (November 2000): 511–21, https://doi.org/10.1353/dem.2000.0010.

49 "Financial Security Becomes One of the Most Attractive Qualities in a Partner as Americans Enter 2022," PR Newswire, February 1, 2022, https://prnewswire.com.

50 "The Decline of Marriage and Rise of New Families: Marriage." Thirty-eight percent of Americans with a high school education or less say financial stability is a "very important" reason to get married, as compared with 21 percent of college graduates. Fifty percent of African Americans and 46 percent of Latinos, as compared to 25 percent of Whites, list financial stability as a "very important" reason to get married.

51 Although half of nonmarital children are born to cohabiting parents, the majority of nonmarital parents are not romantically involved by the time the child is five years old. Sara McLanahan and Audrey N. Beck, "Parental Relationships in Fragile Families," *Future of Children* 20, no. 2 (Fall 2010): 17, https://doi.org/10.1353/foc.2010.0007.

52 See Nicholas Zill, "Even in Unsafe Neighborhoods, Kids Are Safer in Married Families," Institute for Family Studies, February 23, 2015, https://ifstudies.org.

53 W. Bradford Wilcox, "Marriage Makes Our Children Richer—Here's Why," *The Atlantic*, October 29, 2013, https://theatlantic.com (noting that "young adults are at least 44 percent more likely to have graduated from college if they were raised by their married parents").

54 Carmen DeNavas-Walt, Bernadette D. Proctor, and Jessica C. Smith, "Income, Poverty, and Health Insurance Coverage in the United States: 2011," U.S. Census Bureau, September 2012, https://census.gov; "Child Poverty Rates and Family Structure," National Conference of State Legislatures, October 3, 2012, https://ncsl.org.

55 Wendy Manning, "Cohabitation and Child Well-Being," *Future of Children* 25, no. 3 (2015): 51.
56 Manning, "Cohabitation and Child Well-Being," 59; Nicholas Zill, "Substance Abuse, Mental Illness, and Crime More Common in Disrupted Families," Institute for Family Studies, March 24, 2015, https://ifstudies.org.
57 Manning, "Cohabitation and Child Well-Being," 59. See also Trevor Stammers, "Teenage Pregnancies Are Influenced by Family Structure," *British Medical Journal* 324, no. 7328 (January 2002): 51, https://doi.org/10.1136/bmj.324.7328.51a (noting that "young people aged 14–17 who live in a two parent family are less likely to have ever had sexual intercourse than young people living in any other family arrangement, even after adjusting for potentially confounding factors such as race, age, and socioeconomic deprivation").
58 Manning, "Cohabitation and Child Well-Being," 58 (finding that "children born to cohabiting parents have more problems with peers, more aggressive behaviors, more internalizing problems, and more negative teacher assessments than do children born to married parents").
59 Wendy Sigle-Rushton and Sara McLanahan, "Father Absence and Child Well-Being: A Critical Review," in *The Future of the Family*, ed. Daniel Patrick Moynihan, Timothy M. Smeeding, and Lee Rainwater (New York: Russell Sage Foundation, 2004), 120–21.
60 R. Kelly Raley, Megan M. Sweeney and Daniela Wondra, "The Growing Racial and Ethnic Divide in U.S. Marriage Patterns," *Future Child* 25, no. 2 (2016): 90, https://doi.org/10.1353/foc.2015.0014. Only 14 percent of White women ages thirty-five to forty-nine have never been married as compared to 43.6 percent of African American women of the same age. Rachel M. Shattuck and Rose M. Kreider, "Social and Economic Characteristics of Currently Unmarried Women with a Recent Birth: 2011," *American Community Survey Reports* (May 2013), https://www2.census.gov.
61 In 2017, for example, 57 percent of Whites and 63 percent of Asian Americans were married as compared to 48 percent of Latinos and 33 percent of African Americans. Among individuals ages twenty-five and older, those with a bachelor's degree or higher (66 percent) were more likely than those with some college experience (56 percent) or with a high school diploma or less education (54 percent) to be married. Horowitz, Graf, and Livingston, "Marriage and Cohabitation in the U.S." See also Kim Parker and Renee Stepler, "As U.S. Marriage Rate Hovers at 50 percent, Education Gap in Marital Status Widens," Pew Research Center, September 14, 2017, https://pewresearch.org.
62 Jeremy Greenwood, Nezih Guner, Georgi Kocharkov, and Cezar Santos, "Marry Your Like: Assortative Mating and Income Inequality," *American Economic Review, American Economic Association*, 104, no. 5 (May 2014): 348–53, https://nber.org; Carbone and Cahn, *Marriage Markets*; Tyler Cowen, "The Marriages of Power Couples Reinforce Income Inequality," *New York Times*, December 24, 2015, https://nytimes.com.

63 See Edin and Kefalas, *Promises I Can Keep*.
64 Brady E. Hamilton, Joyce Am. Martin, Michelle J. K. Osterman, "Births: Preliminary Data for 2015," *National Vital Statistics Report* 65, no. 3 (2016): 10, http://cdc.gov. (reporting that 16 percent of children born to Asian American mothers, 29 percent of children born to White mothers, 53 percent of children born to Latina mothers, and 70 percent of children born to African American mothers in 2015 were nonmarital). See also Shattuck and Krieder, "Social and Economic Characteristics of Currently Unmarried Women," 4.
65 Forty-three percent of married parents versus 20 percent of single parents and 15 percent of cohabitating parents have a bachelor's degree. Livingston, "The Changing Profile of Unmarried Parents." The nonmarital birth rate for college-educated women is 9 percent, as compared to 57 percent for women with less than a high school diploma. Shattuck and Krieder, "Social and Economic Characteristics of Currently Unmarried Women," 4.
66 Carmen Solomon-Fears, "Nonmarital Childbearing: Trends, Reasons, and Public Policy Interventions," CRS Report for Congress, 2008, 15–16 (reporting that in 2007, 41 percent of women with nonmarital children had incomes below the poverty level). Livingston, "The Changing Profile of Unmarried Parents" ("Just 8% of married parents are living in poverty").
67 Eight percent of married parents are living below the poverty line as compared to 16 percent of unmarried parents living with a partner and 27 percent of single parents. Livingston, "The Changing Profile of Unmarried Parents." Manning, "Cohabitation and Child Wellbeing," 55 ("Cohabitating parents are more likely to be poor, less likely to be employed, and their median household income is about 50 percent lower than that of married parent families"); Sarah McLanahan, "Fragile Families and the Reproduction of Poverty," *Annals of the American Academy of Political and Social Science* 621, no. 1 (January 2009): 111–131, https://doi.org/10.1177/0002716208324862 (finding that children of unmarried parents have fewer parental resources).
68 Campbell and Kaufman, "Racial Differences in Household Wealth" (citing Thomas M. Shapiro, *The Hidden Cost of Being African American: How Wealth Perpetuates Inequality* [Oxford: Oxford University Press, 2004]).
69 Solangel Maldonado, "Parents' Social Capital and Educational Inequality," *Fordham Law Review* 90, no. 6 (2022): 2613; Annette Lareau, *Unequal Childhoods: Class, Race and Family Life*, 2nd Ed. (Berkeley, Los Angeles: University of California Press, 2011); Claire Cain Miller, "Class Differences in Child-Rearing Are on the Rise," *New York Times*, December 17, 2015, https://nytimes.com.
70 Obergefell v. Hodges, 576 U.S. 644, 669 (2015) ("marriage [is] the basis for an expanding list of governmental rights, benefits, and responsibilities" under state law and "is also a significant status for over a thousand provisions of federal law"); Goodridge v. Dep't of Public Health, 798 N.E.2d 941, 956–57 (Mass. 2003) (describing the numerous federal and state benefits available to married couples).
71 Vivian E. Hamilton, "Family Structure, Children and Law," *Washington University Journal of Law Policy* 24, no. 1 (2007): 10; Maldonado, "Illegitimate Harm," 372–73.

72 Elizabeth F. Emens, "Intimate Discrimination: The State's Role in the Accidents of Sex and Love," *Harvard Law Review* 122, no. 5 (March 2009): 1307, 1374.
73 Russell K. Robinson, "Racing the Closet," *Stanford Law Review* 61 (April 2009): 1463, 1500–1502 (discussing government policies that have reduced the pool of eligible Black male partners).
74 Cedric Herring, "Scarce Jobs and Racial Differences in the Decline of Marriage among Men in the United States, 1980–2000," *American Journal of Sociological Research* 6, no. 3 (2016): 74, https://doi.org10.5923/j.sociology.20160603.03 (citing William Julius Wilson, *The Truly Disadvantaged* [Chicago: University of Chicago Press, 2012]).
75 Adrienne D. Davis, "Regulating Polygamy: Intimacy, Default Rules, and Bargaining for Equality," *Columbia Law Review* 110, no. 8 (December 2010): 1970–75; Adrien K. Wing, "Polygamy from Southern Africa to Black Britannia to Black America: Global Critical Race Feminism as Legal Reform for the Twenty-First Century," *Journal of Contemporary Legal Issues* 11, no. 2 (2001): 811, 857–63.
76 Lisa Diamond, *Sexual Fluidity: Understanding Women's Love and Desire* (Cambridge, MA: Harvard University Press, 2009); Robert Epstein, Paul McKinney, Shannon Fox, and Carlos Garcia, "Support for a Fluid-Continuum Model of Sexual Orientation: A Large-Scale Internet Study," *Journal of Homosexuality* 59, no. 10 (November 2012): 1365–81, doi:10.1080/00918369.2012.724634; Esther D. Rothblum, "Sexual Orientation and Sex in Women's Lives: Conceptual and Methodological Issues," *Journal of Social Issues* 56, no. 2 (Summer 2000): 196, https://doi.org/10.1111/0022-4537.00160.
77 Ralph Richard Banks, *Is Marriage for White People? How the African American Marriage Decline Affects Everyone* (New York: Plume, 2012).
78 Cynthia Feliciano, Belinda Robnett, and Golnaz Komaie, "Gendered Racial Exclusion among White Internet Daters," *Social Science Research* 38, no. 1 (March 2009): 9–54, https://doi.org/10.1016/j.ssresearch.2008.09.004.
79 Richard V. Reeves and Edward Rodrigue, "Single Black Female BA Seeks Educated Husband: Race, Assortative Mating and Inequality," The Brookings Institution, April 9, 2015, https://brookings.edu.
80 Belinda Robnett and Cynthia Feliciano, "Patterns of Racial-Ethnic Exclusion by Internet Daters," *Social Forces* 89, no. 3 (March 2011): 807; Gerald A. Mendelsohn, Lindsay Shaw Taylor, Andrew T. Fiore, and Coye Cheshire, "Black/White Online Dating: Interracial Courtship in the 21st Century," *Psychology of Popular Media Culture* 3, no. 1 (2014): 2–18; Celeste Vaughan Curington, Ken-Hou Lin, and Jennifer Hickes Lundquist, "Positioning Multiraciality in Cyberspace: Treatment of Multiracial Daters in an Online Dating Website," *American Sociological Review* 80, no. 4 (August 2015): 764–88, https://doi.org/10.1177/0003122415591268; Ken-Hou Lin and Jennifer Lundquist, "Mate Selection in Cyberspace: The Intersection of Race, Gender, and Education," *American Journal of Sociology* 119, no. 1 (July 2013): 183–215. But see George Yancey, "Crossracial Differences in the Racial Preferences of Potential Dating Partners: A Test of the Alienation of African

Americans and Social Dominance Orientation," *Sociological Quarterly* 50, no. 1 (Winter 2009): 121–43, https://doi.org/10.1111/j.1533-8525.2008.01135.x (finding that while only 49.6 percent of African American women stated that they were willing to date White men, 57.4 percent of White men stated that they were willing to date African American women).

81   Horowitz, Graf, and Livingston, "Marriage and Cohabitation in the U.S."
82   Banks, *Is Marriage for White People?*
83   Perez v. Sharp, 32 Cal.2d. 711, 722 (1948).
84   Amanda Bennett, "(Black) Girl, Unnoticed." *Huffpost*, November 10, 2015, https://huffpost.com.
85   For examples and discussion of racial microaggressions, see Derald Wing Sue, Christina M. Capodilupo, Gina C. Torino, Jennifer M. Bucceri, Aisha M. B. Holder, Kevin L. Nadal, and Marta Esquilin, "Racial Microaggressions in Everyday Life: Implications for Clinical Practice," *American Psychologist* 62, no. 4 (2007): 271–86, doi:10.1037/0003-066X.62.4.271.
86   Monnica T. Williams, Matthew D. Skinta, Renee Martin-Willett, "After Pierce and Sue: A Revised Racial Microaggressions Taxonomy," *Perspectives on Psychological Science* 16, no. 5 (September 2021): 991–1007, https://doi.org/10.1177/1745691621994247 (citing studies).
87   Thomas Healy, "Stigmatic Harm and Standing," *Iowa Law Review* 92 (February 2007): 417.
88   Erving Goffman, *Stigma: Notes on the Management of Spoiled Identity* (Englewood Cliffs, NJ: Prentice-Hall, 1963), 4.
89   R.A. Lenhardt, "Understanding the Mark: Race, Stigma, and Equality in Context," *New York University Law Review* 79, no. 3 (June 2004): 803, 817 (citing sources).
90   Lenhardt, "Understanding the Mark," 817.
91   Courts have recognized the law's stigmatization of racial minorities. Plessy v. Ferguson, 163 U.S. 537, 562 (1896) (Harlan, J., dissenting) (arguing that a law requiring Whites and Blacks to ride in separate railroad cars places a "badge of servitude" upon Blacks); Strauder v. West Virginia, 100 U.S. 303, 308 (1880) (recognizing that law prohibiting African Americans from serving on juries "is practically a brand upon them, affixed by the law, an assertion of their inferiority, and a stimulant to that race prejudice"); Healy, "Stigmatic Harm and Standing," 428–36 (discussing cases). For further discussion on how the law has contributed to stigma, see Healy, "Stigmatic Harm and Standing," 451–52.
92   Russell K. Robinson, "Perceptual Segregation," *Columbia Law Review* 108, no. 5 (June 2008): 1093; Healy, "Stigmatic Harm and Standing," 453–58.
93   Peggy Davis, "Law as Macroaggression," *Yale Law Journal* 98, no. 8 (1989): 1565–66; Sue et al., "Racial Microaggressions in Everyday Life"; Jennifer Crocker, Brenda Major, and Claude Steele, "Social Stigma," in *Handbook of Social Psychology*, 4th ed., ed. Daniel T. Gilbert, Susan T. Fiske, and Gardner Lindzey (New York: McGraw Hill, 1998), 504, 516–17; Angela Onwuachi-Willig and Jacob Willig-Onwuachi, "A House Divided: The Invisibility of the Multiracial Family,"

Harvard Civil Rights–Civil Liberties Law Review, 44 (Winter 2009): 240–41 (listing microaggressions interracial couples endure).

94 Lenhardt, "Understanding the Mark," 840.
95 Amanda Machado, "How the U.S. Taught Me That Spanish Was Shameful," *NBC News*, March 26, 2019, https://www.nbcnews.com.
96 Tanya Hernandez, *Racial Innocence: Unmasking Latino Anti-Black Bias and the Struggle for Equality* (Boston: Beacon Press, 2022).
97 Lenhardt, "Understanding the Mark," 842. Of course, not all stigmatized persons have low self-esteem. "Although the experience of being devalued, stereotyped, and targeted by prejudice may take a toll on self-esteem, academic achievement, and other outcomes, many people with stigmatized attributes have high self-esteem, are happy, and appear to be quite resilient despite their negative experiences." John F. Dovidio, Brenda Major, and Jennifer Crocker, "Stigma: Introduction and Overview," in *Social Psychology of Stigma*, ed. Todd F. Heatherton, Robert E. Kleck, Michelle R. Hebl, and Jay G. Hull (New York: Guilford Press, 2003), 2.
98 Wendy Wang and Kim Parker, "Record Share of Americans Have Never Married: As Values, Economics and Gender Patterns Change," Pew Research Center, September 24, 2014, https://pewresearch.org (looking at 25–34-year-olds and finding that "among never-married white, Hispanic and Asian American young adults, the ratio of employed men to women is roughly equal—100 men for every 100 women").
99 Reeves and Rodrigue, "Single Black Female BA."
100 J. Weston Phippen and National Journal, "'Marrying Down' Costs Educated Women $25K a Year," *The Atlantic*, October 7, 2015, https://theatlantic.com.
101 Reeves and Rodrigue, "Single Black Female BA."
102 Wendy Wang, "The Rise of Intermarriage: Rates, Characteristics Vary by Race and Gender," Pew Research Center, February 16, 2012, https://pewresearch.org.
103 While at least 40 percent of Millennials receive financial support from their parents, African Americans and Latinos are significantly less likely to receive such support. They are instead expected to help support their parents, who tend to have few assets. Mel Jones, "Why So Many Minority Millennials Can't Get Ahead," *The Atlantic*, November 29, 2015, https://theatlantic.com. Almost 50 percent of Whites as compared to 10 percent of African Americans receive help from a family member for a down payment on a home. Jones, "Why So Many Minority Millennials"; Michael Fletcher, "Study Ties Black-White Wealth Gap to Stubborn Disparities in Real Estate," *Washington Post*, February 26, 2013, https://washingtonpost.com. Thirty-six percent of Whites as compared to 7 percent of African Americans receive an inheritance, and the amount that Whites inherit is about ten times larger than what African Americans receive. Thomas M. Shapiro, Tatjana Meschede, and Sam Osoro, "The Roots of the Widening Racial Wealth Gap: Explaining the Black-White Economic Divide," Research and Policy Brief (February 2013), https://doi.org/10.13016/pvyx-ebny. Intergenerational wealth

transfers "account for more of the racial wealth gap than any other demographic and socioeconomic indicators." Kriston McIntosh, Emily Moss, Ryan Nunn, and Jay Shambaugh, "Examining the Black-White Wealth Gap," *Brookings Institution Blog*, February 27, 2020, https://brookings.edu; Naomi R. Cahn, "Dismantling the Trusts and Estates Canon," *Wisconsin Law Review* 2019, no. 2 (2019): 165, 189 (arguing that "the intergenerational transmission of wealth is 'integral to the future perpetuation of racial inequality across generations' in a number of ways: 1) 'education, experiences, friendships, and contacts,' including college tuition; 2) lifetime support, such as qualifying for a first home; and 3) gifting and inheriting assets" and noting that "intergenerational transfers (whether through gift or bequest) accounts 'for at least 50%—and perhaps more than 80%—of the net worth of families in the United States.'").

104 Friends and family have told me that their partner's 401K, home ownership, or the college fund their partner's parents had saved for future grandchildren made them more attractive. Some people are willing to advertise their interest in a financial security or recognize that such traits make them more attractive. For example, several ads in a college alumni magazine's Personals page read:

> -ATTRACTIVE AND AFFECTIONATE: Looking for a man of means.
> -LASIK SURGEON: Featured in NY Times/Wall Street Journal. Dartmouth, Columbia, Harvard, Emory, NYU degrees. Seeks smart, skinny SWF 30 for marriage, $10,000 donation to your charity for intro!
>
> Columbia Magazine Summer 2012 p. 62.

105 Some graduates from elite institutions seek graduates of similarly elite schools. See Right Stuff Dating ("The Ivy League of Dating"), accessed September 7, 2023, https://rightstuffdating.com.
106 Phippen and National Journal, "'Marrying Down' Costs."
107 "Between 10 and 16 percent of the country's income inequality is due to the "growing correlation of earned incomes received by husbands and wives." Phippen and National Journal, "'Marrying Down' Costs."
108 Carbone and Cahn, *Marriage Markets*.
109 Reeves and Rodrigue, "Single Black Female BA"; Phippen and National Journal, "'Marrying Down' Costs" (reporting that "seven out of 10 Black children born into families in the middle quintile of the income spectrum will actually earn less than their parents as they become adults").
110 Banks, *Is Marriage for White People*?
111 Maldonado, "Parents' Social Capital," 2613.
112 Maldonado, "Parents' Social Capital."
113 Solangel Maldonado, "Romantic Discrimination and Children," *Chicago Kent Law Review* 92, no. 1 (2017): 105, 130.
114 Maldonado, "Romantic Discrimination and Children," 130 (quoting Isabel Sawhill, "Celebrating Single Mothers by Choice," The Brookings Institution, May 8, 2015, https://brookings.edu).

115 Maldonado, "Romantic Discrimination and Children," 130 (quoting Kimberly Seals Allers, "There Is a Single Mother Hierarchy, and It Needs to Stop," *Washington Post*, June 10, 2016, https://washingtonpost.com).
116 Shervin Assari, "Parental Education Better Helps White than Black Families Escape Poverty: National Survey of Children's Health," *Economies* 6, no. 2 (May 2018): 30. https://doi.org/10.3390/economies6020030.
117 Bonilla-Silva, "From Bi-Racial to Tri-Racial."
118 Tanya Katerí Hernandez, *Racial Subordination in Latin America: The Role of the State, Customary Law, and the New Civil Rights Response* (New York: Cambridge University Press, 2012); Christina A. Sue, "The Dynamics of Color: Mestizaje, Racism and Blackness in Veracruz, Mexico," in *Shades of Difference*, 114.
119 Sue, "The Dynamics of Color," 116.
120 Sue, "The Dynamics of Color," 117.
121 Hernandez, *Racial Innocence*.
122 Cynthia Feliciano, Rennie Lee, and Belinda Robnett, "Racial Boundaries among Latinos: Evidence from Internet Daters' Racial Preferences," *Social Problems* 58, no. 2 (May 2011): 189–212, https://doi.org/10.1525/sp.2011.58.2.189.
123 Hernandez, *Racial Subordination in Latin America*.
124 Erica Morales, "Parental Messages Concerning Latino/Black Interracial Dating: An Exploratory Study among Latina/o Young Adults," *Latino Studies* 10, no. 3 (September 2012): 314–333, https://doi.org/10.1057/lst.2012.24; George Yancey, *Who Is White? Latinos, Asians, and the New Black/Nonblack Divide* (Boulder, CO: Lynne Rienner Publishers, 2003).
125 Yancey, *Who Is White?*, 70.
126 Shauna B. Wilson, William D. McIntosh, and Salvatore P. Insana II, "Dating across Race: An Examination of African American Internet Personal Advertisements," *Journal of Black Studies* 37, no. 6 (July 2007): 964–82, https://doi.org/10.1177/0021934705282375 (explaining caste and exchange theories).
127 Wilson, McIntosh, and Insana, "Dating across Race," 976.
128 David M. Buss and David Schmidt, "Sexual Strategies Theory: An Evolutionary Perspective on Human Mating," *Psychological Review* 100, no. 2 (1993): 204, https://doi.org/10.1037/0033-295x.100.2.204.
129 Wilson, McIntosh, and Insana, "Dating across Race," 976.
130 Bonilla-Silva, "From Bi-Racial to Tri-Racial."
131 Emens, "Intimate Discrimination," 1373.

CHAPTER 6. WORKING TOWARD EQUALITY

Epigraph: Celeste Vaughan Curington, Jennifer Hickes Lundquist, and Ken-Hou Lin, *The Dating Divide: Race and Desire in the Era of Online Romance* (Berkeley: University of California Press, 2021), 215.

1 Siham Yahya, "My Family Would Crucify Me! The Perceived Influence of Social Pressure on Cross-Cultural and Interfaith Dating and Marriage," *Sexuality & Culture* 18 (January 2014): 759–72.

2   Daniel Cox, Juhem Navarro-Rivera, and Robert P. Jones, "Race, Religion, and Political Affiliation of Americans' Core Social Networks," Public Religion Research Institute (PRRI), August 3, 2016, https://prri.org (reporting study finding that 91 percent of individuals in Whites' core social networks are White).
3   Russell K. Robinson, "Perceptual Segregation," *Columbia Law Review* 108, no. 5 (June 2008): 1093; Russell K. Robinson, "Structural Dimensions of Romantic Preferences," *Fordham Law Review* 76, no. 6 (2008): 2787.
4   Fetishization of racial minorities is quite common on dating platforms. David Eng, *Racial Castration: Managing Masculinity in Asian America* (Durham, NC: Duke University Press, 2001); Robin Zheng, "Why Yellow Fever Isn't Flattering: A Case against Racial Fetishes," *Journal of the American Philosophical Association* 2, no. 3 (2016): 400–419, doi: 10.1017/apa.2016.25; Curington, Lundquist, and Lin, *The Dating Divide*, 92, 99, 120, 158–61, 172–73; Jevan Hutson, Jessie G. Taft, Solon Barocas, and Karen Levy, "Debiasing Desire: Addressing Bias and Discrimination on Intimate Platforms," *Proceedings of the ACM on Human-Compute Interaction* 73 (November 2018): 5, https://doi.org/10.1145/3274342.
5   Nancy Leong and Aaron Belzer, "The New Public Accommodations: Race Discrimination in the Platform Economy," *Georgetown Law Journal* 105 (January 2017): 1271; Sonu Bedi, *Private Racism* (New York: Cambridge University Press, 2020).
6   Bedi, *Private Racism*.
7   California Civil Code, § 51(b) (2015) (emphasis added).
8   Bedi, *Private Racism*, 9; Robinson, "Structural Dimensions"; Hutson et al., "Debiasing Desire."
9   Abram Brown, "Race Protests Are Forcing Dating Apps to Reconsider the Value of Their 'Ethnicity Filters,'" *Forbes*, June 2, 2020, https://forbes.com.
10 Brown, "Race Protests."
11 Zhiqiu Benson Zhou, "Compulsory Interracial Intimacy: Why Does Removing Ethnicity Filter on Dating Apps Not Benefit Racial Minorities?," *Media, Culture & Society* 44, no. 5 (2022): 1034–43, https://doi.org/10.1177/01634437221104712.
12 Brown, "Race Protests"; Carlyn Beccia, "Should Dating Apps Allows 'Ethnicity Filters?,'" Medium, March 6, 2022, https://medium.com.
13 Hutson et al. "Debiasing Desire," 7.
14 Hutson et al. "Debiasing Desire," 7.
15 Gerald A. Mendelsohn, Lindsay Shaw Taylor, Andrew T. Fiore, and Coye Cheshire, "Black/White Online Dating: Interracial Courtship in the 21st Century," *Psychology of Popular Media Culture* 3, no. 1 (2014): 2–18.
16 Mendelsohn et al., "Black/White Online Dating," 13.
17 "Black People Meet," Black People Meet, accessed February 28, 2023, https://blackpeoplemeet.com; "About Us," Elite Singles, accessed February 28, 2023, https://elitesingles.com/about-us (a dating website targeting educated professionals); "About ChristianMingle.com," *Christian Mingle*, February 28, 2023, https://about.christianmingle.com (a dating website and app targeting single Christians);

"Senior Match," Senior Match, accessed February 28, 2023, https://seniormatch.com (dating website and app for individuals over 50). "The Right Stuff," Right Stuff Dating, accessed February 28, 2023, https://rightstuffdating.com (for graduates and faculty of a "select of excellent universities and colleges").
18 "Black People Meet."
19 "Jdate," Jdate, accessed February 28, 2023, https://jdate.com.
20 Orly Lobel, *The Equality Machine: Harnessing Digital Technology for a Brighter, More Inclusive Future* (New York: Public Affairs, 2022), 258.
21 Hutson et al., "Debiasing Desire," 6–7.
22 Hutson et al., "Debiasing Desire," 5, note 17.
23 U.S. Const. amend. I. Although a Mrs. Murphy owner does not have a constitutional right to advertise their discriminatory preferences when seeking a potential tenant (see United States v. Hunter, 459 F.2d 205 (4th Cir. 1972); Ragin v. N.Y. Times Co., 923 F.2d 995 (2d Cir. 1991)), an individual date-seeker has stronger constitutional protections than a Mrs. Murphy owner. A Mrs. Murphy owner is engaged in speech in connection with a commercial transaction—the rental of housing—in which the constitutional protections are weaker than in noncommercial settings such as dating. Central Hudson Gas & Elec. Corp v. Public Service Commission of N.Y., 447 U.S. 557, 563–64 (1980) ("the Constitution accords a lesser protection to commercial speech than to other constitutionally guaranteed expressions"). While dating platforms are engaged in commercial activities—they often charge for their use or receive revenue from advertisers—and thus cannot discriminate or advertise discriminatory preferences, individual date-seekers are typically not engaged in commercial transactions and thus enjoy stronger constitutional protections to express their preferences.
24 Hutson et al., "Debiasing Desire," 13.
25 U.S. Const. amend. I.
26 Ollie Locke and Jack Rogers, "How One Gay App Is Fighting Racist Body-Shamers," *The Advocate*, January 4, 2018, https://advocate.com; Sonia Elks, "Gay Dating App Announces Zero Tolerance of Racism, Transphobia," Reuters, September 18, 2018, https://reuters.com; Brian Mayes, "Why Is It Okay for Online Daters to Block Whole Ethnic Groups?," *The Guardian*, September 29, 2018, https://theguardian.com.
27 47 U.S.C. § 230(C)(2)(A) (emphasis added).
28 Comment by Sara Bronin at Latina Law Scholars Virtual Workshop, June 13, 2022. See also Cecilia Rouse, Jared Bernstein, Helen Knudsen, and Jeffery Zhang, "Exclusionary Zoning: Its Effect on Racial Discrimination in the Housing Market," *The White House* (blog), June 17, 2021, https://whitehouse.gov; William A. Fischel, "An Economic History of Zoning and a Cure for Its Exclusionary Effects," *Urban Studies* 41, no. 2 (February 2004): 331.
29 Several states and municipalities have attempted to end single-family zoning. Margaret Barthel and Jennifer Ludden, "The U.S. Needs More Affordable Housing—Where to Put It Is a Bigger Battle," NPR, February 11, 2023, https://npr

.org; Susan Du and Liz Navratil, "Court Orders Minneapolis to Cease Implementation of 2040 Plan," *Minneapolis Star Tribune*, June 15, 2022, https://www.startribune.com; Jon Healey and Matthew Ballinger, "What Happened with Single Family Zoning in California," *Los Angeles Times*, September 17, 2021, https://latimes.com.

30. Michelle D. Layser, "How Federal Tax Law Rewards Housing Segregation," *Indiana Law Journal* 93, no. 4 (Winter 2018): 915.

31. Richard Rothstein, *The Color of Law: A Forgotten History of How Our Government Segregated America* (New York: W. W. Norton, 2018), 204–6 (discussing John Boger's proposal); Richard Kahlenberg, "An Economic Fair Housing Act," The Century Foundation, August 3, 2017, https://tcf.org; Richard Kahlenberg, "The Walls We Won't Tear Down," *New York Times*, August 3, 2017, https://nytimes.com.

32. Richard Kahlenberg, Halley Potter, and Kimberly Quick, "A Bold Agenda for School Integration," The Century Foundation, April 8, 2019, https://tcf.org.

33. Justin Steil and Michael Lens, "Public Policies to Address Residential Segregation and Improve Health," Health Affairs Health Policy Brief, April 27, 2023, doi: 10.1377/hpb20230321.466701; Lisa Sanbonmatsu, Jens Ludwig, Lawrence F. Katz, Lisa A. Gennetian, Greg J. Duncan, Ronald C. Kessler, Emma Adam, Thomas W. McDade, and Stacy Tessler Lindau, "Moving to Opportunity for Fair Housing Demonstration Program: Final Impacts Evaluation," U.S. Department of Housing and Urban Development Office of Policy Development and Research (November 2011), https://www.huduser.gov.

34. Raj Chetty, Nathaniel Hendren, and Lawrence F. Katz. "The Effects of Exposure to Better Neighborhoods on Children: New Evidence from the Moving to Opportunity Experiment," *American Economic Review* 106, no. 4 (April 2016): 855–902; David D. Troutt, "Cities, Fair Housing, and Gentrification: A Proposal in Progressive Federalism," *Cardozo Law Review* 2, no. 3 (2019): 1177, 1178–82; Bethany Y. Li, "Now Is the Time! Challenging Resegregation and Displacement in the Age of Hypergentrification," *Fordham Law Review* 85, no. 3 (2016): 1189; Genee S. Smith, Hannah Breakstone, Lorraine T. Dean, and Roland J. Thorpe Jr., "Impacts of Gentrification on Health in the U.S.: A Systemic Review of the Literature," *Journal of Urban Health* 97, no. 6 (December 2020): 845–56, doi: 10.1007/s11524-020-00448-4; Ruby Kish, "Inequitable Gentrification: A Form of Exclusionary Zoning That Violates the New Jersey Constitution," *Rutgers CLiME*, May 15, 2019, https://clime.rutgers.edu.

35. Kahlenberg, Potter, and Quick, "A Bold Agenda for School Integration"; Amended Complaint, Latino Action Network v. New Jersey, No. MER-L-001076–18 (N.J. Super. Ct. Law Div. Aug. 2, 2019).

36. Peter Bergman, "The Risk and Benefits of School Integration for Participating Students: Evidence from a Randomized Desegregation Program," IZA Institute of Labor Economics, June 2018, https://iza.org.

37. Paul Tractenberg, Allison Roda, and Ryan Coughlan, "Remedying School Segregation: How New Jersey's Morris School District Chose to Make Diversity Work,"

The Century Foundation, December 12, 2016, https://tcf.org; Anthony J. LoPresti, Comment, "Blurring the Lines: How Consolidating School Districts Can Combat New Jersey's Public-School Segregation Problem," *Seton Hall Legislative Journal* 45, no. 1 (2021) 235–60.

38 Beverly Daniel Tatum, *Why Are All the Black Kids Sitting Together in the Cafeteria? And Other Conversations About Race*, rev. ed. (New York: Basic Books, 2003).
39 Kahlenberg, Potter, and Quick, "A Bold Agenda for School Integration."
40 Jeremy Ashkenas, Haeyoun Park, and Adam Pearce, "Even with Affirmative Action, Blacks and Hispanics Are More Underrepresented at Top Colleges than 35 Years Ago," *New York Times*, August 24, 2017, https://nytimes.com.
41 Grutter v. Bollinger, 539 U.S. 306, 312–14 (2003); Lee C. Bollinger and Geoffrey R. Stone, *A Legacy of Discrimination: The Essential Constitutionality of Affirmative Action* (New York: Oxford University Press, 2023); Valerie Straus, "Why Race-Based Affirmative Action Is Still Needed in College Admissions," *Washington Post*, January 30, 2022, https://washingtonpost.com.
42 Grace Kao, Kara Joyner, and Kelly Stamper Balistreri, *The Company We Keep* (New York: Russell Sage Foundation, 2019); Micere Keels and Keshia Harris, "Intercultural Dating at Predominantly White Universities in the United States: The Maintenance and Crossing of Group Borders," *Societies* 4, no. 3 (June 2014): 366, https://doi.org/ 10.3390/soc4030363.
43 Students for Fair Admissions Inc. v. President & Fellows of Harvard College, 143 S. Ct. 2141 (2023).
44 Olufemi Ogundele, Opinion: "How to Fix College Admissions: Learn from Those of Us Doing the Work Already," *New York Times*, July 5, 2023, https://www.nytimes.com (emphasis added).
45 Students for Fair Admissions Inc., 143 S. Ct. at 2176 (emphasis in original).
46 Students for Fair Admissions Inc., 143 S. Ct. at 2176 (emphasis in original).
47 Elise C. Boddie, "Racial Territoriality," *UCLA Law Review* 58 (October 2010): 401.
48 "Household Travel in America," U.S. Department of Transportation Federal Highway Administration, November 7, 2014, https://fhwa.dot.gov.
49 Deborah Archer, "Transportation Policy and the Underdevelopment of Black Communities," *Iowa Law Review* 106, no. 5 (July 2021): 2125, 2146; Sarah Schindler, "Architectural Exclusion: Discrimination and Segregation through Physical Design of the Built Environment," *Yale Law Journal* 124, no. 6 (April 2015): 1934, 1961–63; Jason Henderson, "Secessionist Automobility: Racism, Anti-Urbanism, and the Politics of Automobility in Atlanta, Georgia," *International Journal of Urban and Regional Research* 30, no. 2 (June 2006): 293, 299–300, https://doi.org/10.1111/j.1468-2427.2006.00662.x; James W. Loewen, *Sundown Towns: A Hidden Dimension of American Racism* (New York: The New Press, 2005), 255; Lior Jacob Strahilevitz, "Exclusionary Amenities in Residential Communities," *Virginia Law Review* 92, no. 3 (May 2006): 437, 487–88.
50 Archer, "Transportation Policy," 2133.

51 For example, to reduce harm to the environment from automobiles. "Public Transportation's Role in Responding to Climate Change," U.S. Department of Transportation, Federal Transit Administration, January 2010, https://transit.dot.gov
52 "Propinquity Effect," *American Psychological Association Dictionary*, accessed September 11, 2023, https://dictionary.apa.org; Amie M. Gordon, "The Role of Familiarity in Attraction," *Psychology Today*, March 27, 2022, https://www.psychologytoday.com.
53 Tanya K. Hernandez, *Racial Innocence: Unmasking Latino Anti-Black Bias and the Struggle for Equality* (Boston: Beacon Press, 2022).
54 Harry T. Edwards, "The Growing Disjunction between Legal Education and the Legal Profession," *Michigan Law Review* 91, no. 1 (October 1992): 34.
55 Masterpiece Cakeshop, Ltd. v. Colorado Civil Rights Commission, 138 S. Ct 1719, 1727 (2018).
56 Fulton v. City of Philadelphia, 141 S. Ct. 1868, 1881–82 (2021).
57 303 Creative LLC v. Elenis, 143 S. Ct. 2298 (2023).
58 In his concurring opinion in *Dobbs*, Justice Clarence Thomas stated that "in future cases," the Supreme Court "should reconsider all of [its] substantive due process precedents, including *Griswold*, *Lawrence*, and *Obergefell*." Dobbs v. Jackson Women's Health Org., 142 S Ct. 2228 (2022) (Thomas, J., concurring). *Griswold v. Connecticut*, 381 U.S. 479 (1965), recognizes the right of married people to use contraception, and *Lawrence v. Texas*, 539 U.S. 558 (2003), recognizes the right of adults to engage in private, consensual sexual acts.
59 Respect for Marriage Act, Pub. L. 117–228, 136 Stat. 2305 (2022).
60 "Governor Murphy Signs Legislation Protecting Interracial Marriage in New Jersey Statutory Law," State of New Jersey Governor Phil Murphy, September 5, 2023, https://nj.gov (statement of Governor Phil Murphy).
61 Rothstein, *The Color of Law*.

INDEX

adoption and adoption agencies, 8, 77–79, 188n71
Adoptions from the Heart, 188n71
advertising, discriminatory, 73–75, 82, 87, 186n39, 186nn41–42, 187n44
African American men: college-educated, 120, 123, 125, 159n40; exclusion from dating pool, 28; gay African American men, dating patterns of, 25–26; intermarriage patterns of, 17; military policies denying marriage to White European women, 54–55; pool of marriageable, 9, 119–20, 123, 125; racial hierarchy and, 28; same-race preference of, 24; stereotyping of, 25–26, 30–32; White women and, 22, 34
African Americans: African American/White individuals, marriage patterns of, 17; citizenship of, 60; court testimony of, 64; interracial dating preferences of, 16–19, 22–25, 120; interracial marriage patterns of, 3, 16, 17, 52, 175n115; marriage opportunities and, 9, 117, 119–20, 123–25, 159n40; "marry down," social/economic costs of, 123–25, 212n109; other minority groups and, 62; racial hierarchy and, 4, 8, 22–25, 27–32, 59, 62; same-race preference of, 24, 120; as single parents, 117; social mobility as motivator for, 129; stereotyping of, 5, 25–26, 28, 30–32, 63–64, 126; term "Black," use of, 151n2; workplace segregation and, 106–7. *See also* African American men; African American women; anti-miscegenation laws; educational segregation; housing discrimination; racial discrimination and bias; residential segregation; spatial segregation
African American women: Asian American men and, 24, 119; college-educated, marriageability of, 23, 120, 123, 125–26, 159n40; interracial marriage rate of Asian women vs., 3, 17; Latino men and, 24, 119; rejection by other racial groups, 28–32, 119, 120; same-race preference of, 24, 120; skin tone and, 29–31; stereotyping of, 28, 30–32, 126; White men and, 4, 21–24, 28–29, 34; willingness to consider partners of other races, 9, 24, 119–20, 124
Airbnb, 70–71, 88, 90, 132
#AirbnbWhileBlack, 88
Alabama: anti-miscegenation law, 40, 168n2; racial categorization in, 41
American Indians: anti-miscegenation laws and white sexual relations with, 2, 38, 46, 52, 59–62, 179n171; anti-miscegenation policies of tribes toward African Americans, 62; citizenship of, 175n123; court testimony of, 64; custom marriages of White men with, 42, 43, 49, 59, 170n34, 171n48; educational segregation and, 57; gender and intermarriage, 17, 158n36; interracial marriage patterns of, 3, 16, 17, 52, 158n36, 175n115; other minority groups and, 62; Pocahontas exception and Whiteness,

219

41–42, 56, 59–60; racial hierarchy and, 38; racial stereotyping of, 179n162; use of term, 151n7
Anderson, Elijah, 107
anti-discrimination laws. *See* Civil Rights Act of 1964; employment discrimination; Fair Housing Act; freedom of association; housing discrimination
anti-miscegenation laws, 8, 37–65; African Americans as targets of, 13, 61, 179n171; American Indians as targets of, 2, 38, 46, 52, 59–62, 179n171; Asians as targets of, 38, 42–44, 53, 170n42, 179n171; educational segregation and, 57–59, 103; federal laws, 48–49, 53; history of, 1–2, 39–40; immigration laws and, 61–62; Japanese Americans as targets of, 40–41; Jim Crow era, 55; long-term effects of, 3, 5–6, 10, 12, 36, 52; *Loving v. Virginia* (1967) ending, 2–3, 36, 37–39; Mexican Americans as targets of, 2, 44–46, 52; military policies, 43–44, 53–55, 61–62, 176n128; Pocahontas exception, 41–42, 44, 56, 60; post–Civil War, 40; public accommodations and, 56–57; racial hierarchy and, 59–61; residential segregation and, 55–56; social beliefs of racial inferiority and, 52, 53; state laws, 48, 52–53, 168n2; Supreme Court construing term "White," 48–52. *See also* racial categories; *individual states*
Arbery, Ahmaud, 109
Archer, Deborah, 143
Arizona, interracial marriage prohibitions and exceptions, 60–61
Arkansas, racial categorization in, 41
Asia, immigration from: Asian women, exclusion of, 43, 171n49; citizenship, ineligibility for, 53; education level of immigrants, 179–80n177; exclusion ended (1965), 61; immigration laws, 48, 53, 61–62, 64, 180n178, 180n182; "mail order" brides, 62, 180n183; military servicemembers wishing to marry Asian women, 44, 53–54, 61–62, 176n128
Asian American men: African American women and, 24, 119; exclusion from dating pool, 28; gay Asian American men, dating preferences of, 25; intermarriage patterns of, 17; Latina women and, 24; racial hierarchy and, 23–24, 28; stereotyping of, 25–26, 30–31, 70, 122; White women and, 4, 22, 24, 34, 43–44, 53, 171n50
Asian Americans: anti-miscegenation laws and, 1, 38, 42–44, 48–52, 53, 170n42, 179n171; Asian/White individuals, marriage patterns of, 16–17; bias against African Americans, 119, 128, 144; court testimony of, 64; COVID pandemic and, 52, 64; dating platforms and, 70, 89; dating preferences of, 5, 22–25, 27–32, 62, 144; educational segregation and, 57–58; interracial marriage patterns of, 3, 16–19, 52, 117, 119–20, 124–26, 128, 158n38, 175n115; as "model minority," 61, 64; naturalization and, 49, 53; other minority groups and, 62; racial categorization of, 15, 62; racial hierarchy and, 59–62; racial mobility gained from White partner, 128; same-race preference of, 24, 54, 162n78; stereotyping of, 25–26, 30–32, 61, 64, 70, 122; as unassimilable, 64, 180n182. *See also* Asian American men; Asian American women
Asian American women: college-educated, 124–25; interracial marriage patterns of, 3, 17, 124, 158n35; Latino men and, 24; racial preferences of, 23; same-race preference of, 162n78; stereotyping of, 30; White men and, 4, 22, 23, 34, 54–55, 59, 61–62, 124, 180nn182–83

Asiatic Barred Zone Act (1917), 48
assimilation, 11, 17, 48, 51–52, 61, 64, 180n182
associational freedoms. *See* freedom of association
assortative mating, 20–21, 117, 124–25, 144

Bad Hombres: From Colonization to Criminalization (documentary), 15
Banks, Richard, 78, 119
Bardwell, Keith, 1, 2
Barocas, Solon, 85
bars and clubs as venue for meeting romantic partners, 12, 66, 71–72, 85, 132–35, 186n30
Bedi, Sonu, 6, 83, 132
Belzer, Aaron, 84, 85, 131–32
Bernstein, David, 87–88
Black Codes (post-Reconstruction), 63. *See also* Jim Crow era
Black People Meet (dating platform), 133–34
Blacks. *See* African Americans
Bloomfield, New Jersey, racial profiling in, 108
Boddie, Elise, 107, 108
Boger, John, 137
Bonilla-Silva, Eduardo, 7, 113, 127, 129
Bridges, Ruby, 57
Bronin, Sara, 136
Brown v. Board of Education (1954), 55, 57–59, 101
Buchanan v. Warley (1917), 55–56, 93
Bumble (dating platform), 89, 135
Bush, George H. W., 64
Butler, Eleanor (Irish Nell), 39–40, 168n8

Cable Act (1922), 175n122
California: anti-miscegenation law, 2, 43, 45–47, 52, 171n47, 181n192; educational segregation, 57, 172n65; housing law, 74; Mexican Americans, intermarriage of, 45–47, 181n192; public university study on racial preferences in dating, 28–29, 31–33, 106; Unruh Civil Rights Act, 132
Caucasians. *See* Whites
Chappy (dating platform), 89, 135
Charleston Rifle Club (South Carolina), 72
Cheektowaga (suburb of Buffalo, New York), mall access in, 109–10
children: anti-miscegenation laws and, 42; assortative mating, effects of, 125; financial support of, 125–27, 141, 205–6n45, 211n103; of free women married to enslaved men, 39–40, 168n8; marriage benefits and, 6–7, 112–13, 115–18, 125–27, 206n51, 206n53, 207nn57–58, 208n64, 208n67; of nonmarital homes, 5, 116, 118, 125–27, 206n51, 208n65; racial mobility and, 127–29. *See also* educational segregation; multiracial individuals: mixed-race children
China, immigration from, 48, 180n177
Chinese ancestry, 41, 42–44, 57, 60, 171n49, 178–79n162. *See also* Asian Americans
Chinese Exclusion Act (1882), 48
citizenship laws, 38, 44, 48–50, 53–54, 60, 146, 172n56, 175nn122–23
Civil Rights Act of 1964: Title II, 71, 85; Title VI, 78; Title VII, 71, 76–77, 186n35
cohabitation: bias and preference, 13, 16; financial constraint as reason for not marrying, 203n10; law discouraging, 5; marriage vs., 116–18, 205–6n45, 206n51, 207n58, 208n65, 208n67; rate of interracial, 157n26; same-sex, 25–26
colleges and universities: access to, 91, 104–6, 140–42; California public university study on racial preferences in dating, 28–29, 31–33, 106; legal reforms for racial diversity, 140–42; meeting spouse while attending, 105–6;

students' dating preferences, 16, 23, 26–29, 31–33, 105–6
colonial American interracial intimacy, 39–40. *See also* Pocahontas exception
Combating Redlining Initiative (U.S. Department of Justice), 99
Communications Decency Act (1996), 87, 136, 190n103
contractual prohibitions under Section 1981, 84
COVID-19 pandemic, 52, 64
Cox, Mary, 40
Craigslist, 73–74, 88–89
criminal cases, racial stereotyping in, 63, 64, 181–82n196, 182n198
Curington, Celeste Vaughan, 130

Date Hookup (dating platform), 22
dating bias and preferences, 4–5, 14; college students, 16, 23, 26–29, 31–33, 105–6; implicit biases, 34–35; individual rejection and psychic injury, 120–21; racial hierarchy and, 27; racial privilege and status, 33–34; skin tone and attractiveness, 29–32, 160n61, 163n113; social disapproval and, 13, 16, 29, 32–33, 38, 130. *See also* dating platforms; interracial intimacy; *specific racial groups*
dating platforms: constitutional protections of date-seekers, 215n23; facilitation of discriminatory conduct by, 132–34; First Amendment rights and, 134–36; freedom of intimate association and, 86–88; gendered racial hierarchy of, 8; legal reform and, 131–34; most common way to meet romantic partners, 20, 79, 105; observations about, 27–29, 164n114; physical attraction and personality, 29–32, 163n113; psychic harm and, 80–82, 90, 134, 136; as public accommodations, 84–86, 131–33; race filters, 6, 67–70, 79, 82–84, 131–33, 136; racial hierarchy and, 22–23, 27; racial preferences and, 20, 27, 67–70; regulation of discrimination and, 79–90; Section 1981 prohibitions and, 84. *See also* sexual racism
dating studies and surveys: California public university study on racial preferences in dating, 28–29, 31–33, 106; Gallup poll (2005) on interracial dating, 16, 156n23; online vs. offline data sources, 26–27; stated preferences, truthfulness of, 19–21, 24
Davis, Sylvester, 45–46
Davis, Viola, 30
Denbeaux, Mark, 108
Department of Housing and Urban Development, U.S., 93
Department of Justice, U.S., 98
Detroit, school busing in, 102
divorce, 113, 125
Dobbs v. Jackson Women's Health (2022), 146, 218n58
domestic workers, exemption from employment discrimination laws, 8, 66, 71
Duru, Jeremi, 63

economic inequality, 3, 7, 123–27. *See also* income levels and financial security
economic mobility, 127–29; Asian immigrants and, 61; law as constraint on, 6. *See also* income levels and financial security
education: of Asian immigrants, 179–80n177; college-educated African American women, marriageability of, 23, 120, 123, 125–26; financial stability and, 124; implicit bias and, 35; interracial dating patterns and, 21–23; interracial marriage patterns and, 3, 17–18, 158–59n40; legal reforms and, 146–47; magnet schools for K-12 students, 139, 142; marriage and financial security linked to, 105–6, 117, 120, 123–24, 207n61, 212nn104–5; sexual racism

lessened by, 120; teaching history of slavery and segregation, 146–47. *See also* colleges and universities
educational segregation, 9, 91; achievement gap, 104; anti-miscegenation laws and, 57–59, 103; "apartheid schools," 92; Asian Americans, categorization of, 62, 177–78n150; effects of, 38, 103–4; higher education, access to, 104–6, 140–42; K–12 public schools, 101–3, 139–40; legal reforms to address, 139–40, 146–47; Mexican Americans, categorization of, 62, 172n64, 178n150; psychic harm and, 59; Puerto Ricans, categorization of, 62; school busing to desegregate, 101–2. *See also* colleges and universities
eHarmony (dating platform), 67, 69
Elite Singles (dating platform), 67–68
Emens, Elizabeth, 3, 68, 118, 129
emotional harm. *See* psychic harm
employment agencies, 76–77, 84, 87
employment discrimination: domestic workers exception, 8, 66, 71; employment agencies not to facilitate, 76–77, 84, 87; implicit bias and, 35; legal exceptions to, 6, 71; prohibition of, 66, 71, 91; racial stratification in jobs, 9. *See also* workplace segregation
Equal Employment Opportunity Commission (EEOC), 77
Equal Protection Clause, 40, 58, 106
Eurocentric standards of beauty and skin tone, 14, 27, 29–31
European ethnic groups: formerly labeled as non-Whites, 11; Latin America seeking Whites as immigrants from, 128; U.S. military permitting marriage of servicemembers with, 54
exclusion. *See* anti-miscegenation laws; racial hierarchy; racial preferences; segregation; *specific types of segregation*

exclusionary zoning: effect on romantic preferences, 6; from race-based zoning to, 93; segregation resulting from, 9; single-family zoning, 99–100, 136–37, 215n29. *See also* redlining
Expatriation Act (1907), 175n122

Facebook, 73, 191n114
facilitation of discriminatory conduct: adoption, 78–79, 80; dating platforms, 66–67, 83–85, 89–90, 131–34; educational segregation, 36, 58; employment agencies, 76–77, 80, 84, 87; freedom of association and, 76–79, 86–88; law's role in, 9, 12, 36, 73–74, 91–111, 112; public accommodations, 132; residential segregation, 36, 76–77, 79–80, 84, 87, 92, 95–96, 136–37
Fair Housing Act (1968), 70, 73–74, 76, 87, 95, 97, 100, 186n35
Fair Housing Council v. Roommate.com (9th Cir. 2008), 73–74
federal funding, discrimination prohibitions related to, 77–79, 188n72
Federal Housing Administration (FHA), 94
Felder, Raoul Lionel, 113
Feliciano, Cynthia, 127
femininity, 30–31
Filipinos, admission to United States and intermarriage of, 43, 62, 171n49, 175n121
First Amendment, 66, 100, 134–36, 146. *See also* freedom of association
Floyd, George, 132
foster care, 78
Fourteenth Amendment, 40, 141. *See also* Equal Protection Clause
freedom of association, 66–90; adoption agencies and, 77–79; as American value, 145; dating platforms and, 86–88; discriminatory advertising and, 73–75; employment agencies and, 76–77; facilitation of discrimination and, 76–79;

as rationale for racial discrimination, 8; realtors and, 76; Supreme Court's and lower courts" recognition of, 72–73
freedom of speech. *See* First Amendment
Fudge, Marcia, 98
Fulton v. City of Philadelphia (2021), 145

Gallup polls, 16, 26, 34, 156n23
Gates, Henry Louis, 108–9
gay men and women. *See* same-sex relationships
gendered racial hierarchy, 4, 8, 13–36, 61–62. *See also* sexual racism
Gentleman's Agreement (1908), 48
gentrification, 138
Gen Z, 114, 204n11
Georgia, racial categorization in, 41
Gibson, State v. (Ind. 1871), 56
Goffman, Erving, 121–22
Gomez, Laura, 63
Gong Lum v. Rice (1927), 58
Goodridge v. Dep't of Pub. Health (Mass. 2003), 116
Grindr (dating platform), 82, 89, 132, 135
Griswold v. Connecticut (1965), 218n58

harassment, racial, 96, 108–9, 143
Harpalani, Vinay, 61
Hart-Celler Act (1965), 61
HER (dating platform), 89
Hernandez, Tanya, 63, 101, 127
Hindus, racial categorization of, 40, 46, 50–51
historically Black colleges and universities (HBCUs), 91
Home Owners' Loan Corporation, 94
"honorary white" status, 7, 113, 127–29, 154n39
Hornet (dating platform), 89, 191n108
Horton, Willie, 64
housing discrimination: facilitation of, 76, 79–80, 87; permissible exceptions, 8–10, 66, 70, 76, 100–101, 183n3, 184n15, 187nn55–56; prohibition of, 66, 70–71, 82–83, 91; roommate exemption, 70, 73–74, 87–88, 89. *See also* Fair Housing Act (1968); residential segregation
Housing Opportunities Made Equal of Virginia, Inc., 75
Humphrey, Beth, 1
Hutson, Jevan, 85

Immigration Act (1917), 48
Immigration Act (1924, aka Johnson-Reed Act), 48, 53–54, 62
Immigration Act (1990), 180n178
immigration laws: Asian women as target of, 43–44, 171n49; Chinese Exclusion Act (1882), 48; discriminatory effect of, 37–38; effect on interracial intimacy, 48, 53–55; long-term effects of, 36; military servicemembers marrying Asian foreign nationals, 43–44, 53–55, 61–62, 176n128; racial hierarchy of, 61–62; repeal of race-based laws (1965), 52
implicit biases, 5, 34–35, 53, 83, 105, 110, 121
income levels and financial security: American Indian custom marriage based on White men's economic interests, 42–43, 49, 59, 170n34, 171n48; children and, 125–27, 141, 211–12n103; interracial marriage patterns and, 7, 17–18, 159nn43–44; laws restricting racial minorities' access to, 36; marriage opportunities related to, 117, 120, 123–24, 203n10, 206n50; of married couples, 117, 123, 205–6n45; racial wealth gap, 100; sexual racism lessened by money, 120; wealth of white men compared to men of other races, 124
India, immigration from, 50, 179–80n177. *See also* Asian Americans
In re. See name of party
intermarriage. *See* interracial marriage
interracial intimacy: assortative mating, 20–21; in colonial era, 39–40; law's

role in shaping opportunity for, 91–111, 130, 131–34; parental approval/disapproval of, 4–5, 16, 32–34, 38; patterns of opportunity for, 19–27; persistence of racial hierarchy and inequality and, 1–8, 48, 92; sexual encounters, 31; social acceptance of, 2, 13, 16, 29, 32–34, 38, 130, 169n20. *See also* dating bias and preferences; freedom of association; interracial marriage; racial preferences; *specific racial groups*
interracial marriage, 16–19; educational attainment and income in, 3, 17–18, 23, 158–59n40; history of ban on, 1–2; laws banning and punishing (anti-miscegenation), 1, 6, 8, 37–65; public acceptance of, 2, 13; racial hierarchy and, 27; rate of, 3, 17, 157n26, 175n115, 192n8; religious ban on, 1; same-sex couples, 18–19; skin tone and, 18; as ultimate indicator of assimilation, 11, 17; with White partners, social mobility of, 128. *See also* anti-miscegenation laws; interracial intimacy; *specific racial groups*
Irish Americans, 11, 14, 15
Italian Americans, 11, 14, 15

Jackson, Ketanji Brown, 105
Japan: immigration from, 48–50; military servicemembers wishing to marry women from, 43, 54, 62, 176n128
Japanese Americans: anti-miscegenation laws and, 40–41; scandal of intermarriage with White women, 171n50; Supreme Court ruling not White, 49–50. *See also* Asian Americans
Jarvie, Danielle, 92, 101
JDate (dating platform), 12, 133
Jim Crow era, 15, 55, 62, 133
Johnson-Reed Act. *See* Immigration Act (1924)
"Juan Crow" practices, 45

Kahlenberg, Richard, 100
Kentucky: church banning interracial couples from joining, 1; housing ordinance excluding persons of color, 55–56, 93
Keodara, Sinakhone, 89
King, Martin Luther, Jr., 108
Kirby v. Kirby (Ariz. 1922), 44–45

Lassiter, Matthew, 102
Latin America: preference for lighter skin tone and European phenotype in, 127–28; restrictions on immigration from, 48–49, 59; terms for population from, 14. *See also* Latinos; Mexican Americans
Latina women: Asian American men and, 24; college-educated, 125–26; interracial dating/marriage patterns, 119; racial preferences of, 23; same-race preferences and, 162n78; White men and, 4, 22, 23, 124
Latino men: African American women and, 24, 119; Asian American women and, 24; racial hierarchy and, 23–24; White women and, 4, 22, 24
Latino People Meet (dating platform), 12
Latinos: ancestry of, 14; anti-miscegenation laws and, 38; bias against African Americans, 4, 34, 119, 127–28, 144; educational segregation and, 3, 57, 61, 91–92, 101, 103–6, 139–41; encouraging children to marry Whites, 5, 7, 33, 127; financial resources improved by marriages to Whites, 159nn43–44; implicit biases of, 35; with Indigenous ancestry, 18, 44–46; interracial marriage patterns of, 3, 16–19, 62, 124, 127, 159n43, 175n115; "Latino," "Latina," and Latinx," use of term, 14; Latino/White individuals, marriage patterns of, 17, 159n46; marriage benefits and, 117; other minority groups

and, 62; racial hierarchy and, 22–24, 62; racial mobility and, 127–28; racial preferences and, 7, 27–28, 32, 127–28, 144; as racial vs. ethnic group, 14–15; residential segregation and, 61, 91–93, 95, 98–101; as single parents, 117; spatial segregation and, 107–8, 143; stereotyping of, 63–64; workplace segregation and, 106–7. *See also* Latina women; Latino men; Mexican Americans

Lawrence v. Texas (2003), 218n58

law's role, 37–65; in artificial line between public and private discrimination, 6; in creating racial categories, 50–51; exceptions to anti-discrimination laws, 6–7; influence on choices of long-term intimate partners, 6–8, 63–65, 131; Jim Crow era, 15, 55, 62, 133; propinquity effect created by, 144; in shaping family forms, 5, 8; in shaping opportunity for interracial intimacy, 91–111, 130; in shaping racial hierarchy, 6–8, 10–11, 37–38, 41, 48, 59–62, 122; in shaping social norms and beliefs, 12, 63–64; White supremacy acknowledged, 52, 178n162. *See also* anti-miscegenation laws; legal reform

Lee, Erika, 61

Lee, Rennie, 127

legal reforms, 10–12, 130–47; colleges campuses, racial diversity at, 140–42; dating platforms, 131–34; educational reform to teach about slavery and segregation, 146–47; freedom of speech and, 134–36; limitations of, 144–47; Mrs. Murphy exception, 137–38, 215n23; public transportation, expansion of, 142–43; residential segregation, 136–39; school assignment system for K-12, 139–40; Section 8 vouchers, 138; single-family zoning, 136–37, 215n29

Lenhardt, Robin, 56, 122

Leong, Nancy, 84, 85, 131–32

Levitt, William, 95

Levy, Karen, 85

LGBT/LGBTQ. *See* same-sex relationships

liberty interests vs. equality, 145–46

life satisfaction, 9, 112, 113, 117

Lin, Ken-Hou, 130

Lobel, Orly, 112, 134

Lopez, Ian Haney, 37, 63

Louisiana, interracial marriage in, 1, 169n18

Louisville, Kentucky: housing discrimination, 55–56; race-based zoning, 93

Loving v. Virginia (1967), 2–3, 36, 37–39, 42, 47, 55, 59

Lum, Martha, 57–58

Lundquist, Jennifer Hickes, 130

marriage and marriage-like relationships: benefits of, 6–7, 9, 11, 112–18, 125–27, 205n43, 206n53, 207nn57–58, 208n67, 208n70; cohabitation vs. marriage, 116–17, 205–6n45, 206n51, 207n58, 208n65, 208n67; decrease in rate of marriage, 113; educational attainment and income as influence on patterns of, 17–18, 23, 105–7, 203n10; emotional security of, 119–20; financial security of, 117, 123–24, 203n10, 206n50; racial hierarchy limiting access to, 11, 207nn60–61; weddings and wedding industry, 113. *See also* interracial marriage

marriage licensing, racial categorization for, 45–46, 48, 65, 131

Marriage Pact, The, 106, 140

Martin, Trayvon, 109

Martinez, George, 41, 44

Maryland, marriage of white woman (Irish Nell) to enslaved Black man in, 39–40, 168n8

masculinity, 30–31; hypermasculinity, 25–26

Masterpiece Cakeshop v. Colorado Civil Rights Commission (2018), 145

Match (dating platform), 22, 67–68
Maynard v. Hill (1888), 114
McCarran-Walter Act (1952), 55, 61
McKay, Terence, 1
Meister v. Moore (1877), 170n38
men: assortative mating and, 21; attractive partner as priority for, 21, 29–30; economic prerequisites before seeking to marry, 113–14; femininity as priority for, 30; marriage benefits of, 205n43; marriage opportunities for well-educated and financially secure men, 120. *See also* African American men; Asian American men; Latino men; masculinity; White men
Metropolitan Life Insurance Company, 95
Mexican Americans: anti-miscegenation laws and, 2, 44–46, 52; federal laws aimed at excluding Mexicans, 48–49; intermarriage with Whites (1924–1933), 52, 175n115; intermarriage with Whites (westward expansion era), 59; racial categorization of, 2, 15, 44–48, 62, 171n53, 172n64, 173n71, 178n150; racial stereotyping of, 63–64, 181n192; spatial segregation and, 133. *See also* Latinos; Treaty of Guadalupe Hidalgo
Mexico, anti-Black racism in, 127
military policies on racial intermarriage, 43–44, 53–55, 61–62, 176n128. *See also* War Brides Act
Millennials, 114, 204n11, 211n103
Milliken v. Bradley (1974), 102
Mississippi: educational segregation in, 57–58; opposition to interracial marriage in, 1; racial categorization in, 41
Missouri, interracial marriage prohibitions and exceptions in, 60–61
mixed-race children. *See* multiracial individuals
mixed-race marriage. *See* interracial marriage

mobility. *See* economic mobility; social mobility
Moran, Rachel, 60
Movoto (real estate site), 76
Mrs. Murphy exception, 6, 70, 73–75, 87, 100–101, 137–38, 215n23
mulattoes, 39, 43
Multi-Ethnic Placement Act (1994, amended 1996), 78
multi-family dwellings, exception to Fair Housing Act. *See* Mrs. Murphy exception
multiracial individuals: mixed-race children, 4, 7, 33, 39, 54, 55, 58, 154n39; partial Whiteness, effect of, 16–17, 22, 27–28; slavery and, 39–40

National Association of Realtors, 99; Code of Ethics, 96
National Fair Housing Alliance, 76
Native Americans. *See* American Indians
Naturalization Act of February 18, 1875, 172n56
naturalization laws. *See* citizenship laws
Nevada, marriage between Whites and Asian or Chinese persons prohibited, 170n42, 171n47
Newark, New Jersey, residential segregation in, 93–94, 108, 147
New Jersey: anti-discrimination in employment laws, 71; educational segregation in, 102–3; public accommodation law, 185–86n29; residential segregation and, 147; same-sex marriage and interracial marriage recognized by state law, 146; school assignment system, reform of, 139–40; spatial segregation and, 108, 143, 196n72, 198n94
New York (state): educational segregation in, 57, 103; employment agencies facilitating discrimination in, 77; residential segregation in, 95; spatial segregation in, 109

New York City's public transportation system, 142–43

Obergefell v. Hodges (2015), 114–17, 145, 146, 218n58
Ogundele, Olufemi, 141–42
Oh, Reginald, 57, 58
OkCupid (dating platform), 22–23, 26, 67–69
Omi, Michael, 28
online dating platforms. *See* dating platforms
Oregon, interracial marriage prohibitions and exceptions, 42, 60–61, 169n17
Orfield, Gary, 92, 101
Ozawa v. U.S. (1922), 49–51

Pace v. Alabama (1883), 40
Pacific Islanders, 15, 19, 68, 69
parental approval/disapproval of interracial relationships, 4–5, 16, 32–34, 38
parenthood: adoptive parent's racial preferences, 77–78; race gap of married parents, 117; single (nonmarital), 5, 116, 118, 125–27, 206n51, 208n65. *See also* children
Parkchester (Bronx, New York), 95, 194n40
Parks, Rosa, 55
Pascoe, Peggy, 37
passing as White, 25, 128. *See also* "honorary white" status
Perez, Andrea, 45–46
Perez v. Sharp (Cal. 1948), 2, 46–47
Pew Research Surveys: on African Americans seeking committed romantic relationships, 120; on financial security as factor in getting married, 203n10; limitations on survey size, 26; on single motherhood, 116
Philippine Independence Act (1934), 175n121
Plainfield School District (New Jersey), 103, 198n94

Plenty of Fish (dating platform), 67–68, 87
Plessy v. Ferguson (1896), 56
Pocahontas exception, 41–42, 56, 60
police: implicit bias and, 35; stops of African American males, 6
pornography sites, 31
Powell, Lewis, 72
private clubs. *See* bars and clubs
privilege, 33–34. *See also* White privilege
propinquity effect, 144
psychic harm: dating platforms and, 80–82, 90, 134, 136; discriminatory advertising and, 74–75, 80, 82; educational segregation and, 59; racial discrimination in intimate sphere producing, 36; racial hierarchy inflicting, 9, 11, 112, 120–22; racial preferences and, 112, 118–23, 129; racial stigma and group harm, 121–23, 210n91, 211n97; sexual racism and, 81–82, 120–21
public accommodations, 56–57; dating platforms as, 84–86, 131–32; discrimination prohibited, 66, 70–71, 145–46, 185n28; sexual racism and, 84–86
public transportation, expansion of, 109–10, 142–43
Puerto Ricans, racial categorization of, 62

racial categories: African Americans defined by law, 169n23; American Indian exception, 41–42; Asians, 42–44; Congress and Supreme Court determining, 48–52; educational segregation and, 59; federal laws contributing to, 48; Latinos, 14–15; law's definition of, 37; marriage license application requiring, 65, 131; Mexicans, 2, 15, 44–48, 62, 171n53, 172n64, 173n71, 178n150; one-drop rule, 47; politics of, 41–44; scientific approach to, 50–51; as socially and legally constructed, 15, 37, 41, 46. *See also* anti-miscegenation laws; gendered

racial hierarchy; racial hierarchy; racial purity; *specific racial groups*
racial discrimination and bias: 2021 study on discrimination against African Americans, 13; criminal cases and, 63, 64, 181–82n196, 182n198; dating platforms/market and, 67–70, 79–90, 132, 134; Latinos subject to, 15; legally permissible areas of, 6, 8; in Mexico, 127; microaggressions, 121, 130, 210n85, 211n93; persistence of, 12, 96–99; racial profiling, 108–9. *See also* anti-miscegenation laws; facilitation of discriminatory conduct; housing discrimination; psychic harm; racial stereotypes; racial stigma; White supremacy; *specific areas of segregation (employment, housing, education, etc.)*
racial harassment and violence, 96, 108–9, 143
racial hierarchy: courts allowing states to impose, 60–61; in dating market, 4, 11, 12, 16, 21–26, 120, 124; educational segregation perpetuating, 58; harms caused by, 9, 11, 112, 120–22; immigration laws and, 61–62; intimacy patterns reinforcing, 7–8, 11; Latino acceptance of, 127; law's role in shaping, 6–8, 10–11, 37–38, 41, 48, 59–62, 122; marriage and marriage-like relationships limited by, 11, 118, 207nn60–61; minority groups' views of other minority groups, 62; options in absence of, 10–11; parents' views of children's interracial relationships and, 5, 7, 33–34, 127; race filters reinforcing, 132–33; racial preferences reinforcing, 144–45; same-race preferences and, 11–12, 135; social entrenchment of, 35, 63, 128–29. *See also* gendered racial hierarchy; racial preferences; *specific racial groups*
racial inequality: access to committed relationships/emotional security, 119–20; access to financial security, 123–25; educational segregation's long-term effects, 103–4; long-term effects of, 36, 38–39, 107–11; perpetuation of, 1–8, 10–11, 48, 92, 112–29; psychic injury and, 120–21; romantic preferences and, 5, 34–35. *See also* racial discrimination and bias; racial hierarchy; racial preferences
racially restrictive covenants, 9, 94–96, 141, 193n33, 194n36, 194n42
racial preferences, 21–35; in adoption, 78–79; children and, 126–27; in dating market, 21–26, 82, 112, 127; gay men and women, 25–26; group harm and, 122–23; harmful effects of, 112, 118–23, 129; implicit bias, 5, 34–35, 53, 83, 105, 110, 121; intimate choices affected by, 3, 6–7, 19–27, 112; legal reforms and, 134–35; marriage opportunities and, 119–20, 124–25; observations about, 27–29, 62, 130; physical attraction and personality, 29–32, 163n113; psychic harm and, 112, 118–19; racial hierarchy reinforced by, 144–45; racial privilege and status, 33–34; religion reinforcing, 108; religious preferences vs., 22; social disapproval of interracial intimate relationships, 2, 13, 16, 29, 32–34, 130; social inequality and, 127–29; spatial segregation and, 107–11. *See also* dating platforms; interracial marriage; racial discrimination and bias; racial hierarchy; racial stereotypes; same-race preferences; *specific racial groups*
racial purity: anti-miscegenation laws as way to maintain, 2; segregation as way to maintain, 56, 58; slavery raising issue of, 39–40; state constitutions and laws to maintain, 178–79n162. *See also* anti-miscegenation laws; Whiteness; White supremacy
racial stereotypes: African Americans, 5, 25–26, 28, 30–32, 63–64, 126; Asian

Americans, 25–26, 30–32, 61, 64, 70, 122; compatibility assessment based on, 5; criminal cases and, 63, 64, 181–82n196, 182n198; implicit bias and, 35; Latinos and, 63–64; law's role in perpetuating, 63–64; masculinity and femininity, 25–26, 30–31; Mexican Americans, 63–64, 181n192; race filters on dating platforms validating and preserving, 133–34; racial hierarchy fueled by, 29; segregation and, 38; social and cultural, effect on romantic preferences, 8, 160n53; standards of beauty and skin tone, 14, 27, 29–31, 173n71. *See also specific racial groups*

racial stigma: of African Americans and Asian American men, 28; group harm and, 121–23, 210n91, 211n97; parental objections to children intermarrying and, 33; psychological harm of, 118–19; racial preferences creating, 112; same-race preferences and, 11–12. *See also* skin tone; *specific racial groups*

Reagan, Ronald, 64

realtors' facilitation of housing discrimination, 76, 84, 87

redlining, 9, 91, 93–94, 97–98, 141

religious preferences: ban on interracial marriage, 1; racial vs., 22; spatial segregation of religion, 108, 200n124

Republicans: opposition to interracial marriage, 1, 2; opposition to single parenthood, 116

residential segregation, 3, 55–56, 91, 92–100; 1968 to present day, 96–101; African American neighborhoods, 195n60; effect on romantic preferences, 6, 55–56; history before 1968, 92–96; home valuation, 94, 96–98, 100, 195n61; legal reform and, 136–39; Mexican Americans and, 45; Mrs. Murphy exception, 6, 70, 73–75, 87, 100–101, 137–38, 215n23; persistence of, 10, 12, 96–99; race-based zoning to exclusionary zoning, 93; racially restrictive covenants, 9, 94–96; racial steering, 9, 76, 91, 96, 99, 141; redlining, 9, 91, 93–94, 97–98, 141; segregated schools as by-product of, 102, 137; single-family zoning, 99–100, 136–37, 215n29; state-sanctioned harassment and violence to maintain, 96. *See also* exclusionary zoning

Respect for Marriage Act (2022), 146

Rhimes, Shonda, 30, 165n127

Rice v. Gong (Miss. 1927), 57–58

Richmond, Virginia, housing ordinance, 56

Robinson, Russell, 9, 25–26

Robnett, Belinda, 127

Rodriguez, In re (W. D. Tex. 1897), 44

Roemer, Neoshia, 151n7

Roldan, Salvador, 43

Rolfe, John, 42, 60

romantic segregation, 9

Roommate.com, 73–74

Rothstein, Richard, 93, 98, 99; *The Color of Law: A Forgotten History of How Our Government Segregated America*, 147

Rudder, Christian, 27, 68

Runyon v. McCrary (1976), 72

same-race preferences, 9, 119; dating platforms and, 68; racial hierarchy and, 11–12; rationales for, 144–45; same-sex relationships and, 25; servicemembers of Japanese ancestry seeking to marry Japanese national, 54; Whites and, 12, 21–23, 135, 162n78. *See also specific racial groups*

same-sex relationships: dating platforms and, 85; interracial dating patterns of, 4, 25–26, 32; interracial marriage and cohabitation patterns of, 4, 18–19; marriage laws and, 114–16, 145–46; racial hierarchy and, 4, 25–26; same-race preferences, 25; sexual racism in, 120

Schindler, Sarah, 109
school segregation. *See* educational segregation
Schwemm, Robert, 74, 75
Section 8 vouchers, 138
Section 1981 prohibitions, 84
segregation: failure to teach history of, 146–47; Jim Crow era, 15, 55, 62, 133; law's role in, 9, 91–111; long-term effects of, 36, 38–39, 107–11; preventing social interactions among races, 38, 130, 176n136, 176n141, 177n146; spatial, 107–11, 142–43. *See also* educational segregation; residential segregation; spatial segregation; workplace segregation
Seton Hall Law School, 108, 147
sexual racism: dating platforms enabling, 6, 8, 66–70, 79, 80, 82–84, 132–34, 136; in LGBTQ dating market, 120; limiting marriage opportunities, 9; psychic harm and, 81–82, 120–21; public accommodations laws and, 84–85; voluntary efforts to address on dating platforms, 88–90. *See also* racial stereotypes; skin tone
sexual strategies theory, 129
Shelley v. Kramer (1948), 95–96
single-family zoning, 99–100, 136–37, 215n29
skin tone: dating platforms filtering for, 67; gay minority men and, 25; interracial dating and, 8, 27, 29–31; interracial marriage and, 18, 120; Latinos/Mexican Americans and, 14, 63, 127, 173n71, 181n192; psychic harm from discrimination based on, 81–82, 121; racial stigma and group harm based on, 122–23; Supreme Court rejecting as way to make racial determination, 49–50
slavery: criminality attributed to African Americans based on, 63; failure to teach history of, 146; Irish Nell's descendants and lawsuits to establish freedom based on white ancestor, 39–40, 168n8; legacy's effect on rate of intermarriage, 3, 6, 8, 121–22; racial purity as issue for, 39–40; state Slave Codes, 63
social clubs. *See* bars and clubs
social distance: dating platforms exacerbating, 16, 134; interracial intimacy as indicator of, 3, 19; law's role in facilitating, 6, 38, 52; minority member attempting to distance self from racial stereotype, 123, 128; between White and African American college students, 28. *See also specific types of segregation*
social justice, 9, 112
social mobility: Asian Americans and, 61; intermarriage with White facilitating, 128–29; Latinos and, 127–28; law as constraint on, 6; racial privilege and status's effect on, 33–34. *See also* assimilation; economic mobility; racial hierarchy
social norms and beliefs: anti-miscegenation laws and, 52, 53; interracial intimacy and, 2, 13, 16, 29, 32–34, 38, 130; law's role in shaping, 12, 63–64; racial hierarchy entrenched in, 63. *See also* dating bias and preferences; racial hierarchy; racial preferences
South Carolina: anti-miscegenation law, 168n2
South Dakota: marriage between Whites and Asian persons prohibited, 171n47
spatial segregation, 107–11, 142–43, 200n124
State v. See name of party
steering, 9, 76, 91, 96, 99, 141
stereotypes. *See* racial stereotypes
Stevens v. United States (10th Cir. 1944), 60
strip clubs, 30
Students for Fair Admissions v. Harvard (2023), 103, 106, 141

Stuyvesant Town (New York City), 95, 194n41
Sue, Christina, 127
Supreme Court, U.S.: baker's right to refuse to make custom cake for same-sex couple, 145; educational segregation upheld by, 57; freedom of speech favored over freedom from discrimination, 145–46; marriage upheld between White man and American Indian woman, 170n38; no federal constitutional right to abortion, 146; race-conscious admissions policies as violation of Fourteenth Amendment, 103, 106, 141–42; racial classifications and categorizing who is White, 49–52; religious liberty interests of foster care agency favored over rights of same-sex couples to be foster parents, 145; same-sex marriage entitled to equal treatment, 114–17, 145. *See also specific cases*

Taft, Jessie, 85
Texas: racial intermarriage prohibited in, 169n17; segregated schooling of children of Mexican descent, 172–73n68
Thind, U.S. v. (1923), 50–52
Thomas v. Dosberg (N.Y. App. Div. 1996), 72–73
303 Creative LLC v. Elenis (2023), 145
Tinder (dating platform), 89
Title VII. *See* Civil Rights Act of 1964; employment discrimination
Traynor, Roger, 46–47
Treaty of Guadalupe Hidalgo (1848), 2, 44, 48
Troutt, David, 104
Trump, Donald, 64, 182n206
Tydings-McDuffie Act (1934), 175n121

Uber, 88–89, 132
Undesirable Aliens Act (1929), 48–49

U.S. v. See name of opposing party
U.S. Census: categorization of Hispanics or Latinos by, 14–15, 18, 49, 155n9; definition of American Indian, 151n7; racial identification as "some other race" on, 155n8, 156n11; same-sex couples in interracial relationships, 18–19

Villazor, Rose, 53, 54, 97
Virginia: anti-miscegenation law and Pocahontas exception, 41–42, 44, 56, 60; banishment of White in interracial marriage, 39; extramarital sex of Whites with Black partners in, 39; marriage license application requiring racial designation, 65; Racial Integrity Act (1924), 41

War Brides Act (1945, amended 1947), 54–55, 61, 176n127, 176n133
Washington (state), recognition of marriages between White men and American Indian women, 61
wealth. *See* income levels and financial security
Westfield School District (New Jersey), 103, 198n94
Westminster v. Mendez (9th Cir. 1947), 45
Where White People Meet (dating platform), 12
White men: African American women excluded by, 4, 21–23, 28–29, 34, 119; Asian American women and, 4, 22, 23, 34, 54–55, 59, 61–62, 124, 180n183; custom marriages with American Indians, 42, 43, 49, 59, 170n34, 171n48; income when married to African American or Latina women, 18; Latina women and, 4, 22, 23, 124; racial hierarchy and, 22; racial preferences of, 4, 22; religious preferences of, 22; same-race marriage, income level in, 18; wealth of, 124

Whiteness, 27–30; definition of, 39–40; Pocahontas exception, 41–42, 56, 59–60. *See also* Eurocentric standards of beauty and skin tone

White privilege, 153n36, 202n3; "honorary white" status and, 7, 113, 127–29, 154n39; intermarriage with non-white and loss of, 33–34; intermarriage with White, social mobility of, 128–29; racial exclusion and, 113

Whites: ethnic groups classified as, 15; implicit biases and, 5, 34–35; interracial dating patterns of, 4–5, 16–19, 24–25; legal determination of who qualified as, 37–41; Mexican Americans treated as, 44–49, 59; racial anxiety of White college students, 105; racial hierarchy in dating, 8, 21–29; same-race preferences and, 12, 21–23, 135, 162n78; term "White," use of, 151n2; wealth gap and, 100. *See also* anti-miscegenation laws; White men; Whiteness; White privilege; White supremacy; White women

White supremacy, 55, 58–59, 63, 108, 144–45; laws acknowledging, 52, 178n162

White women: African American men and, 22, 34; Asian American men and, 4, 22, 24, 34, 43–44, 53, 171n50; income level in marriage with African American or Latino men, 18; Latino men and, 4, 22, 24; "marry down," less likely for, 124; parental or social disapproval of interracial dating or marriage, 34; same-race preference of, 22–23, 162n78

Wiggins, Cynthia, 109–10

Winant, Howard, 28

women: interracial marriage rate of Asian vs. African American women, 3, 17; loss of citizenship for marrying men ineligible for citizenship, 53; masculinity as priority for, 30–31; parental disapproval of interracial dating or marriage of daughters, 33–34; skin tone and, 29–31. *See also* African American women; Asian American women; gendered racial hierarchy; Latina women; parenthood; White women

workplace segregation, 91–92, 106–7, 110. *See also* employment discrimination

Wyoming, marriage between Whites and Asian persons prohibited, 171n47

zoning: for public schools, 102–3; single-family, 99–100, 136–37, 215n29. *See also* exclusionary zoning; residential segregation

Zoosk (dating platform), 67, 87

Zwolinski, Matt, 90

ABOUT THE AUTHOR

Solangel Maldonado is the Eleanor Bontecou Professor of Law at Seton Hall University School of Law, where she writes and teaches in the areas of family law, gender, race, and their intersections. She is an associate reporter of the American Law Institute's *Restatement of the Law: Children and the Law* and co-editor of *Family Law: Cases and Materials* and *Family Law in the World Community: Cases, Materials, and Problems in Comparative and International Family Law*.